House of Hospitality

House of Hospitality

BY DOROTHY DAY

Our Sunday Visitor Publishing Division
Our Sunday Visitor, Inc.
Huntington, Indiana 46750

Text of *House of Hospitality* by Dorothy Day originally published in 1939 by Sheed & Ward, Inc. All additional texts in this edition — including the Preface, the Introduction, the footnotes, and For Further Reading — copyright © 2015 by Our Sunday Visitor Publishing Division, Our Sunday Visitor, Inc. Published 2015.

20 19 18 17 16 15   1 2 3 4 5 6 7 8 9

ISBN: 978-1-61278-815-9 (Inventory No. T1621)
eISBN: 978-1-61278-375-8
LCCN: 2014952457

Cover design: Amanda Falk
Cover art: Photo of Dorothy Day courtesy of the Department of Special Collections and University Archives, Marquette University Libraries. Background image courtesy of Shutterstock.

PRINTED IN THE UNITED STATES OF AMERICA

TABLE OF CONTENTS

Preface

Heartfelt thanks to Our Sunday Visitor for bringing back into print Dorothy Day's *House of Hospitality*. Originally published in 1939, *House of Hospitality* recounts the early days of the Catholic Worker movement, founded by Peter Maurin and Dorothy. This republication is particularly timely, coinciding as it does with the Church's efforts toward a "New Evangelization" and with Pope Francis' emphasis on the works of mercy, justice, and care for the poor. It also provides further support for our ongoing efforts to have her canonized as a saint.

The life and work of Dorothy Day provide an excellent source for a renewed sense of commitment to the Gospel and our Christ-centered faith, both for those who continue to practice the faith and for those who may have left or drifted away. *House of Hospitality* contains the seeds of her authentic understanding of the Gospel and the role of the Church in the world that will be more fully articulated in her later works. Dorothy Day's faith always radiates out from the person of Christ, through participation in the Church through word and sacrament, to formation of a community that is open and ready to serve all who come, especially those most in need.

It is difficult to read the book without marveling at the movement of the Spirit in the comings and goings of people; the struggles to sustain the food lines, shelter, farm, and newspaper; and in their strivings for social change. Trust in divine Providence and openness to the gift of every moment — even in the midst of loneliness, sadness, vulnerability, and self-doubt — miraculously mark these early days of the movement.

Examining how we live morally is fundamental to the renewal of our faith. Love of God was never an abstract ideal for Dorothy, but was inseparable from love of neighbor and the spiritual and corporal works of mercy. Welcome and hospitality, all the imperatives of the Sermon on the Mount, were central to her, not just the prerogative of saints but a call directed at every Christian. Although these early days are filled with the presence of nuns, priests, believers, unbelievers, servers, and served (even bishops), she exemplified the apostolate of the laity.

Pope Francis has exhorted the Church to be "poor and for the poor." Dorothy Day believed in and labored for such a Church. Her experience of life in God was inseparable from her choice of a life of voluntary poverty, of living with the poor, and of accepting each person for who they are, being a loving presence for the life and human dignity for which God created us, and seeing the face of Christ in all who come to the door.

In the early 1990s, my predecessor, Cardinal John O'Connor, after careful consultation with those who knew and worked with her, initiated her cause for canonization. We believe she is a saint for our time. As a layperson, a woman, a single mother, a model of devotion to the Church and her saints, and with her commitments to peace, justice, life, and the works of mercy, she is an inspiration for all of us who, like her, face contemporary national and international trials of war, injustice, racism, abortion, and social, political, and economic challenges. Dorothy Day can help us transcend superficial labels of left and right, liberal and conservative, more government or less. She can help us return to the mercy and forgiveness of Christ, our beginning and end, the wellspring from which we can create, as Peter Maurin said, a society where it is easier to be good.

Near the end of chapter ten, Dorothy describes walking by a group of unemployed men who are lined up to receive breakfast provided by the Worker. She finds it difficult to even speak to them, seeing the depth of their "patient misery and despair." Rather she would take their hands, and pray:

> Forgive us — let us forgive each other! All of us who are more comfortable, who have a place to sleep, three meals a day, work to do — we are responsible for your condi-

tion. We are guilty of each other's sins. We must bear each other's burdens. Forgive us and may God forgive us all!

We need her for our Church. We need her for our time. We need her for each other.

CARDINAL TIMOTHY M. DOLAN
Archbishop of New York
September 5, 2014
Feast of Blessed Mother Teresa

Introduction

House of Hospitality:
Discovering the
"Downward Path of Salvation"

By Lance Byron Richey

During the summer of 1939, while the world drifted towards the catastrophe of total war, Dorothy Day's diaries are almost silent, and the handful of entries remarkably mundane. Her normal routine of travel and speaking. The difficulties and occasional drunkenness of her companions at the Catholic Worker house. A short meditation on the nature of sin. Then, almost in passing, she mentions on July 30 that she has "been working all month at the proofs of the new book and a last chapter." She obviously completed her work, since *House of Hospitality* was published in August, only days before the outbreak of the Second World War.

House of Hospitality is in many respects only a first draft of Day's account of her initial encounter with Peter Maurin in 1933 and the early experiences of the Catholic Worker movement they founded, which would find mature expression more than a decade later in her masterpiece of spiritual autobiography, *The Long Loneliness*. But here the style of writing is highly journalistic, the structure amorphous and only generally chronological, and the subject matter quotidian (for Day and her companions, at least). As Day explains: "The following pages are jottings written down during journeys, notes kept for my own comfort, information, clarification, or publication.... A great many of these notes were not written for publication, but for my own self in moments of trouble and in moments of peace and joy" (p. 48).

The occasional character of the material — and the lack of any narrative unity (or even a discernible structure) — is painfully apparent throughout the work. Despite its literary shortcomings, Day defends the value of the book as a historical document: "Some will think, perhaps, that it is premature to present this sketchy material on the movement that the *Catholic Worker* has become to our friends and readers; but on the other hand, it may be a very useful volume to those thousands who wish to know more about the work we are doing in the lay apostolate" (p. 48). Day would have been as surprised as anyone to discover that, over three-quarters of a century later, interest in that work would be, if anything, even greater than when she wrote those lines.

Dorothy Day was born in New York City to a non-practicing Episcopalian family on November 8, 1897. Because her father was in the newspaper business, they moved several times during her youth. The family was living in Oakland, California, when the Great Earthquake of 1906 destroyed the city of San Francisco and ended her father's employment there. He eventually found a new position in Chicago, where Day grew to young adulthood, attending the University of Illinois at Urbana–Champaign for two years before leaving to move with her family back to New York in 1916, where she followed her father into journalism.

Unlike the rest of her family, though, Day had been radicalized during her college days and felt a strong sense of solidarity with the industrial proletariat and an affinity for the Socialist Party that claimed to speak for them. In the decade between her arrival in New York City and her conversion to Catholicism in 1927, she lived the life of a political radical to the fullest. Settling among the working poor on the Lower East Side, Day wrote for various radical newspapers, worked as a nurse during the Influenza Pandemic, and then dove into the Bohemian intellectual culture in Greenwich Village. Over the next few years she experienced several love affairs, a failed marriage, and had an abortion (which she fictionalized in her autobiographical novel, *The Eleventh Virgin*, in 1924). Not surprisingly, by the mid-1920s Day felt her life had spun out of control and began to withdraw from the radical literary and political scene.

When she settled into a common-law marriage with Forster Batterham in 1925, her life seemed to be taking on a recognizable form, which an unplanned (but welcomed by her) pregnancy the next year promised to complete. Instead, it brought to a head the religious crisis which had been building in Day's life since childhood, and had only been masked by the frantic political and literary activity of the previous decade. Her decision to have their daughter, Tamar Teresa, and then herself baptized in the Catholic Church shattered her marriage. By late 1927 she found herself adrift once again, a single mother (with a somewhat sordid and radical past) belonging to a conservative Church and alienated from her former associates, who rejected Catholicism as a reactionary and outdated religion.

For the next five years, Day supported herself as a writer, including a short and unsuccessful stint as a screenwriter in Hollywood and a period in Mexico, where she wrote somewhat sentimental and romanticized articles on its religious culture for Catholic periodicals such as *Commonweal* and *America*. Eventually, a childhood illness of Tamar and the worsening effects of the Great Depression forced her to return to America, where she continued to scrape together a living as a freelance writer while she struggled to find a way to reconcile her newfound religious faith and her commitment to radical politics and the poor. In early December 1932, she went to Washington, D.C., to cover the Hunger March on the Capitol. "The feast of the Immaculate Conception was the next day and I went out to the National Shrine and assisted at solemn high Mass there.

And the prayer that I offered up was that some way would be shown me, some way would be opened up for me to work for the poor and the oppressed. When I got back to New York, Peter Maurin was at the house waiting for me" (p. 28).

Peter Maurin, a French peasant twenty years older than Day, had spent his youth as a Christian Brother in France before immigrating to Canada. By the time an editor at *Commonweal* referred him to Day, he had already spent over two decades wandering around North America reflecting on the social teaching of the Catholic Church (such as it was at the time) and, like Day, seeking to find a way to use the Catholic tradition to challenge the dehumanizing effects of urban industrialism in modern society. Though not a scholar in the modern sense of the term, Maurin was widely read in theology, philosophy, history, and economics, and he introduced Day to a world of ideas and possibilities of which the narrow ethnic Catholicism she had previously experienced was completely unaware.

Recognizing her talents as a journalist and her receptivity to being "indoctrinated" in his ideas, Maurin pushed her to begin a newspaper to disseminate his thoughts about the reform of society along agrarian and Catholic lines. Thrilled to have finally found an outlet for both her political and religious impulses, Day scraped together several hundred dollars and published the first issue of *The Catholic Worker* newspaper on May 1, 1933. Maurin intended himself to be the sole author for the paper, with Day serving as editor and publisher, and was not pleased when the first issue included other voices, not all in agreement with his. Nevertheless, he ultimately accepted the role of teacher, muse, and columnist in the paper, which always bore his unmistakable imprint but ranged beyond his somewhat narrow and nostalgic ideals of a "back to the land" retreat from modern society.

At the same time, Maurin also encouraged Day to begin practicing the works of mercy herself as a response to the suffering caused by the Depression. She began, as she tells us in

House of Hospitality, by taking in or acquiring lodging for several poor women she encountered, which quickly grew into a full-time job of caring for and feeding the poor in her neighborhood, all while editing and publishing the newspaper and supporting herself as a freelance writer. This became the St. Joseph House, the first Catholic Worker community.

Through the newspaper, Day became the public face of the Catholic Worker movement. The paper's circulation grew rapidly, from 2,500 copies in May 1933 to 20,000 by year's end, and to 100,000 by 1936. While these numbers would fluctuate for the remainder of the decade, depending on the popularity of the causes which Day would champion, it remained the dominant voice for Catholic social teaching in the United States and beyond, with subscriptions coming in from Europe, Asia, and even Africa. Following Day's example, readers established a string of Catholic Worker houses across the nation to meet the needs of the poor and to, in the words of Maurin, "build a new society within the shell of the old."

Day remained incredibly active throughout the decade, bringing her journalistic experience to bear when covering strikes, protests, and the daily inhumanities which governments and individuals alike inflict upon the poor, all the while encouraging her readers and the leaders of the Church to respond both individually and corporately to these evils. At its best, her writing evokes the muckraking journalism of the Progressive Era, by which she had made her living in the early 1920s, prior to her conversion. In *House of Hospitality*, though, a new and more profound element appears in her writing, as she attempts not simply to describe and denounce these injustices, but also to penetrate the mystery of human suffering and death, which she beheld on a daily basis.

Indeed, death and madness stalk the pages of *House of Hospitality*, especially the death of the young. Joe Bennett, fellow Catholic worker, dead at twenty-four. Fred Brown, the unemployed seaman, also struck down at twenty-four. An unnamed child whose funeral procession passed by the Catholic Worker house. The prostitute Lucille, dying from syphilis at age twenty-three and abandoned in a shed until Day's companions discovered and cared for her until her death. Those with delusions of persecution, Bernard Adelson of himself, Mr. Breen of the Church. Sarah Harding, shrieking from her window in the middle of the night until she is taken away to Bellevue. The mentally ill who appeared on her doorstep daily for food, clothing, and shelter. The names pour out endlessly in her writings, as do the struggles and sufferings behind each one.

As *House of Hospitality* shows clearly, by the end of the 1930s the physical and emotional stresses of the Catholic Worker movement had stripped Day of any romantic illusions about the poor she might have ever entertained. Likewise, the economic hardship caused by the Great Depression seemed destined to continue indefinitely, guaranteeing a never-ending stream of poor and broken souls demanding her help. The pressure of her responsibilities as a mother, writer, editor, speaker — all piled atop her work of feeding and clothing the poor, whose numbers seemed only to increase — was enormous. Frequently, we find Day, overwhelmed but undefeated, struggling to make sense of it all: "As I sit I am weeping. I have been torn recently by people, by things that happen. Surely we are, here in our community, made up of poor lost ones, the abandoned ones, the sick, the crazed and the solitary human beings whom Christ so loved and in whom I see, with a terrible anguish, the body of this death" (p. 125).

Surrounded by such misery, Day responded in the only way she could, forcing a solution by an act of will rather than discovering one through an act of the mind:

> Love and ever more love is the only solution to every problem that comes up. If we love each other enough, we will bear with each other's faults and burdens. If we love enough, we are going to light that fire in the hearts of others. And it is love that will burn out the sins and hatreds that sadden

us. It is love that will make us want to do great things for each other. No sacrifice and no suffering will then seem too much. (p. 267)

And in responding thus, she began to understand fully for the very first time her favorite passage from Dostoevsky's *The Brothers Karamazov*, where Father Zosima, confronted by a woman who dreams of distributing all her wealth and serving the poor but holds back for fear of the opinion of others, reveals the beautiful but terrible truth of the Christian life: "Love in action is a harsh and dreadful thing compared with love in dreams" (p. 166).

In retrospect, August 1939 seems an especially propitious moment for her to offer an initial account of the founding and nature of the Catholic Worker movement. The months leading up to the publication of *House of Hospitality* (or following it — the precise date is unclear) coincided with Day's discovery of the rigorous and heroic (some said perfectionist) spirituality of the Canadian Jesuit Onesimus Lacouture. In the Lacouture Retreat (which she attended almost annually from the early 1940s until the late 1960s), Day began to acquire a theological vocabulary to interpret her conversion and work which would bear fruit in *The Long Loneliness*. Day would write there of her initial experience of what she termed simply "the Retreat": "Though still I saw through a glass darkly, I saw things as a whole for the first time with a delight, a joy, an excitement, which is hard to describe. This is what I expected when I became Catholic. This is what all my reading had led me to expect in the way of teaching and guidance in the spiritual life."

If Day was on the cusp of profound interior changes in 1939, her work with the Catholic Worker movement was also facing equally profound external challenges. Over the next several years, the wartime economic boom, the closure of many

Catholic Worker houses due to the conscription or enlistment of young men, and the deep internal divisions caused by Day's radical pacifism would threaten the very existence of the movement. Under the psychological and spiritual pressures brought on by the war, Day herself would withdraw from the Catholic Worker movement for six months in late 1943 for an extended period of prayer and reflection, before making a final and irrevocable commitment to it. Despite her refusal to participate in it, the war proved as transformational for Day as it was for the world as a whole. She emerged from it with a hard-earned spiritual maturity that found its perfect expression in *The Long Loneliness*, and that would see her and the Catholic Worker movement through the challenges confronting them in an increasingly affluent, secularized, and militarized postwar America.

In this postwar environment, *House of Hospitality* was quickly forgotten, both by Day (who rarely made any mention of it) and the public at large (since it was never reprinted after its first appearance). The reasons for its oblivion are not hard to find. As a theological meditation on the origins of the Catholic Worker movement, it was definitively superseded by *The Long Loneliness*. As an account of her day-to-day existence in the 1930s, it is less detailed than her recently published diaries, *The Duty of Delight*. Stylistically, it lacks the narrative unity and polish of *Loaves and Fishes*. By any objective measure, *House of Hospitality* stands on the periphery of Day's canon, not at its heart.

Nevertheless, *House of Hospitality* remains an essential document for understanding Dorothy Day. Over seventy-five years after its appearance, it has the unique ability to take us back to the moment when Day had not yet mythologized for herself the origins of the Catholic Worker movement or her own conversion. Separated as we are from her by time, death, and the legend that has grown around her life, this nearly forgotten book offers us a glimpse, not of a legendary social activist or of a saint, but rather of a single mother living among and fighting on behalf of the poor, trying (and often failing) to make sense of the injustice and death she confronted daily. Eventually, the meaning of her experiences would become clearer, but in *House of Hospitality* they remain wrapped in mystery. In reading this, her *minor opus*, we can share in that mystery, walking with Day along the first steps of the journey that she called "the downward path of salvation" (see p. 283).

Note About the Text

The text herein is a reproduction of the 1939 edition of *House of Hospitality*. With the exception of minor typographical errors, the original text (with Dorothy Day's sometimes idiosyncratic style and spelling) and formatting have been preserved in its entirety. Scripture references in brackets have been provided by the editor.

All notes in the text are by the editor and are limited to those figures and events which can assist the modern reader to appreciate the literary and theological sources of Day's spirituality, and the breadth of her influence in the Catholic intellectual, social, and ecclesial circles of her day. No effort has been made to identify the countless persons mentioned in the text that worked in or were served by the Catholic Worker community. Their identities, known now only to God, will surely be revealed in the Last Judgment.

Foreword

1

THE story of the *Catholic Worker* begins with Peter. If it were not for Peter there would be no *Catholic Worker*. If it were not for Peter there would be no Houses of Hospitality and Farming Communes. Peter has changed the life of thousands of people. I met Peter Maurin in December, 1932, right after the Hunger March staged by the Communists.

This is the way the movement Peter now heads began. For five years after my conversion to the Catholic Church I had been living a quiet and studious life. I had earned my living by working as bookseller, cook, research worker, synopsist, dialogue writer and newspaper correspondent. I had been to Hollywood, to Mexico, to Florida, and a good part of the time I had lived in New York.[1]

In the fall of 1932 I had been writing articles for *America* and the *Commonweal,* and the first week in December I went to Washington, D.C., to cover the Hunger March of the Unemployed Councils, and the Farmer's Convention. Both were Communist-led.[2]

If the journalists and the police of Washington had been coached in their parts, they could not have staged a better drama,

---

1 For a fuller account of the period between Day's conversion and first meeting with Peter Maurin, see her *The Long Loneliness* (New York: Harper and Row, 1952), 138-166; see also Jim Forest, *All Is Grace: A Biography of Dorothy Day* (Maryknoll, NY: Orbis, 2011), 87-100.

2 During the early 1930s the National Unemployed Council, sponsored by the Communist Party but including many (estimated by Day to be 90 percent) non-communists, staged a series of "Hunger Marches" around the country, including two in Washington, DC (in March and December 1932). Day accurately captures the atmosphere of hysteria and fear of insurrection which surrounded these events, as well as the government's heavy-handed response.

from the Communist standpoint, than they did in the events of that week.

Drama was what the Communist leaders of the march wanted, and drama, even melodrama, was what they got. They weren't presenting their petitions to Congress with any hope of immediately obtaining the cash bonuses and unemployment relief they demanded. (Nevertheless five years later unemployment insurance became part of Social Security legislation.) They were presenting pictorially the plight of the workers of America, not only to the countless small towns and large cities through which they passed, not only to the Senate and the House of Representatives, but through the press to the entire world. And in addition they were demonstrating to the proletariat.

They were saying, "Come, submit yourselves to our discipline, — place yourselves in our hands, you union-workers, you unemployed, and we will show you how a scant 3,000 of you, unarmed, can terrorize authorities and make them submit to at least some of your demands!"

It does not matter that the victory won was only that of marching to the Capitol. To those unarmed marchers who for two days and two cold nights in December lived and slept on an asphalt highway with no water, no fires, no sanitary facilities, with the scantiest of food, surrounded by hysteria in the shape of machine guns, tear and nauseous gas bombs, in the hands of a worn and fretted police force, egged on by a bunch of ghouls in the shape of newspaper men and photographers, — to these marchers, the victory was a real one. They had achieved their purpose.

They had dramatized their plight for the workers themselves and given them a taste of power. They might be booed by police, sneered at by the Vice-President, they might be hungry, unshaven, shivering and exhausted, but they felt a sense of power when they saw a whole capital, the center of their country, mobilized against them.

When they had finally gained permission to march, they set out jauntily, defiantly, conscious of victory, though they were escorted through the streets as prisoners, even as they had been prisoners since Sunday, on blockaded New York Avenue, between the government-owned hillside and the miles of railway tracks on the other side.

They were victors in that they had forced an unfriendly press to play into their hands and give them headlines and pages of dramatic publicity. They were victors in that they had induced the press to excite the police to a brutal and stupid show of force.

I do not blame the harried police, the firemen, the reserves, even though they cursed and bullied and taunted the marchers as though they were trying to provoke a bloody conflict. I blame the press which for a few ghastly headlines, a few gruesome pictures, was ready to precipitate useless violence towards a group of unemployed human beings who were being used as "Communist tactics," as "shock troops" in the "class struggle."

It is true that the Hunger March was led by Communists. But it is also true that ninety percent of the marchers were union men and women or unskilled, unorganized workers who were not Communists, but were accepting for the time being, the leadership of the militant Unemployed Councils, affiliated with the Communist party. "No other leaders presented themselves," they argued, "nothing was being done for us. We accepted this leadership and accepted the means offered by them to dramatize our plight."

2

I went through Union Square in New York the week before, just as the Hunger Marchers were getting ready to pull out for Washington. It was sunny but very sharp and cold and the fresh-ploughed sod of the park had a frozen, barren look.

About twenty-five trucks were lined up at the north end of the square and a few thousand "comrades" were gathered around to "make a demonstration" and see off their friends, the delegates chosen from the various Unemployed Councils of New York. The march on Washington was organized by the National Committee of these Unemployed Councils, and for the past weeks delegates had been setting out from all over the United States, from California, from Washington, Oregon, and all the Middle Western states.

Details of the plan of march were given months before in the *Daily Worker*, the Communist newspaper. For the past months collections had been taken up at all Communist meetings to finance the march, and the trucks were hired for $100 apiece for nine days to take the delegates to Washington and back again. According to the published plan, the delegates were to get to Washington, demonstrating on the way in town and village, parade in Washington, present their petition, and turn about and return to their homes, in the same organized fashion. Discipline was to be maintained, violence was to be avoided, food and lodging were to be requested from the cities en route and from Washington, but all preparations such as the hiring of halls, rooms and food for the delegates were to be made beforehand.

Carl Winter, the secretary of the Unemployed Council of New York, was a mild, serious man of thirty-five or so, said by his companions to be a good organizer and a respected leader. He was a modest man, and refused to be photographed by the newsreel men, urging Anna Burlak, Karl Reeve, and Ben Gold to go before the cameras. Anna Burlak was a tall, blond, handsome girl of twenty-two, one of the leaders of textile workers of New England.

I talked with George Granich, one of the delegates on the march and the pay-off man for the truckmen. George was an old friend of mine. "The New England bunch got in last night," he said, "and they were offered accommodations at the Municipal Lodging House by the city. But to get these accommodations it was necessary to go through all sorts of red tape, and the giving up of one's clothes to be fumigated, so everyone went down to the Manhattan Lyceum and slept wrapped in their blankets on the floor. These delegates are all picked anyway, to withstand hardship on the march. They're a strong bunch and ready to sleep in the trucks if they have to."

An attempt had been made to bar members of the "oppressed races" from the march ("the hundred-percent American police would have had it in for them," Granich said), but the seamen's groups insisted on bringing along Filipino delegates. The marine workers who occupied the first trucks were a colorful group, made up as they were of all races. The sailors wore their tight-fitting dungarees, woven belts, wind-breakers and pulled-down woolen caps.

The line of march as planned, lay through Jersey City, Elizabeth, Newark, New Brunswick, Trenton, Philadelphia, Chester, Wilmington, Baltimore and on to Washington.

I did not follow the progress of the Western group going into Washington, but the progress of the Northern group was typical. There was no trouble for the marchers in any of the cities on the way until they reached Wilmington. There they were holding a meeting in a church and Ben Gold, one of the leaders, was making a speech, when suddenly windows were broken simultaneously on either side of the hall and tear gas bombs were thrown in. The meeting was in an uproar and milled out into the street in anything but orderly fashion, as was natural. There the police took the opportunity to club and beat the marchers. Ben Gold, after being badly beaten, was jailed, and the march went on without him.

On Sunday, with the Hunger Marchers approaching Washington, the city, according to the papers, was in a state bordering on hysteria. There were riot drills of the marines at Quantico; guards at the White House, Capitol, Treasury, power plants, arsenals of the National Guard, the American Legion, countless volunteers, supplemented by 370 firemen, all were armed with machine guns, tear gas, nauseating gas, revolvers, sawed-off shot guns, night sticks, lengths of rubber hose. The newspapers with scareheads and photographs of the radical "army" fanned flames of hostility, and of actual fear in the public.

When I went out with some newspaper men to meet the marchers and to visit their final encampment, I was struck by the fact that perhaps the most frightened of all were the newspaper men. They implored their editors to authorize the purchase of gas masks (thirty dollars apiece) and they kept a good distance away from the marchers, and with their eyes open for the best means of escape should anything happen.

In addition to the marchers, groups of liberals came to the city to give their moral support and to add their petitions to those of the 3,000 marchers. There were delegates from the League of Professional Groups which was formed before the national election to support the Communist candidates and which is now continuing its propaganda to support the Communist movement. Members of this delegation included Malcolm Cowley, one of the editors of the *New Republic*, Matthew Josephson, magazine writer and author of several biographies, James Rorty, poet, John Hermann, novelist and winner of a Scribner prize, Michael Gold, writer for the *Daily Worker*, Charles Rumford Walker, former associate editor of the *Atlantic Monthly*, and others.

When the news came that the marchers were being held prisoners in the half-mile stretch of roadway, fifty feet wide, this group of liberals joined forces with the National Committee for the Defence of Political Prisoners to take legal action to free them. A writ of habeas corpus was taken out and an injunction asked against the city commissioners.

Various women's organizations, pacifist groups, the Fellowship of Reconciliation, Quakers, and others protested against the ludicrous and uncalled-for show of force. There were no Catholic groups protesting.

Only one paper in Washington, the Scripps-Howard *Daily News*, gave a calm, unhysterical account of the situation. It suggested editorially that the marchers were within their rights in wishing to present their petition and that such imprisonment of the marchers and show of force were both unnecessary and unconstitutional.

The other papers screamed of the "mad fanaticism" of the marchers, "fanned to wild fury by the inflammatory speeches of the leaders." *The Star* spoke of razor blades secreted in the shoes of the marchers which could, if kicked with properly, sever arteries of the police. They hinted "they may be armed." And they went on in this way through edition after edition, Sunday and all day Monday.

Then on Tuesday morning it was announced that the marchers were to parade and to leave that night. And so, after this permission to parade had been refused steadily before and since their entry into Washington, they did parade, just as they had set out to do, just as the campaign had been mapped out for them in the *Daily Worker* a month before. The plan was delayed, but not defeated.

The papers did their best to make a riot out of it and failed. They merely presented to public view the Communist leaders who could carry through successfully a planned and disciplined demonstration. And the Washingtonians who lined the streets by the thousands to watch the procession, laughed tolerantly at the songs and slogans, and said admiringly, "They sure have got gumption, standing up against the police that way."

3

I watched that ragged horde and thought to myself, "These are Christ's poor. He was one of them. He was a man like other men, and He chose His friends amongst the ordinary workers.

These men feel they have been betrayed by Christianity. Men are not Christian today. If they were, this sight would not be possible. Far dearer in the sight of God perhaps are these hungry ragged ones, than all those smug, well-fed Christians who sit in their homes, cowering in fear of the Communist menace."

I felt that they were my people, that I was part of them. I had worked for them and with them in the past, and now I was a Catholic and so could not be a Communist.[3] I could not join this united front of protest and I wanted to.

The feast of the Immaculate Conception was the next day and I went out to the National Shrine and assisted at solemn high Mass there. And the prayer that I offered up was that some way would be shown me, some way would be opened up for me to work for the poor and the oppressed.

When I got back to New York, Peter Maurin was at the house waiting for me.[4]

He had come in a few days before and had met my brother and sister-in-law with whom I was living. John was working nights on one of the Hearst papers and Tessa was going to have a baby. John did not earn very much so they had moved in with me.

It was a tenement apartment, four rooms deep and there was a yard in back. There were peach trees and fig trees in the yard, planted by Italian tenants. Privet hedges lined the fences and hid their bleak ugliness. In the summer half the yard was fenced in to protect the beds of petunias that scattered their

---

3 While Day had been involved in radical politics since her time at the University of Illinois (1914-1916), she was never a member of the Communist Party. She did officially join the Socialist Party while in college, but "the meetings were dull, and I didn't attend very many" (*The Long Loneliness*, 47).

4 Peter Maurin (1877-1949) was the decisive influence on Day's conversion, introducing her to Catholic social teaching and providing her a means to synthesize her political convictions with orthodox Catholicism. For a fuller account of his life, see Day and Francis Sicius, *Peter Maurin: Apostle to the World* (Maryknoll, NY: Orbis, 2004). See also Marc H. Ellis, *Peter Maurin: Prophet of the Twentieth Century* (New York: Paulist, 1981).

fragrance even there between the canyons of buildings. Both on the Fourteenth Street and Fifteenth Street side, the buildings were five and six stories high. Next door and down the block the gardens were the same, and the Italians used to sit and smoke their pipes under the stunted trees at night.

We were on the first floor and in the basement below was a barber shop with an organ in the rear where the Italian barber used to play sad tunes at night when his work was finished. Germans and Italians lived next door and upstairs.

I slept in the noisy front room, noisy because people came in all night and slammed the outside door and stamped up and down the bare steps. The milkman started the noise again at four in the morning. But one gets used to these things.

In the second room my daughter Teresa slept.[5] Teresa was six. There was just room there for a bed and dresser. It was also a passage to the next room, which was in turn a passage to the kitchen. John and Tessa slept in the room next to the kitchen. The kitchen was also our sitting room, library and dining room, but we were not as crowded as most of our neighbors. We had to heat the place with gas. The front room was a north room, and cold. The kitchen was heated by the cooking and by the gas oven, an expensive form of heat (the poor are always extravagant) and it was a south, sunny room, so we lived in it all winter, only using the bedrooms for sleeping purposes.

Tessa and John were twenty-one and twenty-two years old then. They were happy and carefree and didn't mind being crowded and having lots of company. And Tessa was Spanish.

It was because she was Spanish and hospitable that she welcomed Peter when he came. John is more reserved.

They often talk of that first night Peter Maurin walked in. He was wearing a khaki shirt and shabby stained pants and an

---

5   Tamar Teresa Hennessy (1926-2008). Day's decision to have Teresa baptized into the Catholic Church, followed by herself in 1927, led to the dissolution of her common-law marriage with Teresa's father, Forster Hennessy. See *The Long Loneliness*, 132-151.

overcoat, the pockets of which were crammed with books and papers. When he started looking for something he pulled glasses out of his pocket (glasses which he bought along the Bowery for thirty cents and which magnified) and perched them halfway down his nose. For a year or so he wore a pair which had one ear-piece missing so they sagged on one side of his face.

On this night however, he did not stop to look for papers. He came in brusquely and wanted to know where I was. Hearing that I would be back in a day or so, he started indoctrinating Tessa.

Holding out one finger, from a position of vantage in the middle of the floor he began reciting his phrased essays, enunciating them so that one could almost see them clear and black against a page.[6]

"People go to Washington,
  asking the Federal Government
  to solve their economic problems.
  But the Federal Government
  was never meant
  to solve men's economic problems.
  Thomas Jefferson says,
  'The less government there is
  the better it is.'
  If the less government there is,
  the better it is,
  the best kind of government
  is self-government.
  If the best kind of government
  is self-government,
  then the best kind of organization

---

6   Maurin's free-verse "essays" have remained a staple of the *Catholic Worker* paper, and are collected in Peter Maurin, *Easy Essays* (Catholic Worker Reprint Series; Eugene, OR: Wipf & Stock, 2010).

is self-organization.
When the organizers try
to organize the unorganized,
they often do it for the benefit
of the organizers.
The organizers don't organize themselves.
And when the organizers don't organize themselves,
nobody organizes himself.
And when nobody organizes himself,
nothing is organized."

Tessa was making supper, trying to find John's tie, and being hospitable and listening with one ear. This probably sounded anarchistic to her, caught in passing as it were, but her father is an anarchist so she felt quite at home with Peter. Tessa herself was a Communist.

Peter spoke and still speaks with a strong accent, but Tessa also was used to accents. Peter came from Languedoc near the border of Spain twenty-five years ago. Even his type was familiar to her, short and sturdy, shoulders broad and powerful, features hewed as though out of rock.

John confessed afterward that he thought of an anarchist friend, truly unbalanced, whom I tried to avoid and said that if he had been home alone he would not have told Peter that I would be back in a few days.

But nothing could have kept Peter from finding me, once he had made up his mind. He had read some articles I had written in the *Sign* and the *Commonweal* and had determined that I should start on his program of social reconstruction.

If I had not said those prayers down in Washington — if I had not been reading the lives of the saints, canonized and as yet uncanonized, St. John Bosco and Rose Hawthorne for instance — I probably would have listened, but continued to write rather than act.

4

It has taken us years to pry Peter's story from him. He deals with ideas and considers personalities unimportant, and it has only been little by little and day by day that we have gained a knowledge of his background. He was born in a small village in the southern part of France, and his own mother died when he was nine years old. His father married again and there were twenty-three children in the family. Every now and then Peter tells us about the communal aspects of life in a little village; the bake-oven which all the villagers used; the flour mill. They had a big stone house and the sheep were housed on the first floor and the family on the second. When Peter was a young man he became a cocoa salesman travelling all over France. Finally, he reached Paris where he associated with the radicals of the day and continued his studies. He first came to Canada as a homesteader, but when his partner was killed in a hunting accident he gave it up and began wandering around the country doing whatever work came to hand. He has worked in steel mills, coal mines, lumber camps, on railroads. He has dug ditches and sewers, and worked as janitor in city tenements. He has taught French, and has always continued studying. Always he was an agitator, speaking on street corners and in public squares, indoctrinating the men with whom he came in contact in lodging houses, coffee shops and along the wayside.

"We must study history," he says, "in order to find out why things are as they are. In the light of history we should so work today that things will be different in the future." Journalists, he believes, should not merely report history, but make history by influencing the time in which they write. In other words they should be propagandists and agitators as he himself has always been. He started to write, he says, because he could not get enough people to listen to him, and his writing was influenced, technically at least, by the works of Charles Péguy, who also wrote in short phrased lines. St. Augustine had used this technique in writing his meditations, finding it a help to break up the sentences into phrases that catch the eye.

Peter always had sheaves of these writings in his pockets, and he began visiting the offices of Catholic papers and magazines trying to get them printed. At times he mimeographed copies of his work and distributed them himself. Always he emphasized voluntary poverty and the works of mercy as the techniques by which the masses could be reached, and he lived as he taught. He has the simplicity of a saint or a genius, believing that everyone is interested in what he has to teach, believing that everyone will play his part in the lay apostolate.

He was living at that time in Uncle Sam's hotel down on the Bowery where he paid fifty cents a night for his room. Today, as he travels all over the country, speaking at colleges and seminaries, he still lives in flop houses, sleeps in bus stations, and eats in dingy lunchrooms on the "Skid Rows" of the country. He possesses only the clothes that he wears and the books that he has in his pocket. He has no desk at which to write, no office — in fact, no home except the Catholic Worker Houses of Hospitality throughout the country. He is the most completely detached person that it has ever been my privilege to meet.

When we met he had been working in a boys' camp up near Mount Tremper, New York, for four years, cutting ice in winter, quarrying rock, and doing odd jobs about the camp. He was working without pay but when he came to New York, Father Scully, who had charge of the camp, gave him a dollar a day to live on. After weeks of stimulating discussion around Union Square he would go back to the camp to continue his studying and his writing. These years seem to me to have been years of preparation for the work that he is doing today. He had drawn up a program of action which was simple and comprehensive. He feels it is not enough merely to bring the workers propaganda by way of a newspaper, pamphlets, and leaflets. One must combine this with the direct action of the works of mercy: feeding the hungry, clothing the naked, sheltering the homeless, in order that one may instruct the ignorant, counsel the doubtful, and comfort the afflicted. The corporal and the spiritual works, according to Peter, must go hand in hand, and getting out the *Catholic Worker* and distributing literature were to Peter performing spiritual works of mercy.

In order to carry on this work, he said, we needed hospices such as they had in the Middle Ages, and he always referred to these hospices as "Houses of Hospitality." In regard to this he wrote the following in an early issue of the paper:

THE DUTY OF HOSPITALITY

People who are in need
*   and are not afraid to beg*
*   give to people not in need*
*   the occasion to do good*
*   for goodness' sake.*

Modern society calls the beggar
*   bum and panhandler*
*   and gives him the bum's rush.*

But the Greeks used to say
*   that people in need*
*   are the ambassadors of the gods.*

Although you may be called bums
*   and panhandlers*
*   You are in fact the Ambassadors of God.*

As God's Ambassadors
*   you should be given food, clothing and shelter*
*   by those who are able to give it.*

Mahometan teachers tell us
*   that God commands hospitality.*

And hospitality is still practised
　　in Mahometan countries.

But the duty of hospitality
　　is neither taught nor practiced
　　in Christian countries.

THE MUNICIPAL LODGINGS

That is why you who are in need
　　are not invited to spend the night
　　in the homes of the rich.

There are guest rooms today
　　in the homes of the rich
　　but they are not for those
　　who need them.

And they are not for those
　　who need them
　　because those who need them
　　are no longer considered the Ambassadors
　　of God.

So people no longer
　　consider hospitality to the poor
　　as a personal duty.

And it does not disturb them a bit
　　to send them to the city
　　where they are given the hospitality
　　of the "Muni"
　　at the expense of the taxpayer.

But the hospitality that the "Muni"
　　gives to the down and out
　　is no hospitality

because what comes from the taxpayer's pocketbook
does not come from his heart.

BACK TO HOSPITALITY

The Catholic unemployed
  should not be sent to the "Muni."

The Catholic unemployed
  should be given hospitality
  in Catholic Houses of Hospitality.

Catholic Houses of Hospitality
  are known in Europe
  under the name of Hospices.

There have been Hospices in Europe
  since the time of Constantine.

Hospices are free guest houses;
  hotels are paying guest houses.

And paying guest houses or hotels
  are as plentiful
  as free guest houses or Hospices
  are scarce.

So hospitality like everything else
  has been commercialized.

So hospitality like everything else
  must now be idealized.

HOUSES OF HOSPITALITY

We need Houses of Hospitality
  to give to the rich
  the opportunity to serve the poor.

We need Houses of Hospitality
to bring the Bishops to the people
and the people to the Bishops.

We need Houses of Hospitality
to bring back to institutions
the technique of institutions.

We need Houses of Hospitality
to show what idealism looks like
when it is practiced.

We need Houses of Hospitality
to bring Social Justice
through Catholic Action
exercised in Catholic Institutions.

HOSPICES

We read in the Catholic Encyclopedia
that during the early ages of Christianity
the hospice (or the House of Hospitality)
was a shelter for the sick, the poor,
the orphans, the old, the traveler
and the needy of every kind.

Originally the hospices (or Houses of Hospitality)
were under the supervision of the bishops who
designated priests
to administer the spiritual and temporal affairs of
these charitable institutions.

The fourteenth statute of the so-called
Council of Carthage held about 436
enjoins upon the bishops
to have hospices (or Houses of Hospitality)
in connection with their churches.

PARISH HOUSES OF HOSPITALITY

Today we need Houses of Hospitality
    as much as they needed them then
    if not more so.

We have Parish Houses for the priests
    Parish Houses for educational purposes
    Parish Houses for recreational purposes
    But no Parish Houses of Hospitality.

Bossuet says that the poor
    are the first children of the Church
    so the poor should come first.

People with homes should have
    a room of hospitality
    so as to give shelter to the needy
    members of the parish.

The remaining needy members of the parish
    should be given shelter in a Parish Home.

Furniture, clothing and food
    should be sent to the needy
    members of the Parish
    from the Parish House of Hospitality.

We need Parish Homes
    as well as Parish Domes.

In the new Cathedral of Liverpool
    there will be a Home as well as a
    Dome.

HOUSES OF "CATHOLIC ACTION"

Catholic Houses of Hospitality
    should be more than free guest houses
    for the Catholic unemployed.

They could be vocational training schools
    including the training for the priesthood
    as Father Corbett proposes.

They could be Catholic reading rooms
    as Father McSorley proposes.

They could be Catholic Instruction Schools
    as Father Cornelius Hayes proposes.

They could be Round-Table Discussion Groups
    as Peter Maurin proposes.

In a word, they could be
    Catholic Action Houses
    where Catholic Thought
    is combined with Catholic Action.

5

But while Peter read aloud his inspired lines on hospitality we had as yet no office. I had worked on the first issue of the paper at the kitchen table after supper, at the library, sitting in the park in the afternoon with Teresa.

Peter's idea of hospices seemed a simple and logical one to me, hospices such as they had in the Middle Ages for the poor and the wayfarer and which we certainly very much needed today. But I liked even better his talks about personal responsibility. He quoted St. Jerome, that every house should have a "Christ's room" for our brother who was in need. That "the coat which hangs in one's closet belongs to the poor." Living in tenements as I had for years I had found many of the poorest practising these teachings.

I was familiar enough with the hospitality of the Communist, with the voluntary poverty of the Communist. At a meeting that very week of the farmers' delegation, coming back from Washington and going back to their homes in the Middle West and New England, the chairman had called upon the audience to provide hospitality for the delegates.

"Who has an empty bed in their homes?" he wanted to know. "Who will put up one of the comrades for the next few days?" And hundreds of hands were raised.

It was like the Christian gesture put forth by the *Daily Worker* during the seamen's strike two years ago when the editors called upon the readers to provide Christmas dinners to the strikers, and so many responded that two thousand were fed. In the old days many of my friends had hitch-hiked around the country organizing for unions and for Communist affiliates, and they were always put up in homes of the workers and shared their poverty with them.

If one worked for one's fellows it was obvious that one had to embrace voluntary poverty, though the Communist would not call it by that name. Even now when we talk of it in the *Catholic Worker* as an indispensable means to an end, they claim that we are trying to lower the standard of living of the masses.

But of course it was getting out a labor paper which caught my imagination, popularizing the teachings of the Church in regard to social matters, bringing to the man in the street a Christian solution of unemployment, a way of rebuilding the social order.

Peter brought up the idea of the paper the first time I met him and he kept harping on it, day after day. He told me I needed a Catholic background, and he came day after day with books and papers and digests of articles which he either read aloud or left with me to read.

I was doing some research then on peace, for a women's club, and was in the library until three every afternoon. And every day when I got home I found Peter waiting to "indoctrinate" me. He stayed until ten when I insisted he had to go home. He followed Tessa and me around the house, indoctrinating. If we were getting supper, washing dishes, ironing clothes, or washing them, he continued his conversations. If company came in he started over again from the beginning.

Teresa had measles that winter, and Peter followed the doctor around, commenting on the news of the day, hopefully looking for a stray apostle. He approached the plumber, the landlord when he came to collect the rent, the grocery clerk. When he had to stay away because so small a house had to be kept in peace and quiet during sickness, he spent his time at the Rand school, making a digest of Kropotkin's *Fields, Factories and Workshops* for me.[7]

It was impossible to be with a person like Peter without sharing his simple faith that the Lord would provide what was necessary to do His work. Peter had counted on some priest to provide a mimeograph machine to get out the first issues of the paper, but nothing came of it. So I began planning a printed edition. It would cost only fifty-seven dollars to get out 2,500 copies of an eight-page paper and I had some money coming in from articles. When I spoke of the work to Father Purcell, then editor of the *Sign*, he held up Father Ahearn of Newark for ten dollars and Sister Peter Claver[8] for one dollar and handed me that. They were the first contributors to the work. Father McSorley,[9] of the Paulists also helped by giving me work and advice.

Later that winter, Peter had to go up to the camp where he had been working for the past four years to put in some time cutting ice. He came down for a Catholic Industrial Conference

---

7   Peter Kropotkin (1842-1921), Russian nobleman and one of the main theorists of modern anarchism. His ideas had a seminal influence on Day and deeply affected the voluntaristic and non-hierarchical structure of the Catholic Worker movement.

8   Sister Peter Claver, C.PP.S. (1899-2004), famously the first contributor to the *Catholic Worker* paper, also introduced Day to the Retreat Movement of Father Onesimus Lacouture, S.J.

9   Rev. Joseph Augustine McSorley, C.S.P. (1874-1963), a prolific author in his own right, served as a spiritual adviser for Day and as an "official adviser" of the Catholic Worker movement for the Archdiocese of New York during much of the 1930s.

which was held at the Astor in February but returned again for another few months. When the paper came out on May 1, 1933, he was still in the country.

The first issue was sold in Union Square on May Day. Two hundred thousand Communists and trade unionists paraded, gathered in the Square and dispersed all during that long hot day. A friendly priest sent a young convert, Joe Bennet, and two other young Catholics, to help sell copies. The two latter fled in short order. The sarcasm and questionings as to the place of a Catholic paper in Union Square was disconcerting. Joe, tall, gaunt and crippled, stayed throughout the day.

He is dead now, poor Joe, and he did not want to die. He was only twenty-four and he enjoyed every moment of living, enjoyed it seriously, with great earnestness. His faith was a tremendous thing to him and he wanted to do great things for God. But he had rheumatic fever and he suffered much, and his frail body could not stand the strain of his energetic desires. He worked with us for a time, later for Father Purcell in Alabama, and then two years ago, he came back to us to die.

That first issue took up the question of the cooperatives, of the Negro in labor, of the trade unions, of the unemployed. One of Peter's essays which caught all eyes, dealt with the dynamite of the Church.

> Albert J. Nock says,
>   "The Catholic Church
>   will have to do more
>   than to play
>   a waiting game:
>   she will have to make use
>   of some of the dynamite
>   inherent in her message."
>
> To blow the dynamite
>   of a message,

is the only way
to make that message
dynamic.

Catholic scholars
have taken the dynamite
of the church;
they have wrapped it up
in nice phraseology,
have placed it
in an hermetically
sealed container,
placed the lid
over the container,
and sat on the lid.

It is about time
to take the lid off
and to make
the Catholic dynamite
dynamic."

6

About this time my brother got a job as city editor of the Dobbs Ferry *Register* and moved there, so in a month or so I rented the store downstairs which the barber had vacated. At first, however, the first floor apartment was the office. The rent was twenty-five a month, too high for a heatless place. But there was always hot water and the house was clean. There were no desks, no files, no typewriters even, because I had sold mine to pay the second printing bill.

An expressman, a Communist, contributed the first furnishings in the way of an old desk and a filing cabinet. Someone else brought in an old typewriter. We let our wants be known in the columns of the paper and soon plenty of furniture began coming in. At times we were better furnished then than we are now. Often too people who had been evicted, who had lost their furniture and now were in a position to start housekeeping again, came to us in need of furniture and we were stripped bare again.

With the second issue of the paper, Dorothy Weston, who was only twenty-one, joined me. She had studied at Manhattanville, Fordham and Columbia, had a brilliant mind and was intensely interested in the work. Soon others came, a young Canadian, a New Englander, an unemployed real estate operator, a convert Jew, a Lithuanian boy of eighteen,[10] a bookkeeper, a former policeman, an Armenian refugee, a German distributist, and we had an editorial force, a circulation department and a very active group of propagandists.

A pot of stew and a pot of coffee were kept going on the coal range in the kitchen and all who came in were fed. We worked from early morning until midnight.

Teresa and I slept in the middle room between the kitchen and the store. In the summer we could also move a typewriter into the back yard and write or receive callers out there.

Homes had to be found for the men — some had been sleeping in Central Park — so we rented an eight-dollar-a-month apartment near Tompkins Square, a rat-ridden place, heatless and filthy, abandoned even by slum dwellers.

The paper's circulation increased from 2,500 to 20,000 in six months, but since it is a monthly it was not the paper alone which kept us busy. Neighbors came in needing clothes and we had to go to friends and readers begging for them.

---

10   Stanley Vishnewski (1916-1979), who would remain with the St. Joseph Catholic Worker house the rest of his life, also wrote a memoir covering the early years of the movement. See his *Wings of the Dawn* (New York: Catholic Worker, 1984).

People were being evicted on all sides. We had to find other apartments, help get relief checks for them, borrow pushcarts and move them.

We cooked, cleaned, wrote, went out on demonstrations to distribute literature, got out mimeographed leaflets, answered a tremendous correspondence, entertained callers. Bishop O'Hara, Bishop Busch, Monsignor Ryan,[11] Father Virgil Michel,[12] Father Parsons, Father Benedict Bradley, Carleton Hayes, Parker Moon, Jacques Maritain,[13] and many other visitors, — priests, laymen, seminarians, students, workers and scholars came to visit us day after day, even as they do now. They came to see what we were doing and they taught us much. Subscriptions came in from India, China, Italy, France, England, Germany, Africa, Australia, from countries all over the world. A *Catholic Worker* was published in England and another in Australia. The Canadian *Social Forum*, *The Christian Front*, *The Sower* (American), *The Right Spirit*, the Chicago *Catholic Worker*, these are more children.

By the time we had gotten out six issues of the paper the need to start a hospice for women made itself felt. With the seventh issue of the paper we announced its beginning. We called upon Saint Joseph to help us and we went to the curates of our parish, Father Seccor and Father Nicholas. They interested young working women who pledged their help. Among themselves they collected quarters to pay the rent. Girls who lived in unheated, cold-water flats gave their quarters to the extent of

---

11   Rev. Msgr. John A. Ryan (1869-1945), Catholic moral theologian and pioneer of Catholic social teaching in the Church in America.

12   Rev. Virgil Michel, O.S.B. (1888-1938), pioneer of the Liturgical Movement in the United States. Day, embracing his thought, introduced the Divine Office into community worship at a time when the Rosary (which she also prayed daily) was almost the sole form of public prayer for the laity.

13   Jacques Maritain (1882-1973), one of the foremost Catholic philosophers of the twentieth century and a leading voice for engagement with the modern world during this period. His writings were an important influence on the early Catholic Worker movement, and were in turn recommended regularly to readers of the paper.

fifteen dollars. Ten dollars came from a priest and ten dollars more came from a husband, who, from the bedside of his dying wife, sent this donation as one he knew she would be glad to make for the opening of a home for unemployed women. It was really not a house that we were opening up, but an apartment in the neighborhood, steam-heated, with a good big bath and six large rooms, five of which could be used as bedrooms. One room was even large enough to contain four beds. The rent was fifty dollars a month. The kitchen was large enough to be used as a small sitting room.

In the seventh issue of the paper we announced the opening and wrote:

"So far three beds are all that have been obtained although fifteen are needed. We also have four blankets, two of them donated by a woman the members of whose family are unemployed, save for one son who is working for ten dollars a week. She washed the blankets herself and sent them down to the office with prayers for the success of the new venture. Another woman, unable to afford to buy things herself, canvassed among her friends until she found one who voluntarily bought ten sheets and pillow slips. Another one of our readers sent in two sheets, another sent curtains and a blanket, and she is the mother of a large family and could well use them herself.

"The winter is on us and we can wait no longer. Even without furniture we have opened the doors. We will borrow blankets for the time being and use those of the editors. They can roll themselves in coats and newspapers, which are said to be very warm, though we are sure they are also very noisy. However, we hug to ourselves the assurance that all these things, such as blankets, will be added unto us, so we are not dismayed. Come to think of it, there are two rugs on the *Catholic Worker* floor which, if energetically beaten out, will serve as covers.

"Christ's first bed was of straw."

7

A year later we moved to an eleven-room house on Charles Street, where the women occupied the third floor, the men the second, and the offices the first. The dining room and kitchen were in the basement, the only warm part of this cold house which had no furnace and had to be heated room by room. A year after that we were offered the use of an old rear tenement house on Mott Street and here we are today.[14]

Throughout the country there are twenty-three hospices, each one now accommodating anywhere from a few people to one hundred and fifty. There are "cells" made up of interested readers who are personally practising voluntary poverty and the works of mercy. There are bread lines run at many of the houses so that now about five thousand a day are fed. In New York City over a thousand come every morning to breakfast.

We have fed workers during strikes. We have been out on picket lines. We have spoken at meetings all over the country to workers, unemployed, unorganized and organized, to students, professors, seminarians, priests and lay people. Through these contacts we have reached thousands more who have become lay apostles.

And now there are four farming communes, which are a step towards clarifying Peter's fourth step in his four point program — labor papers, round-table discussions, houses of hospitality, and farming communes. As Peter says there is no unemployment on the land. As St. Thomas said, "A certain amount of goods is necessary for a man to lead a good life." On the land there is a possibility of ownership. There is the possibility for a man to raise his own food. There is room for the

---

14   The original address of the St. Joseph Catholic Worker House was 144 Charles Street, relocating to 115 Mott Street in 1936, then to 221 Chrystie Street from 1950 to 1958, then to 39 Spring Street and back to 175 Chrystie Street over the following decade, before finally settling at its current address of 36 East First Street in 1968.

family on the land. In our endeavor to de-proletarianize the worker, as Pius XI advised in his encyclical *Forty Years After*,[15] we have advocated not only de-centralized industry, cooperatives, the ownership by the workers of the means of production, but also, the land movement.

The following pages are jottings written down during journeys, notes kept for my own comfort, information, clarification, or publication. They are random notes published now while we are in the midst of the work, in the heart of the conflict.

At any time the work is likely to be interrupted by visitors. Often I have written only a few paragraphs, or a few pages, only to be called away to deal with some problem of human misery.

Some will think, perhaps, that it is premature to present this sketchy material on the movement that the *Catholic Worker* has become to our friends and readers; but on the other hand, it may be a very useful volume to those thousands who wish to know more about the work we are doing in the lay apostolate. A great many of these notes were not written for publication, but for my own self in moments of trouble and in moments of peace and joy. So one cannot say that this is really the story of the *Catholic Worker* movement. That remains for some more disinterested person to cover. This Foreword is to give some background for these pages, most of which make up a notebook kept casually over a period of five years. I present it with apologies.

As St. Teresa of Avila[16] said in giving an account of her first foundation:

"If our Lord should give me grace to say anything that is good, the approval of grave and learned persons will be suf-

---

15   *Quadregisimo Anno* was issued by Pope Pius XI in 1931, commemorating and updating the foundational document of Catholic social teaching, Leo XIII's *Rerum Novarum* (1891).

16   St. Teresa of Ávila (1515-1582), Spanish mystic and reformer, foundress of the Discalced Carmelites. St. Teresa's forceful but warm personality appealed greatly to Day, who named her daughter after her.

ficient; and should there be anything useful, it will be God's, not mine; for I have no learning, nor goodness.... I write also as if by stealth and with trouble because thereby I am kept from spinning; and I live in a poor house and have a great deal of business. If our Lord had given me better abilities and a more retentive memory I might then have profited by what I heard or read, and so, if I should say anything good our Lord wills it for some good; and whatever is useless or bad, that will be mine … in other things, my being a woman is sufficient to account for my stupidity."

House of
Hospitality

ONE

1

"PYTHAGORAS used to divide his disciples' days into three parts: the first was for God and spent in prayer; the second for God and spent in study and meditation; the third for men and the business of life.

"Thus all the first two-thirds of the day were for God.

"And as a matter of fact, it is in the morning, before the distraction of our intercourse with men, that we must listen to God.

"But let us be precise. 'What,' you will ask me, 'is the meaning of listening to God? Must I, like the contemplatives of Hindustan, listen to him from dawn to midday with head bent between my hands or with eyes raised to Heaven? What am I to do in reality?'

"Here is my answer. You are to write....

"St. Augustine begins his Soliloquies thus: 'I was a prey to a thousand various thoughts and for many days had been making strenuous efforts to find myself, myself and my own good, and to know the evil to avoid, when on a sudden — was it myself? Was it some other? Was it without or within me? I cannot tell, yet above all things ardently longed to know: — at all events, suddenly it was said to me: "If you find what you are seeking, what will you do with it? To whom will you confide it?" — "I shall keep it in my memory," answered I. "But is your memory capable of treasuring up all that your mind has conceived?" — "No, certainly it cannot." "Then you must write." — But how can this be done, seeing that you believe your health unequal to the labor of writing? These things cannot be dictated; they demand the most complete solitude. "That is true; I know not, then, what to do." "Listen! Ask strength, ask help to find what you seek. Then write it, that this offspring of your mind may animate and strengthen you...." '

"Now, I ask you, do you think that these things happen only to St. Augustine?"

— *Père Gratry's* The Well-Springs.[17]

But I am a woman, with all the cares and responsibilities of a woman, and though I take these words of Père Gratry and of St. Augustine to heart, I know that what I write will be tinged with all the daily doings, with myself, my child, my work, my study, as well as with God. God enters into them all. He is inseparable from them. I think of Him as I wake and as I think of Teresa's daily doings. Perhaps it is that I have a wandering mind. But I do not care. It is a woman's mind, and if my daily written meditations are of the people about me, of what is going on, — then it must be so. It is a part of every meditation to apply the virtue, the mystery, to the daily life we lead.

I shall meditate as I have been accustomed, in the little Italian Church on Twelfth Street, by the side of the open window, looking out at the plants growing on the roof, the sweet corn, the boxes of herbs, the geraniums in bright bloom, and I shall rest happy in the presence of Christ on the altar, and then I shall come home and I shall write as Père Gratry advises, and try to catch some of these things that happen to bring me nearer to God, to catch them and put them down on paper.

It is something I have wanted to do, which I have done sketchily for some years. Usually I have kept a notebook only when I am sad and need to work myself out of my sadness. Now I shall do it as a duty performed joyfully for God.

And because I am a woman involved in practical cares, I cannot give the first half of the day to these things, but must meditate when I can, early in the morning and on the fly dur-

---

17   Rev. Auguste-Joseph-Alphonse Gratry (1805-1872), French theologian and spiritual writer. The work referenced is *The Wellsprings* (trans. S. J. M. Brown; New York: Benziger, 1931).

ing the day. Not in the privacy of a study — but here, there and everywhere — at the kitchen table, on the train, on the ferry, on my way to and from appointments and even while making supper or putting Teresa to bed.

2

We have begun. The first and second issues of *The Catholic Worker* are off the press. Peter's constant indoctrination, his simple program of life has caught hold, on my life at least. All winter he came to us as a teacher. John and his wife, Teresa and I, were living together for this past year: now their baby is born, John has a job editing a paper in Dobbs Ferry and they have moved up there. Thinking of Peter's "voluntary poverty" as the foundation of the new work I am undertaking, I gave them most of the furniture and there remains only a bed, a table and two chairs. The two front rooms with the table and two chairs are the offices; the bedroom has nothing but the bed in it. A Communist truck driver around the corner who is in the moving business is bringing me in a file case and desk today. We possess one typewriter, which belongs to my assistant.

Teresa is spending most of the summer on my sister's farm and I am free for work. Already I have assistance, as before the second issue of the paper was off the press, Dorothy Weston came in and volunteered her services. She lives uptown but a good part of the time she spends her nights down here. She likes to work half the night.

Peter has returned for the past few months to the camp up the Hudson where he has been working for the past seven years, studying and writing and sleeping in a shack and living on a few dollars a week. He will come down for occasional round-table discussions and street speaking, but he is an agitator, not an editor, and his job will be to speak and to write.

3

It is another hot day and people go about gleaming in the sun, walking slowly as though to move were a feat in endurance. Children sit on the front steps with nothing on but a rag to cover them. Women return from markets with laden shopping bags, fruit, salads, hot weather vegetables, walking as though they were half asleep. Even at six-thirty when I go out to Mass there is a heavy haze in the air.

But the little yard back of the office is cool and fresh because Mrs. Riedel hoses it first thing in the morning and mops down the back steps. The petunias and four o'clocks are in bloom — the gorgeous cerise color the Mexican Indians so love and which they use in their serapes and woven rugs and chairs and baskets. The fig tree has little figs on it and the wild cucumber vine in the 14th Street yard across the way is spilling over the fence. There is a breeze out here and it is pleasant to have early morning coffee and the paper outside.

It is one of the compensations of poverty to have such a garden. In the front the street is slummish. At night one walks warily to avoid the garbage that is hurled out of the windows in sacks. There are odors, foul odors often, out in front. I will not be so realistic as to more than hint at them. But out behind the house there is the fresh green smell of growing things.

One bathes in a white tub next to the kitchen sink, and one is thankful that it is indeed a white tub instead of two slate wash tubs with the panel between removed. It is the only white tub in the house and the snobbish landlord put it in, in consideration of the fact that the tenants who lived here before used to live in Tudor City. Poor things, to have to move from Tudor City down to East 15th Street! But there are smells up there too. We were out walking last spring and exploring down below the arrogant heights and we were delighted to be assailed by the stockyard smells of a slaughter house. "Delighted," I say? That is class-warrish, to be delighted at some slight sharing of the rich in the miseries of the poor. But I must admit my delight and hug it to me. I do penance through my nose continually.

Yes, I have a white bath tub, but the toilet is in the hall, and since I don't possess a kimono and since I also possess a sense of modesty, I have to dress to go out there. (I suppose my sense of modesty will be questioned for having mentioned the place.) Even so, I must greet Mr. Rubino, or pause to gossip with Mrs. Riedel as I go in or out. Some more penance. But these are little things.

Joe Calderon called up this morning. "This is Operator 78960," he said mysteriously with his betraying Brooklyn accent. "Calling to report that this noon I am speaking down at Wall Street again, and that I can't get up to the office to get bundles of *The Catholic Worker* because I'm already laden down with my stand. Did I tell you I made a nice stand with metal legs? It can't break. I can't fall off — yes, I suppose I can fall off, but I'll be careful."

"Don't be too careful," I urged him. "Your exuberance is catching."

Joe fell off his soap-box the first time he spoke some time ago, and just lately he fell through it. It was borrowed from a Socialist too, but the Socialist was a good fellow and didn't mind. So now there is a specially constructed stand with metal legs. Joe has worked in an office on the Stock Exchange for the last five years and after work has gone over to the downtown Fordham school to take classes in scholastic philosophy, economics and sociology. He is a handsome boy, with a big mouth and when he gets excited he talks out of the side of it. His friend Anthony Ullo, also an Italian, is quieter, more reserved, and very determined. They are both very young.

"You see, we believe in the motions of the Holy Spirit," he explained. "And I think that Catholics ought to stand up for the social doctrine of the Church and tell people about it. They need to be told.

"I'm really a convert in a way. We're Italians and naturally Catholics, but I never had any interest in the Church until I was eighteen. Then a teacher in high school where I was going persuaded me to go over and see Sister Peter Claver whom you mentioned in the first number of *The Catholic Worker* as being one of the first subscribers. She's a wonderful woman! She can sit and listen to whatever you have to say by the hour, and then she'll tell you to come back again and tell her some more. The first thing you know, you find yourself going to Mass, and helping out in the boys' clubs in the parish.

"It was the same way with my friend Tony. We weren't friends before though we were in the same parish. He used to go around with the Italians and I used to go with the Jews. So we hadn't gotten together. And then Sister Peter Claver was making a census of the district and she came across him mending his bicycle. They started to talk and she told him to drop around to see her, and she did with him just as she did with me. She just listened. She told him to come back and she went on listening. She's a wonderful person.

"She gave us books to read too. Did you ever read *The Reality of God* and *Religion and Agnosticism* by Baron von Hugel[18]? Or *The Mystical Elements of Religion?* Between Sister Peter Claver and those books I found myself back in the Church.

"Tony was taking law and he works down on Wall Street too. Having a half an hour for lunch we decided we'd begin soap-boxing during our lunch period. He takes fifteen minutes and I take the other fifteen."

To get permission to speak, Calderon went around to the police captain and told him what he wanted to do. The Captain himself has boys at Fordham and he gave Joe the period from one to one-thirty, taking half an hour from the Socialist to do it.

"And was he sore!" Joe said.

---

18   Baron Friedrich von Hügel (1852-1925), influential theologian and spiritual writer. While never censured, he fell under suspicion during the Modernist Crisis under Pope St. Pius X.

Still, he lent them his soap-box.

"His name is Klein, and his mother is Irish, and he says he was a Catholic until he was nine years old and that then he saw the light! Can you beat that? But he's listening to us. In our talks we are following Cronin's *Science of Ethics*. Last Tuesday we started our talks by giving a summary of Father Parsons' *Modern Mind and the Church*. You read it, didn't you? How the disorder is caused by the world losing its organic unity and man his interior unity; how ethics are divorced from business, politics and education; how the Church, the state and the family are working at cross purposes; too much stress laid on money-making and profits. ... We had a big crowd, two or three hundred — in fact, as many as the street in front of us would hold.

"And then we outlined the subjects of our future talks. We told the people that we were going to begin with the reality of God because God was being denied from the soap-box every place else. We were going to argue His existence from design — that's what we did today — and next time from cause and effect; then the argument from motion and finally, the argument of the common consent of mankind.

"Then having pointed out that God is the source and the end of all life, we are going to argue that any government which prevents the attainment of this end can't be accepted, — and that brings us to Communism and Socialism ..."

4

Yesterday we had callers all day. First a traveling salesman came in who had heard about the paper while on his yearly retreat over at Manresa, Staten Island, where copies of it had been distributed.

We discussed the coal situation and the old Homestead strike and the endless battle of labor for recognition in the coal and steel industries.

Then a high school teacher with her troubles in the Teachers' Union and the obstructionist tactics of the Communists in that organization. The last meeting she attended lasted from one until nine at night, and she without lunch, but they were trying to wear out their opponents, so the Communists kept the floor and talked interminably until those not so fervent were worn down and had to go home and then the vote when it was taken was swung in their favor.

Miss K. told too about teaching in summer school and how one little seven-year-old boy, a Serbian, came to school at eleven only to fall asleep immediately on his desk. On questioning him she discovered that he worked in a laundry from seven until ten-thirty every day sorting clothes for twenty-five cents a week! She took the matter up with the school nurse and the employer was brought to court and fined fifty dollars.

But child labor, in spite of laws, still goes on. People are hungry. They themselves conspire with the employer to outwit the Department of Labor inspectors.

Then a red-headed boy came in who said he never had a job since he left school two years ago, and wanted copies of the paper.

Then a member of the Steam-fitters' Union who was passing out handbills calling attention to conditions in the Ebling and Michel Breweries owned by Mr. Rubel (who also has fifty ice plants where he underpays his help), and in Liebman's Brewery, which puts out Rheingold Beer. The handbills are distributed to urge a boycott of these beers. He was going to the Labor Temple that evening, he said, to attend some other union meetings and took fifty copies of *The Catholic Worker* to distribute there.

5

Office hours around here are from eight in the morning until twelve at night. Many visitors come in and always one of us has to be on hand, either Dorothy or I. Little by little we are getting helpers to address our growing mailing list and help us with the truly formidable number of evictions we are asked to handle, not to speak of cooking and cleaning.

Early this morning Dorothy, Tina and I went over to Mrs. N.'s to see about her moving. The marshal was due to come at ten and put her on the street and she didn't want her belongings exposed to the neighborhood. The Unemployed Councils (Communist) are interested in making demonstrations which are a very good thing too, in that they call the attention of the public to the plight of the poor, but most of the time those who are the cause of the demonstrations are much embarrassed. We were afraid they were going to be on hand this morning as they usually show up by the time the furniture gets put on the street, so we wanted to get there early.

With the assistance of two stalwart young fellow-workers we got the moving under way. The janitor of the house where Mrs. N. had been living recommended a house down the street where the landlord didn't mind taking Home Relief vouchers.

The hardest thing to move was a giant rubber plant which reached all the way to the ceiling.

Mrs. N. makes her living by collecting rags and old iron from dump heaps and garbage cans and selling them. She used to be a janitress herself and had a comfortable little apartment in return for taking care of two houses down the street. But she lost her job and now she is sixty-two and there is not much chance of getting anything else. She is all alone save for a huge cat called Rags who is so old he is toothless. When she opened to our knock he was lying on one of the pantry shelves looking on indifferently at all the moving that was going on around him.

For her meals and his, Mrs. N. collects scraps from the First Avenue market, picking up stale vegetables and scraps of meat and fish heads. She does not like to ply her trade of picking rags out of ash cans during the day, so she sets out at night, continuing her work often until early in the morning. Just the night before, the janitress said, she had brought in an iron bed and spring at twelve o'clock, making several trips with them. She had had no bed before, sleeping on a pile of rags in the corner.

Her possessions consisted only of trunks and a couple of large baskets of her belongings, a table and chairs, a kitchen range and some kerosene lamps.

She cooked of course, over a wood fire, even in the hottest weather. She had not been able to afford either gas or electricity.

"But then most of the people around here never use gas or electricity," the janitress said. "I always burn wood myself. I get wood from the Edison people down by the river. They are always giving away free wood. They are awful good."

6

Teresa, aged seven, is very much around the office these first cold days. Since *The Catholic Worker* has moved to the store downstairs, there is ample room for another assistant and her little desk.

She likes even better than sitting at a desk to crawl under the furniture coverings of a set of chairs and sofa the young woman racktender at the Paulist Church sent down as a contribution to our office furniture. There, ensconced in her tent with her little friend Freddy Rubino, I heard her talking the other day.

"There now," she said, "you have committed a mortal sin, and you haven't got God in your heart any more."

Freddy is two years younger than herself. Freddy had a few minutes before kicked his mother in the shins and called her a pig and generally scandalized the neighborhood, though everyone should have been accustomed to witnessing these scenes at least once a day.

Teresa's reproof made Freddy indignant. "He is so there," he insisted. "He's right there."

"No, there's a devil there now."

"I don't want a devil there. I want God there. He is there."

"Well, all you have to do is to say you're sorry and it will be all right."

So that was settled.

Then there was the question of mortal and venial sin. "If you just do it suddenly then it's not a mortal sin, but if you stop to think and do it anyway, then it is. For instance, if I decide I don't want to drink any cocoa milk and don't do it."

"I wouldn't be quite so extreme and rigorous," I told her. "It has to be a serious matter, and I'm sure it's not serious if you don't drink your milk. A cow can live on grass so I guess you can live on the amount you eat."

"What I'd like to live on are cucumbers," Teresa decided. "Or maybe popcorn with ketchup on it."

Her ideas about heaven are just as original as her ideas about food. She has it all worked out with her friends in the back yard as to just what sort of mansion she is going to have in heaven. There will be a beach there with horseshoe crabs and spider crabs and a place where she can fish. And there will be no cities but only country places and there will be no quarrels or fights....

For a while the children were playing ghosts and the two younger ones, Freddy and Teresa, were going around scared. Perhaps she was reassuring herself as well as them when I heard her talking out in the kitchen while they played one rainy afternoon.

They were all having a very good time and feeling very peaceful. I didn't know it then, I was listening, charmed at the angelic dialogue, but I found out afterward that they were mixing soap powder, cocoa and coffee together and making the most delicious little pastries which they were proceeding to cook on an electric grill. It was the peculiar smell which informed me of their doings.

The conversation proceeded thus:

"There are no ghosts. Really there aren't," said Teresa.

"But there are spirits," the little girl from upstairs said.

"God is a Spirit and that's enough," Teresa decided.

I was reminded of a story Mother Clark up at the Cenacle of St. Regis had told me of a little girl who was being instructed for her first Holy Communion. They were asking her what a spirit was and when she could not answer they started asking her questions.

"Has a spirit got eyes or hair?"

"Has a spirit arms or legs?" And so on.

She agreed that a spirit had none of these things but she finally said brightly:

"But a spirit has feathers!"

Thank God for Pope Pius X who urged early Communion.[19] He was the one who said that it was sufficient for a child to know the difference between her daily food and the heavenly food she would receive.

I know that if anyone started asking Teresa any questions she would not be able to answer them. She has an aversion to answering questions. My only knowledge of her spiritual processes is through her conversations, either with other children or with me. She will volunteer information, but she will not have it drawn from her by direct questioning.

There was an article in the *Journal of Religious Instruction* recently about a series of questions asked twenty-five children of Teresa's age and their answers.

I tried out the questions on Teresa and she only scratched her head and acted irritated. Her answers were barely adequate.

---

19 Pope St. Pius X's *Quam Singulari* (1910) lowered the age for receiving Communion to the "age of reason" and encouraged regular reception of the sacrament, which had become irregular for lay Catholics in the modern period.

And yet when I hear her talk, hear her wise little comments on things I say, I feel certain as to her spiritual knowledge.

About prayer, for instance, Freddy said that he did not know how to pray. Questioned by Teresa, he said that he merely repeated prayers after his mother. All he had to do to pray was to think every now and then of God, Teresa told him. "Just remember Him," she said. "Like after I go to Communion in the morning, then lots of times during the day I suddenly remember that I did, I suddenly remember that I've got God. That's a prayer, too."

7

A deer gets trapped on a hillside and every effort is brought to bear to rescue him from his predicament. The newspapers carry daily features.

Mrs. A. with her four children and unemployed husband living on $1.50 a week, is trapped by economic circumstances and everyone is so indifferent that it took three or four afternoons of Mike Gunn's time to see to it that the Home Relief came to the rescue. Though Mike has enough to do with his Labor Guild over in Brooklyn, he was doing his bit as part of our Fifteenth Street Neighborhood Council.

Three little pigs are crowded into a too-small cage, the case is brought into court, the judge's findings in the case being that pigs should not be crowded the way subway riders are. And a family of eight children, mother and father, are crowded in three rooms and the consensus of opinion is that they're lucky to have that and why don't they practice birth control anyway.

One of the Home Relief Workers came in the other day and was voicing just such sentiments. She was absolutely unacquainted with Catholic teaching on birth control and abortion, and we talked on the subject. Though we may not have convinced her, we at least served the purpose, we hope, of toning down her propaganda among unemployed families.

A scavenger hunt is the latest game of "Society." A hilarious pastime, the *New York Times* society reporter calls it, and describes in two and one half columns the asinine procedure of several hundred society and literary figures, guests at a party at the Waldorf-Astoria, surging forth on a chase through the highways and byways of Manhattan Island. "The scavengers' hunt of last night brought an enthusiastic response even from persons whose appetites for diversion are ordinarily jaded. The hunt was a search through the city streets for a ridiculously heterogeneous list of articles."

Any morning before and after Mass and straight on through the day there is a "scavenger hunt" going on up and down 15th Street outside the windows of *The Catholic Worker* and through all the streets of the city. People going through garbage and ash cans to see what they can find in the way of a heterogeneous list of articles. The *Times* does not state what these things were but probably the list was made up of something delightfully and quaintly absurd such as old shoes, bits of string, cardboard packing boxes, wire, old furniture, clothing and food.

If the several hundred guests at the Waldorf had to scavenge night after night and morning after morning, the hunt would not have had such an enthusiastic response.

8

Teresa is now a member of the Fifteenth Street Neighborhood Council and took part in her first eviction the other day. She had a cold and was staying home from school in order to keep out in the air, it being a balmy day, so she had her chance to help.

The Friday before, a Home Relief worker from 22nd Street came to the office to get aid for a woman and child who were being evicted from a dark flat in one of the tenements of William Horn (31 Union Square).

There were five stalwart friends of *The Catholic Worker* in the office at the time, Harry Crimmins, Frank O'Donnell, Tom Coddington, William Walsh and a Mr. Powers from Atlantic City who came to inquire about the work of the paper and stayed to help.

Understanding that the eviction was at three in the afternoon, we sallied forth, but when we got there, the landlord's agent had called off his man, expecting us to do the job of putting the woman out, and thus saving him eighteen dollars.

We refused to move the woman's furniture until it had been brought down by the marshal. We explained to the agent that often a landlord who was unwilling to accept a Home Relief voucher offered to move the family himself, paying five dollars to a neighborhood truckman rather than eighteen to the marshal. This agent stood sneering and scoffing by the door and refused to do anything.

"You have no sympathy for landlords, have you?" he wanted to know.

We assured him that our sympathy was rather with the weaker party. All right then, he would call the marshal! The eviction would be the following Monday at three o'clock.

It was hard to understand his unwillingness to have the poor woman moved. It was as though he delighted in the idea of heaping humiliation on her.

Monday came, and the relief worker hastened around to the office, to tell us that the marshal was about to arrive, though it was only one, not three in the afternoon. Only Harry Crimmins, Teresa, Dorothy Weston and I were in the office, so leaving Dorothy to mind the office, the three of us sallied out.

Several police and huskies were standing at the door of the tenement to greet what they thought was going to be a delegation of Communists, only to meet instead seven-year-old

Teresa, Harry Crimmins and me. They dissolved into thin air. (It is a wonder they wouldn't stay and help us.)

Teresa carried toys, pieces of the baby's crib, parlor ornaments and dishes, and Harry Crimmins and I managed the rest. The Mission Helpers of the Sacred Heart, a community of nuns who run a day nursery and do visiting work in the neighborhood, promised to keep an eye on our evicted friend — she is a Protestant — taking charge of her two-year-old child when she works as a dishwasher for seven dollars a week.

This is only one of the dozen eviction cases we have had in the last month. We have moved Jews, Protestants and Catholics. A German livery stable man loaned us his horse and wagon to move a Jewish neighbor, and Jews, Protestants and Catholics have helped us by contributing clothes, furniture and their services.

9

One afternoon last month we went up to the Municipal Lodging House of the City of New York and looked at the largest bedroom in the world there. The seventeen hundred beds, the eight rows stretching way out to the very end of a pier, two-tiered beds at that, were a grim sight, the collectivization of misery.

The huge vats of stew stirred with a tremendous ladle only emphasized the ugly state which the world is in today. Every night the men stand out on 25th Street in long lines and are hustled through, catalogued, ticketed, stamped with the seal of approval, fed in a rush and passed on to the baths, the doctor, the beds, all with a grim efficiency which gave testimony to the length of time this need has existed for the mass care of the impoverished.

One day last summer, I saw a man sitting down by one of the piers, all alone. He sat on a log, and before him was a wooden box on which he had spread out on a paper his meagre supper. He sat there and ate with some pretense of human dignity, and it was one of the saddest sights I have ever seen.

The attendant who showed us around told of how the lame, the halt and the blind who were being housed at the "muni" were transported in a bus to a place which the Salvation Army runs for such men where they can sit inside all day out of the wind and rain. *But what about Catholic provision for such men? There is none.* The money which the priests at the Holy Name Mission collected through the years went for immediate relief for homeless and hungry men and they were not able to start the building project for the men which they had been planning. Oh, for parish houses of hospitality!

If the largest bedroom in the world was a sad sight the women's dormitory was even sadder. At one end of it there were beds with little cribs by the side of them for women with babies. But women know that if they are forced to accept the hospitality of the city, their older children will be taken from them and only infants left to them, so not many of them go there. Our escort told us of a family which had come in the night before. The family was evicted, and the mother was so sick she had to be carted off to the hospital, and the man, the old grandmother and the three children had to go to the city for relief. The older children were taken to the Children's Aid and the baby left with the grandmother. And what must have been the thoughts of the mother lying in the hospital, wondering where her mother, her children and her husband were spending the night? What but thoughts of hatred and despair that such cruelty and inhumanity can exist today.

(This was written five years ago and last week I paid another visit to the lodging house. Thanks to the Works Progress Administration and the increased amount of money put at their disposal, things have changed for the better. The largest bedroom in the world has been converted into a day shelter for men, where thousands can sit at benches all through the long cold days, playing cards, reading, mending their clothes or just brooding. At the end of the pier there is space partitioned off where men can take showers, have a shave by unemployed barbers, wash and press their clothes, have them mended by unemployed tailors.

Since there are facilities both at 26th Street and South Ferry for the men to stay indoors out of the bad weather, the long lines of men waiting for food are to a great extent done away with. The meals have improved greatly, but complaints of graft are always being made, that those employed by the city sell a lot of the good food provided for the men. Of course, since these charges are made by the men themselves no attention is paid to them.

Since then, too, the women's lodging house has been transferred twice, first to 14th Street, where it occupied three old buildings which were made very comfortable and homelike. Instead of one dormitory there were many smaller rooms with curtains hung at the windows and colored comforters gracing the foot of each bed. The dining room was very attractive and open to all who were in need. One friend of mine who was living on a $2.75 a week food allowance said that she went over there Thanksgiving and Christmas and all she had to do was sign her name on the book before going in to partake of the city's hospitality. She said there was a great spirit of gaiety and cheer. The rumor is that the neighborhood objected to the lodging house. Since then they have moved to 6th Street where they occupy an old building formerly used by the Children's Aid. The women in charge are young and not at all "matronly." There is the same kind spirit. About 150 women can be accommodated. They stay only until transients can be sent back home, until relatives can be located, or until they can be placed on relief. It is a sad thing to see these women and children sitting around all day in the small crowded room on hard benches, waiting hour after hour and not knowing what is going to happen to them.

A Catholic place for women is maintained at St. Zita's on West 14th Street. Here a large laundry provides work for all the women who are taken in. Inasmuch as they are working all day, there is little opportunity for them to get out and try to find other work which will enable them to maintain a home again.

Women in any condition are taken in. On one occasion I was walking across 14th Street and came across an elderly woman who was very drunk. She kept dropping her gloves and her little bundles and falling down when she tried to pick them up. I stopped to help her and she clutched me by the arm and wanted to know where she could get shelter. St. Zita's was only half a block away so I managed to get her to the door where I rang the bell. A kind little nun immediately took her in with no question. What heroic work to care for these sad and difficult cases! And what Christ-like patience it calls for.

The Salvation Army Home on Rivington Street is a four-story building with a dormitory on each floor. There one must pay twenty-five cents a night for a bed, and God help you if you have five cents less than the required amount. Many of the old women who stay there are able to get a day's work now and then which pays for their room, but they never have enough to pay a week's room rent all at once. There is also an Episcopalian place, St. Barnabas' House, which accommodates about fifty women. And now, of course, there is our House of Hospitality. Ours, of course, is like a large family and when the women come to us they come for an indefinite stay. Some of them have been with us for the past four years. We have no rules, any more than the average family has, and we ask no questions. Many of the women have come to us so exhausted by poverty and insecurity that it has taken them months to recover. There are others who will always be victims of shattered nerves, and incapable of holding down any job. Many of them try to help us and participate in the work around the house. Whatever co-operation they give is voluntary. I love to think of that story of Dostoievsky, *The Honest Thief*, which exemplifies true Christ-like charity. One knows that that is a true story and that incidents like that happen often among the poor.)

10

Our lives are made up of little miracles day by day. That splendid globe of sun, one street wide, framed at the foot of East 14th Street in early morning mists, that greeted me on my way out to Mass was a miracle that lifted up my heart. I was reminded of a little song of Teresa's composed and sung at the age of two.

"I'll sing a song," (she warbled)
"Of sunshine on a little house
And the sunshine is a present for the little house."

Sunshine in the middle of January is indeed a present. We get presents, lots of them, around *The Catholic Worker* office. During the holidays, a turkey, a ham, baskets of groceries, five pounds of butter, plum puddings, flannel nightgowns and doll-babies, sheets, wash rags and blankets descended on us. There was even the offer of a quarter of a moose from Canada, but we didn't know where we could put it, so we refused it.

We appealed in our last issue for beds, and eight beds came. Our House of Hospitality for unemployed women is furnished now, and the surplus that comes in we will give to unemployed people in the neighborhood.

As I write, a blanket comes in from Houghton and Dutton, Boston, Massachusetts, sender unknown, but one of our Boston subscribers, no doubt. We threatened in the last number to sleep between newspapers and under rugs, but we didn't have a chance. When it was three below zero we had denuded the house of blankets to the extent of having to use donated overcoats which had just come in, but even this minor mortification was soon denied us.

During this last cold snap one of the girls from the apartment came in to tell us that they could use four more blankets, and that very afternoon a car drove up to the office and four blankets — beautifully heavy ones — were brought in by a chauffeur.

And so it goes. Books, food (two bottles of wine and a box of cigars! — And who sent them? we wonder), clothes and bedding.

But now our cash box is empty. We just collected the last pennies for a ball of twine and stamps and we shall take a twenty-five-cent subscription which just came in to buy meat for a stew for supper. But the printing bill, the one hundred and sixty-five dollars of it which remains unpaid, confronts us and tries to intimidate us.

But what is one hundred and sixty-five dollars to St. Joseph, or to St. Teresa of Avila either? We refuse to be affrighted. (Though of course the printer may be, "oh, he of little faith!")

Don Bosco tells lots of stories about needing this sum or that sum to pay rent and other bills with and the money arriving miraculously on time. And he too was always in need, always asking, and always receiving.

A great many of our friends urge us to put our paper on a business-like basis. But this isn't a business, it's a movement. And we don't know anything about business around here anyway. Well-meaning friends say, "But people get tired of appeals." We don't believe it. Probably most of our friends live as we do, from day to day and from hand to mouth, and as they get, they are willing to give. So we shall continue to appeal and we know that the paper will go on.

It's a choice of technique, after all. People call up offering us the services of their organizations to raise money. They have lists, they send out telephone and mail appeals. They are business-like and most coldly impersonal. Though they may be successful in raising funds for Jewish, Catholic and Protestant organizations and offer us several thousand a week, minus their commission, we can't warm up to these tactics. We learn ours from the Gospels and what's good enough for St. Peter and St.

Paul is good enough for us. Their technique of revolution was the technique of Christ and it's the one to go back to.

And as for getting tired of our appeals, Jesus advocated importunity thus:

"Which of you shall have a friend, and shall go to him at midnight, and shall say to him, friend, lend me three loaves, because a friend of mine is come off his journey to me, and I have not what to set before him. And if he from within should answer and say, trouble me not, the door is now shut and my children are with me in bed and I cannot rise and give thee. Yet if he shall continue knocking, I say to you though he will not rise and give him because he is his friend, yet because of his importunity he will arise and give him as many as he needeth" [Luke 11:5-8].

So our friends may expect us to importune and to continue to ask, trusting that we shall receive.

TWO

1

A FEW nights ago, Sarah Harding who was living two flights upstairs went insane.

It was three o'clock in the morning when it all began and when the neighbors discovered the cause of the shrieks which echoed up and down the block, they laughed grimly, shut down their windows, covered up their ears with their blankets and went back to sleep. They were pushing off the horror from themselves.

When the screaming began they heard it in their sleep for a moment, separated it from the occasional night howlings of dog or cat, recognized it for what it was, and awoke.

Windows were pushed up, lights were turned on. What was it all about?

"Perhaps someone is having a baby," Mrs. Bloch who lived across the hall said. We were both peering out of our doors. "I remember when I had mine —"

Every woman in every apartment thought of those appalling minutes of agony, those last interminable minutes. They thought of their own animal cries, abstractly, and suddenly remembered how quickly they had forgotten them. How suddenly, as the new life was catapulted into the world, they had felt relieved and joyous.

But not many babies are born at home any more. At the first suggestion of pain, there is that comfortable sense that now the months of waiting are over with, now something definite is about to take place. For the poor the hospitals are cheap. A baby can be brought into the world for thirty dollars in the big wards of any of the hospitals, and for nothing at Bellevue. And oh, the pleasant days of rest afterwards, the neat wards, the relief from all household cares, the children, the shopping, the three meals a day.

It was of these things that all the women in the tenement thought, stirring in their beds restlessly at the continued rasping cries. They thought too, that some woman's husband was being made to pay. Let him suffer a little too! Let him be tormented, shocked, horrified! Let him see his woman becoming an animal, a tortured beast. It is this he has put upon her. This is her share of the business of life and love. And if there are other children in the family — how will they react to this agonizing business? How will they react to the sight of their mother, an abstract, twitching bundle of nerves and flesh, each nerve being probed by agony.

But soon it became obvious that something more was occurring, that these cries were not just the cries of a woman in labor. No woman in childbirth is going to stand in her window and shriek curses, and talk, talk, talk in this fearful fashion. When will she become hoarse? Her throat will be torn out. It will bleed from the knife-like quality of those cries.

To the listeners nearer at hand, no movement, no bustle, came from the apartment where the woman stood wailing at the window. There was no evidence that any normal business of life was being carried on.

One man put his head out the window and shouted, "Aw shut up, you drunken slut!" (He probably was the man who threw milk bottles into the paved yard in back to emphasize his disapproval of the Petroffs who played and sang after midnight.)

His reproof started a new train of conjecture. Perhaps a drunken rout was going on and everyone else had passed out except this woman. Perhaps it was poison liquor. Why didn't someone find out?

"Nobody likes to interfere," Mrs. Bloch whispered. "Perhaps a husband and wife were fighting and he's gone away and left her."

Oh the basic cowardice and inhumanity of man! I remembered how when I was a little girl, another child and I had once been chased around our doll carriages by a fierce dog, and caught at and nipped until our dresses had been torn to ribbons. And I remembered how people witnessing this miserable sight, in their own fear, had not come out to help. We welcomed the policeman who rescued us and I could have kissed his hands with gratitude — those hands guilty perhaps in their turn of other brutalities.

Why didn't someone call the police now? Why didn't somebody do something? Where was the woman? In which apartment? What were her immediate neighbors doing?

The shrieks were continuing. It had been an hour now since they had started.

Then two of our friends began calling to the woman from another window, talking to her, kindly questioning her. Her words came clearer through her cries. There was something about a door being locked, something about a horror issuing from the radio. She was being torn to pieces by her ghastly emotions.

"They are getting an ambulance," someone shouted.

The French people upstairs, now that they knew something definite was being done, banged down their windows, laughing. Some other tenant laughed too. "She'll break my eardrums," he said.

There was the clang of an ambulance on the street. And then the cries died away. Everywhere windows were being banged down. It was five o'clock, still time for a little sleep for those who were calloused by the duration of the turmoil to the thought of this other human being's suffering. They only thought, "We can get another couple of hours' sleep," and sank into oblivion.

In the morning we found out that the woman's name was Sarah Harding, that she was thirty-five years old, was living alone and that a search was being made for someone belonging to her.

She had been taken to Bellevue, and her neighbors who had long been too afraid of her wild despairing glance to speak to her, breathed sighs of relief. It was just an incident in the crowded life of the tenement on East Fifteenth Street.

2

We are an international household. Yesterday afternoon Peter brought in his Armenian friend, Mr. Minas, and asked if he could put up a bed for him. We have the apartment next door as well now, so we got a camp cot to put up in the kitchen after the meetings are over in the evening. Teresa and I each had two blankets, so I took one off each bed for him — one for under and one for over — since a camp cot has no mattress. Now we sit down to table, American, French, Irish, Polish, Jew, Lithuanian, Italian and American.

As for the meetings held every night now, there are all nationalities there too — Ukrainian, Spanish, Italian, German, Belgian, Swiss, English, Scotch, Irish, Russian, Negro, French, Lithuanian, Jew, and now — Armenian. I do not know what Mr. Minas' religion is. I have not asked him. Peter says he was educated in a Jesuit school in Egypt and writes poetry.

Right now he is sitting down in the kitchen getting quotations — the pronouncements of various priests against Fascism. He is also going to distribute our daily supplement through the streets.

Last night Frank took the supplement around to various taverns in the neighborhood, most of which are run by Catholics and one of which down by Tompkins Square is frequented by Russians. At this, the last place he visited, he said they were all in a most affable mood, and after reading the sheet gravely, registered their approval by singing: "Proschai, proschai."

Eileen went over to Sheed and Ward's last night to their monthly disputation and distributed papers there. She says that cars and chauffeurs were lined up in front of the door. Their employers should have invited them inside to partake of Catholic culture.

It is hard to put over the idea of Catholic culture because people are afraid of the word culture in America. They think at once of Shakespeare clubs and Browning societies and they are repelled.

Speaking of Mr. Sheed,[20] one of the things he said when speaking before our group the other night was this:

"The Christians in Russia — and there are Christians in Russia who are allowed to practice their religion after a fashion — say: 'Do not try to save us from the Bolsheviks. They are materialists with material aims, ignoring and denying God and they say so. But the Western Christians are also materialists with material aims denying God — but they don't say so. Leave us alone and perhaps a new Christianity will arise in Russia.'"

3

Margaret, our Lithuanian friend, who comes down from the House of Hospitality to help us every day, is full of stories.

About how she found ten dollars:

"I had been walking about the city for three days," she said, "and not eating very much, so I was hungry. I don't think I'd had anything to eat the day before at all because I was trying to save my last ten cents for carfare. I'd been staying at a rooming house on 57th Street, and then she sold out and I had to go because I was behind in my rent anyway. I went to my cousin's, but her husband doesn't like me, so it was hard to stay there. There was no extra bed, so I slept on my coat in the hallway. I had to get out of the house before he got up, so I didn't get any meals there. So I was hungry.

---

20 Frank Sheed (1897-1982), Catholic convert, writer, and co-founder (with his wife, Maisie Ward) of Sheed & Ward, publisher of *House of Hospitality*.

"I walked around and walked around and, finally, I went into the Paulist Church. I said a prayer there to the Little Flower — I sat there for a while — and then I went out again. Right next door there is a restaurant. I used to go in there when I had a job. So I had a sandwich and a cup of coffee and I said to Jim at the cash register when I went out: 'That's my last dime.' And then I went out and I walked and walked. And suddenly, right up against a building I saw a folded up bill. I didn't know whether it was a dollar bill or not, I got so weak and faint. I was hot and sick from seeing it. I picked it up, but I was scared to pick it up for fear some one would see me and take it from me. I was so scared I shook. I picked it up and held it in my hand tight and walked away fast. I didn't dare to look at it. I walked from 59th Street all the way down to Tenth, but I didn't wait that long to look and see what it was. I opened it and there was *two* five dollar bills, not just one. I was scared. Nothing like that ever happened to me before. I was afraid it was counterfeit and I would get arrested and they wouldn't believe me that I found it. Well, anyway, I met a girl friend of mine and she was hungry too — staying at the Rivington Street place for a quarter a night — so we went and ate finally. And I had enough to pay for room rent again for a few weeks.

"Nothing like that ever happened to me before. I mean like finding money. But other things happened.

"I was thirteen when I started to work. I didn't want to go to school anyway, and my father and brothers were working in the mines and they thought I might as well be working too.

"My father and mother were Lithuanians and were living down below Wilkes Barre in a little mining town. I was born in a company shack, and the shacks were awful. There were so many of them and they were just made of boards, and to keep warm you had to line them with newspapers.

"Well, I went to work in a silk mill when I was thirteen, and pretty soon after a few months or so, I got sick and had to go to the hospital. I was in the hospital two months. And then I did housework for a doctor's wife and then for another family.

"I didn't go home after that. I worked in another silk mill for a few years, and I held lots of other jobs. I even worked in a saloon in Scranton. That was when I was seventeen.

"Then I came up to New York and worked over in Williamsburg in a factory where they made casings for sausages. We had to wear rubber boots up to our knees and big rubber aprons and tie our heads up, but the smell got into our skins. I had to take a bath every night, and then it didn't help.

"I worked there until my hands swelled up till they were like hams, from keeping them in the water with the chemicals all the time. I had to quit and wait until my hands got better and lay off work for a while.

"So then I worked in another silk mill over in Astoria. I had four looms and I got to work at a quarter of seven and laid off at five-thirty at night. I was very fast and I earned a lot of money.

"You couldn't sit down on the job. You had to go walking around and around and around. If you stopped the threads would break and that slowed you up. Some of the girls were slow and could only handle one loom, and that meant they didn't earn much money. Some tended more looms than I did.

"The pay kept going down and down and finally they laid us all off and started making plush. The factory is closed down now.

"Then I worked for a drug supply house and for the Beech-Nut Gum people and for the Royal Gelatine people. Making boxes. That was hard work too.

"And, oh, yes, I was a chambermaid and a waitress. Two of the places I worked in — a Greek place and a Polish place — they never threw anything out. They put back what was left over on the plates into the stew. I never could eat nothing.

"I was thin, but not as thin as I was when I worked in the silk mill. I looked then as if I was falling apart.

"And I worked too in a tobacco plant up in Connecticut. Hanging up tobacco on poles to dry. There were lots of children working in that place, seven, eight and nine years old. They came to work with their mothers and helped around the place, carrying baskets and running errands and helping around.

"Yes, I've had lots of jobs, I can't remember how many.

"I wish I had a job again."

4

One night I went up to the Mothers' Club at St. Barnabas to talk to the women who all live in snug warm houses with their husbands and children around them, their time filled and their life sweetened by the good works their concerted means permit them to do.

They had contributed before ($34.00) — to the work of the House of Hospitality and they took up a collection again of ten dollars.

This morning a contrast. Margaret came in to find a letter from her mother in Pennsylvania saying that her six-year-old child was going to be committed to an institution. Her mother is running a boarding house for miners, and she neglected to watch over or care for the child. The grandmother cannot read or write English, so it was the thirteen-year-old brother's duty to write this piece of news to Margaret. He said she made water in the streets where people could see her, and went around begging in peoples' houses.

We were considering what we could do in the way of keeping the child out of the institution when Mrs. Carleton Hayes called up and told us she was sending a check for twenty dollars which she had collected from among her friends. This would about cover the trip down. We shall see what can be done.

Little duties pile up. I get up at seven-thirty, go to eight o'clock Mass, prepare breakfast for Peter, Mr. Minas, Teresa and myself; go through the mail, do bookkeeping, hand the orders over to Frank and put the letters aside to be answered; read some of the Office of the day and write the daily page to be mimeographed. All the while there are interruptions, people coming in and the telephone. Frank and Eileen come in about ten or eleven o'clock. Peter and Mr. Minas go out. Margaret comes in. Teresa and Freddy play about. Sometimes Teresa does her arithmetic by playing with the money in the cash box and sometimes in the big graphic arithmetic book I bought her. I am keeping her home from school as she has not been well. She reads about a page and a half a day, also some prayers. The rest of the time she plays outside these warm spring days.

This morning at eleven Jimmie Lafki came in to play with the typewriter for an hour. He is sixteen and looks twelve, has not made his first Communion yet and is just out of a state institution where he has been for two years. He was committed up-state, his guardian tells us. It looks to me more as though his aunt wanted to get rid of him. She is a huge, dirty woman weighing over two hundred pounds, whose dirty flannel nightgown always protrudes above her other clothes which she has piled on her in layers. With all that fat to keep her warm you would not think she needed so many clothes. She had come in to us for clothes, sheets and blankets for the boy, and, overcome by his beaten look, I had suggested that the boy come in every day at eleven, just to occupy himself since he was under parole and not attending school.

Jimmy practiced typing, watched how the mimeograph machine worked, had lunch, ran off five hundred copies for us and then sped away with a bundle of books under his arm, including a Catechism.

Then the Home Relief worker, wanting a Confirmation outfit for a twelve-year-old girl; then Charlie Rich, to type some of his spiritual writings. Then Tessa with her dialectic materialism and her baby who is baptized a Catholic, but who she insists is going to grow up a 'Daily Worker' and not a 'Catholic Worker.'

Mr. Minas returns to take out the papers. A "Fascist" drops in to try to whip up hatred for the Jews amongst us.

Then Ade Bethune[21] in with some of her lovely drawings of Don Bosco, St. Catherine of Sienna and the second Corporal Work of Mercy. She stayed to make an impression on the stencil of Don Bosco for the Italians in the neighborhood for Easter Monday, the day after his canonization.

5

A long day full of difficulties. A priest called up and said he was sending over a young woman who had threatened to kill herself. She had already made one attempt, he said she told him, and she was without work and without shelter, having been put out of her room early that morning. We talked to her, gave her breakfast, some clothes and sent her up to the House of Hospitality.... Then another telephone call came for a friend down on 11th Street who was ill and needed a doctor, so we called Dr. Koiransky of Willard Parker, who has volunteered his services for the poor of the neighborhood, and he assured us of his immediate attention. We went down there ourselves and the job from then on was one of feeding the baby, changing him (and he squirmed like an eel), shopping, cooking, washing diapers and such duties until five o'clock came, when someone else could take a turn at caring for the sick girl, who could not move from her bed, but was not sick enough to go to the hospital. Two editors demonstrated their willingness to be both workers and scholars at this job, but it took almost more dexterity than they possessed to change the kid.

Mr. John Erit, who spoke at the third meeting of the Workers' School came in this evening at supper time and showed us how to make Italian spaghetti. There are many kinds of spa-

---

21   Ade Bethune (Adélaide de Bethune: 1914-2002), Catholic artist and longtime associate of Dorothy Day. She designed the masthead for the *Catholic Worker* newspaper, and her work regularly illustrated the paper.

ghetti, but this was the simplest kind, called Castle of San Angelo, because when the soldiers were being besieged there they lived for weeks on it.

Our guest chef worked under disabilities. The pots were not big enough, the fire was slow, but as usual around *The Catholic Worker* office, a little miracle was performed in that twelve people were fed with neatness and dispatch.

On fast days, *The Catholic Worker* staff is fed on Jewish cooking. Mrs. Gottlieb around the corner makes up a pile of potato pancakes or fish, and her cooperation saves the editors a great deal of time and effort.

A Spanish friend threatens to bring in some stewed octopus with ink sauce, but the diners are not very enthusiastic about the prospect.

And speaking of food, Peter Maurin arrived in from the country after an absence of four weeks. Discussing economics, he displayed his grocery and newspaper bills for the month — $9.

Peter is in favor of a big pot on the stove and a continual supply of vegetable soup, constantly renewed from day to day — an idea shared by both Don Bosco and the I.W.W.'s.

After supper we went out to the pushcart market and bought a large pot for 79 cents, a ten-quart one, and while the Workers' School is in session, we shall dine on soup.

A rather monotonous diet, but at the writing, Mr. John Brunini of the *Commonweal* staff offers to come down soon and cook up a meal.

6

This evening Freddy and Teresa helped count the money in the cash box which had been empty for quite a few days.

"*The Catholic Worker* is rich," Teresa kept chortling, forgetting her theory that it is bourgeois to be rich. She immediately wanted to misappropriate some of the funds.

"My birthday is this month — St. Joseph's month," she said, "and I am going to think of all the things I want St. Joseph to ask God to send me."

And she ruminated about a baby goat, a sheep, a pet hen and a few other things which she thought would contribute to her happiness.

We begged her, however, not to ask St. Joseph for them, for if he sent them along, what with his love for animals, we might find them somewhat in the way and not be grateful as we should.

There's a cat, now — a most dilapidated cat, who sat and yawned rudely during a lecture by Father Parsons, the other night. It's a dirty cat, thin-tailed and ungainly.

"But I love him because he is so soff", Teresa said, clutching him to her bosom.

Yes, we are rich this month, and feel ourselves well provided for. And we ask for no greater blessing of St. Joseph during this, his month, than for hearts which become increasingly "soff", as Teresa says, with the love of God.

7

For some time now we have had Adelson with us. Lately he has been staying here in the office at night — sitting up at the table with a blanket around his shoulders — sleeping and writing. Mr. Minas has gotten a room for himself so that he can sleep mornings and recover from the life about here. Adelson sometimes works around the office and then suddenly he will start talking and not stop for hours. Right now as I write he is talking to Frank who is always very patient with him.

"There was one time in my life when I was happy. That was when I was cultivating the garden of my soul. The day was not long enough. I studied. I worked until I had money. I worked on the day shift and the night shift and I slept for two hours and worked again. And when I had saved some money I studied.

I got up at six and I worked all day until night and worked at night until midnight. My soul was a fresh garden.

"And now my garden is laid waste. Now the pigs are rooting in it, it is a shambles. I am an outcast and a pauper, despised of men. I am a man whose heart is broken.

"Once I was as gay as a child. I worked with my two hands for everything. When there was no work I went from factory to factory. When there was a sign on the door 'No Help Wanted' I went in anyway.

"This went on for years. I had a friend who wanted to help me go to school and he came to me and said: 'Are you tired of the struggle? Are you beaten yet?'

"Now I am beaten. I am a soul in anguish. My mind is gone. I know that my mind is crooked. And what can I do about it?

"If I had not been so impatient, if I had not been so proud and eager, I would have been a great political leader. The world would not have been in the condition that it is today. It is all my fault."

When once he begins talking about his responsibility for world conditions, he becomes very incoherent and it is impossible to follow him.

8

We sold *The Catholic Worker* after all the Masses over at the Immaculate Conception Church this morning. I went to the ten o'clock and as I sat in the kitchen before leaving, Peter was holding forth on the necessity of meetings for Harlem every night, hiring a hall, getting professors and drawing large crowds. I told him he was always too optimistic as to the response he would get and that he had much better confine himself to the street meetings. He looked at me meekly and said, "Just as you think best." I mentioned the fact that the professors had enough work on their hands and after giving up their time to our Workers' School here for three months they were due to have a rest. "Oh, rest, rest!" he exclaimed sadly. So I reminded him of their day lectures, books to write, examinations to prepare, their families to watch over, etc. Peter would have everyone give up every activity and go straight to the workers.

Grace and her two children came in to lunch. They are two and four years old and their father hopes that they will grow up to be "good little atheists". The conversation at lunch was between Peter and Charles Rich, who with his Jewish blood is ardent in defense of the faith. The existence of God, St. Thomas Aquinas, intuitive knowledge, St. Augustine — these were the matters discussed, and the children listened spellbound by the vehemence, if not by the content of the speeches. They are often hellions at table but this time they were angels and Grace herself was able to eat her lunch in peace. She was thankful for the conversation despite the subject, but if her husband had been here, he would have snatched the children away by the hair.

Charlie worked in Child's Restaurant for twelve years and was influenced in his conversion by a cook he knew who gave him *The Divine Comedy* to read.

Now he visits his friends, a cook, a porter and a bus boy, and they have sent in a contribution by him and are coming down to see us.

9

"Even if only one person were served and helped by the House of Hospitality, *The Catholic Worker* would be repaid and could feel that its labors were not in vain," said one of the editors during the month, when a bit of wrangling was going on at the apartment.

It was early in the year, when the February blues had taken possession of everyone. The cold permeated, vitality was low, the winter seemed interminable. There was a fuss because one girl likes plenty of fresh air and another one thought she had enough of it during the day, tramping the streets looking for work and wanted a snug airlessness at night. There was a fuss about whether there should be a sign in the bathroom saying: "Wash out the tub."

The editors, too, felt that their strength was not enough to keep up with the duties of each day. Getting out a paper seemed a simple task compared to the innumerable things which came up every day in regard to the ten girls housed down the street; the feeding of the staff and of the countless visitors who came in; the getting ready for the Catholic Workers' School; the doling out of clothes contributed and solicited by willing friends of the paper and needy neighbors respectively.

Yes, life seemed too complicated just a week or so ago. One day there was one problem after another. Minutes and hours and days were taken up with doing everything else in the world except getting out a paper and answering letters in connection with that paper.

And then — it is the way life goes — all difficulties seemed to resolve themselves. Matters were adjusted and now everything runs smoothly again.

During the month about twenty-five women were cared for, some left to take jobs, three were sent away to a rest house for several weeks. The beds were always occupied and yet we never had to turn any girl away. Always, when a new one came in, another, providentially, was leaving for a job.

Sometimes during the month some of the girls dropped into the office to discuss their problems with us, stayed for lunch and remained to clear up the dishes. One of them has offered her services in our common kitchen, God be praised, and now the editors' tasks are lightened by this volunteer help. It is a reward, we are sure, sent as a result of an action of our latest cooperator, Eileen, who, when she came to the office to join the staff, seized pail, ammonia and window rags and went to the House of Hospitality to clean windows, as the first task to be performed for the paper.

The situation of our kitchen helper is dire in the extreme — a baby expected, no husband, no funds, only the shelter afforded her by the House of Hospitality and the food and clothing that she receives from us — yet she thought not of herself on the opening night of the school, but of the workers' school.

"When I listen to Peter Maurin talk," she said, "I feel tears come to my eyes. I was praying all evening that everything would go all right."

THREE

1

ALTHOUGH the Communists and Socialists had their hundreds of thousands out in the streets yesterday, we feel that *The Catholic Worker* made its presence felt, too. Fifteen or more high school and college students, from Manhattan, Fordham, St. John's College, Cathedral College and from City College distributed papers and leaflets in Union Square all afternoon and in the evening up around Columbus Circle and Madison Square Garden.

The man who was selling the I.W.W. paper in Madison Square came up to get a copy from me, and said, "I was a Catholic myself once — I'd like to see your paper." And people of all nationalities were anxious to get it.

One young woman came in this morning who said she had seen a copy in the Square and wanted to find out about the House of Hospitality. She had been living down on Rivington Street and now her money was all gone and she had no place to go. She was telling me about her friend, who was also down and out, who went to take a room, or a bed up in Harlem, was seduced by a young Spanish American and threw herself under a subway train a week later.

Her lips were trembling as she talked (it was only eight-thirty in the morning), so I invited her out to have a cup of coffee.

Last week a colored woman who has been staying up at the Municipal Lodging House came in for a bite to eat. She looked in need of a shelter where she could stay in bed and rest for a few days instead of having to walk the streets from morning to night as the guests of the lodging house have to do.

So that evening I went to talk to the girls to see if it would be all right with them to invite Mary to stay up there. After all, I did not want to run the risk of submitting her to insult on account of her color — nor did I expect too much of the girls in the way of freedom from race prejudice, since I know very well that Catholics of means and better education are not free themselves from it.

I talked to the girls, reminding them how our Lord washed the feet of His disciples the night before He suffered and died for us, and told them how we all should serve each other, whether we are white, black or yellow. The girls were perfectly happy to welcome the new guest, and it was like a special birthday present for the paper to find this continuing of the cooperative spirit among them.

Mary took the paper up to Harlem to distribute for us yesterday, and all the other girls up at the house went to Mass or Communion to offer it up for our special May Day work. Margaret, our cook, despite her condition, for she is expecting her baby in six weeks, went on the subway yesterday, passing out papers from Times Square to Astoria and from Manhattan to Brooklyn. I was much touched and grateful for the help they all gave us.

An old Irishman of 73 came in this morning for his copies of the paper. He lives down in the Bowery and has a thirty-dollar-a-month pension, from which he insists on giving us a dollar. He comes in regularly every month.

2

It was good to sit out in the back yard this afternoon and have tea and I was glad to see Helen Crowe here when I got back. She had been attending a meeting around the corner and she had some work to do, and so came in to use our typewriter. Peter read and argued with her from *The Militant* which calls for a Fourth International, and he, Peter, was arguing for a fifth. I had to keep shushing him so that Helen could get her work done and come out and have tea. We had moved a couch out into the back yard and brought out the rose bush, the hyacinth and the daffodil plants, and the sun was hot and it was delicious.

Peter should be happy now that he has a companion with whom to carry on dialogues. Haig, as he is called, has been staying up at the Municipal Lodging House for some time and Peter wanted to take him in at the office in order to have him to argue with for the school. So now Peter sleeps on a mattress on the floor, and Mr. Haig on Peter's bed. Haig is not a Catholic, but a German Evangelical, or something like that, but he has not practiced any religion since childhood. Peter introduced him to me as an anarchist, but for the purposes of argument, he is a Communist orthodox one night, Left Wing Opposition another night, Socialist another, Fascist, etc.

He is undergoing a course of reading under the supervision of Peter, starting with Christopher Dawson's *The Modern Dilemma*,[22] and he is writing an article for the paper on the Municipal Lodging House. Tonight he is making himself useful by going up to Father Scully's parish to a Holy Name meeting to argue with Peter. It is to be a regular Platonic Dialogue and Peter is revelling in the thought that he has been given the floor for the evening. I am afraid they will be regarded as entertaining rather than instructive. Father Scully's parish, being one of the richest in the city, is not fertile ground to work in as far as I can see. The Psalmist says: "Those who are in honor are without understanding" [paraphrasing Psalm 48:21].

Afterwards they are going up to Harlem to argue from eleven to one, taking the tail-end of what street meetings are going on. Later they hope to get permission from the Police Department to do some speaking.

The best meeting of this week was that at which we had Father Donnelly who is a marvel at explaining dogma. He pays his audience the compliment, or rather does them the honor, of explaining the most difficult doctrines completely. He gives them the very best that he has, and when he wondered, a little

---

22   Christopher Dawson (1889-1970), British Catholic historian and popular author. The work referenced is *The Modern Dilemma: The Problem of European Unity* (London: Sheed & Ward, 1932).

discouraged at some of the questions which came out of the meeting, whether anyone had gotten anything out of his talk, I told him that my feeling was that it was too much expected to-day that people should be articulate. That is, if they are not able to repeat back like parrots what they have been told, it is taken for granted that they have not grasped the subject matter. There are so many dogmas which one can feel and yet not express.

The meeting was crowded to the doors. Late in the evening a drunken Irishman came in and listened for a while open-mouthed, and then got up, waving his hand in farewell.

"I have listened and I've listened," he said, "but, never once have I heard the name of the Mother of God mentioned." And he went disconsolately out of the door.

If Harry Crimmins had been here, his great devotion to the Blessed Mother would have impelled him to rush out after the poor creature and walk the streets with him all night talking of the Blessed Virgin. But as it was the old man got away before anyone could say a word to him.

Another man came up after the meeting and said, "This is one of the worst evenings I have ever spent, how in the world do you stand it."

But the others stood it so well that they stayed and stayed until eleven, instead of going at ten as we try to persuade them to do. There were men from Columbus Circle there, a number of union men from the neighborhood, and all in all, the majority of them people the meetings are intended for.

After the meeting, Father Donnelly, Frank, Tom, Joe, Dorothy and I went across the street to our German cafe where we had limburger sandwiches and bock beer, which were very good. Father Donnelly had to finish part of his Office to the strains of most atrocious jazz coming over the radio.

A Mexican came in the other day with an introduction from a Mexican Jesuit who had been staying in the parish down on Second Avenue and is going back to Mexico this June. Mr.

Frisbie is a very zealous and inspiring man, all afire with zeal for souls. But he is also very funny.

He and his wife are staying in New York so that she can be examined by doctors to find out whether her heart will permit her to live in Mexico City which is too high for most heart cases. But if they cannot stay there, then he is going down to the State of Tabasco where there is only one priest and he in hiding, disguised as a porter. Mr. Frisbie wants to assist him with catechetical work. How his wife's heart will stand that, I do not know.

He very generously offered to go up to speak to the Spanish American group of boys at 112th Street, who have no conception of Catholicism.

I hope he has some effect on them.

3

A few days ago we had quite a time at the House of Hospitality. An old lady who has been staying there, was run down by a truck some time ago and her face badly bruised. The owner of the truck came around and settled with her so that she would not sue, and with the money in her hand she proceeded to get drunk. It took a priest, seven policemen and a steamfitter, and the circulation manager and editor of a paper to get her out of the house and then she won out, and was really victorious.

One old woman who had come in drunk a few months ago was told to go, and why we should waste any more time on Nellie I didn't see. However, I went to St. Zita's and they said they would care for her there. That evening, after having tried in vain twice that day to get her to St. Zita's, and she having consumed four pints, Father Seccor and Harry and I went up. Nothing could be done with her, so Father went out to call a policeman hoping that his uniform would impress her to the extent of accompanying him in a cab to the Home. But one policeman always brings others in his train, and before we knew it, two radio cars had driven up, two policemen from their beats had appeared, and it was indeed an impressive sight to hear the sirens and see the police rushing to protect the House of Hospitality from poor little Nellie.

She finally agreed to get into the cab with one policeman and Father Seccor and Harry, after she had been given the choice of the station house, Bellevue or the Home, but once in the cab she insisted on going to a rooming house where she was known. It was too late by this time to get her in St. Zita's, so they went to the rooming house, going in with her, to impress upon the landlady, who might have been dishonest, that Nellie was not to be tampered with. There she will drink herself out, or go to Chicago, as she said she was going to do with the money.

Yes, there had been a good deal of trouble lately; John with his heart attack, Dorothy sick again and then Nellie on her drunk. It would seem that we lead a disturbed and harassed life, and yet on the whole we are very peaceful. Everything runs really harmoniously and smoothly and our headquarters is a pleasant place of an evening with everyone at his activities. Last night there was no meeting and Mr. Minas sat and wrote poetry in lovely fine Armenian script, smoking his strange-smelling cigarettes; Haig, the German, pondered over Christopher Dawson's latest book; Peter, the Frenchman, plotted his propaganda; Jimmie Raksi, our little Hungarian boy from the reformatory, played with the kitten, having just virtuously attended his Catechism class; Margaret, our Lithuanian, curled her hair in preparation for Sunday, and the rest of us, English, Irish and American, listened to a symphony orchestra play Beethoven.

4

I have been reading a lot of Ozanam[23] lately. He started his religious Conferences of St. Vincent de Paul after the "history

---

23   Blessed Frédéric Ozanam (1813-1853), founder of the Society of St. Vincent de Paul. Beatified in 1997.

conferences" had been carried on for about a year. One of his companions confessed himself to be tired of the "eternal controversies".

The difficulty with Ozanam's group was evidently just the opposite of our main difficulty. Dorothy has been married for the past six months and she and Tom are only in the office a few hours a day. They are both mainly interested in propaganda, the getting out of a paper and pamphlets, and are not much interested in the works of mercy or houses of hospitality except as propaganda centers, with a careful weeding out going on all the time so that only those who agree with us and work with us are kept.

Ozanam's group discarded the propaganda and kept only to the charitable work so that indoctrination did not go hand in hand with charity. We feel that the two must go together since we are trying to change the social order. We have to change the social order so that men will have a chance to become men.

Following Peter's ideas, we are trying to make the workers into scholars and the scholars workers. So we take whoever comes to us as sent by God and do not believe in picking and choosing. If we start eliminating then there is no end to it. Everyone wishes to eliminate someone else. In a group of people living together more or less in community, grievances always pile up which change from day to day and from month to month. Even if we had only picked "intellectuals", young students and propagandists, there would be dissensions and grave differences of opinion. Tom and Dorothy are more at home with the scholars and wish to concentrate more on propaganda. As it is, most of the money is spent on food and shelter and not much is left for the paper and for pamphlets.

But Peter and I feel that the work is more important than the talking and writing about the work. It has always been through the performance of the works of mercy that love is expressed, that people are converted, that the masses are reached.

"Charity should never look behind but always ahead, because the number of her past good deeds is always small, whereas the present and future miseries which she must solace are infinite," Ozanam wrote.

"The faith, the charity of the first ages, they are not too much for our age. Evils equally great must have an equal remedy. The earth has gone cold, and it is for us Catholics to reanimate the vital heat which is being extinguished, to recommence the era of the martyrs. For to be a martyr is a thing within the reach of all Christians. It is to give our lives for God and for our brothers....

"The race of man in our days seems to me like the reveller of whom the Gospel speaks. It, too, has fallen among thieves who stole away its treasure of faith and love. The priests and the Levites have passed and this time, as they were true priests and Levites, they approached and longed to heal the sufferer. But in its delirium it knew them not and repulsed them. In our turn, feeble Samaritans, profane and of little faith though we be, we dare, nevertheless, to accost this great invalid. Perhaps it will not be affrighted at us, so let us try to probe its wounds and to pour oil into them, to whisper in its ears words of consolation and peace, and then, when its eyes re-open, we will put it back into the hands of those whom God has constituted the guardians and physicians of souls.

"When we Catholics reminded these straying brethren of the marvels of Christianity, they used one and all to retort: 'You are right if you speak of the past; Christianity in other times did wonders, but today it is dead. And indeed, you who boast of your Catholicism, what do you do? Where are the works which prove your faith and would make us respect and admit it?' They were justified; this reproach was only too well deserved. Well, then, to work! Let our acts square with our faith. And what were we to do in order to be genuine Catholics if not that which is most pleasing to the eyes of God? Let us then help our neighbor as Jesus Christ did, and put our faith under the protection of charity...."

In season and out of season, he pleaded for "the annihilation of the political spirit in the interests of the social spirit."

5

June 1934

"I said 'Hail Marys' all the while I was picking flowers," Teresa told me this morning when she came in with a bouquet of purple clover, daisies and buttercups to put in front of her much-loved statue of the Child King.

We are in our little house on the beach where I am taking an enforced, and oh, how welcome, vacation because of Teresa's illness. She is all better now, but after three weeks in the hospital and four weeks in what she calls a "conbalescent home" I did not dare bring her back to the city. So here we are, all happy and solitary.

We dine on clams and eels and baked sand shark, and on dock weed of which there are still some tender leaves remaining, and we till the soil to plant flowers, and gather shells, mount seaweed, wade and row and endure sunburn and offer up constant thanksgiving for the beauties all around us.

Today the bay is rough with a constant sound of water, and since the bay is enclosed it is the sound of waterfalls rather than the sound of the surf.

We cannot go to Mass in the morning because the nearest church is five miles away and the chapel up in the village is only open on Saturday nights and Sundays. We strove to get permission to go to a near-by chapel where there is daily Mass for a community of Sisters, but the permission was not given, so we content ourselves with morning prayers, led by Teresa who learned lots of new ones up at her convalescent home in Palenville which is run by the Franciscan Missionaries of Mary.

"The way you learn new prayers," Teresa told me, "is just to say them over night and morning every day for a while. I like learning new ones so you must teach me some."

Her favorite just now is an ejaculatory prayer, which she says comes to her mind often during the day. "By thy holy pitrinity and by thy Immaculate Conception, purify my body and sanctify my soul."

I gather that the peculiar word in the first paragraph means "maternity" and I try to change the prayer for her but she is fond of it the way it is. She is only eight, but quite set in her ways, and if a Sister says a thing, it is so, regardless of what my opinion may be.

The "new" prayer we are learning now is the Song of the Three Children [Daniel 3:52-90], very fitting to say down here on the beach where there is not only sand and sea, but field and woodland; where there is not only the odor of sweet grass and clover, but the salt smell of seaweed and the pleasant odor of decaying sea life.

There is much to do every day. We have to watch the tide, for when it is out, Smiddy will be going down to dig bait and clams and we must accompany him.

Smiddy lives on the beach in a little old shanty eight feet square, just big enough for a narrow cot and an oil stove. It is a place built by one of the neighbors to put fishing tackle and lobster traps in, but no sooner was it built than Smiddy's tent, in which he had lived for some years, was washed away by an unusually high tide and he moved into the shack to take possession from that day to this. Seven years have passed and now it is Smiddy's shack, and he repays the neighbors for allowing him to squat by gifts of clams and fish.

When he needs a haircut, he goes up to the barber with clams. When he wants groceries, he exchanges fish for them. Long years ago he captained a barge, but his young wife died and since then he has been a beachcomber and he has never worked as the neighbors mean the word. Nor had he ever wanted to work except at his clamming and fishing until the WPA came to the island. Then he tried to get a job, and has been indignant ever since at his failure.

Smiddy has known Teresa ever since she was six weeks old and he it was who contributed the lobsters — two dozens of them, trapped by himself — for her baptismal feast. He has always let her help him skin eels, clean fish and dig bait, though she was more of an obstruction than a help when she was one and two years old. He is quite at home with her now as she picks up the foot-long sand worms and black fat clams "to save his back", he says gratefully.

Did I say we were solitary? There is always Smiddy and there are also two Communist children who live up the road and who come down to swim. Teresa has known little Mike since she was two and he three. Even then he was an adventurous youth and, pretending he was a doctor, syringed out her ear by pouring sand in it through a funnel. The little girl, Bunty, is five and she and Teresa have fun playing house and Michael feels out of it, and tries to lord it over them.

They stayed to supper one night last week when they were down on the beach and Michael carried on a long aggrieved monologue:

"I'm going to take a boat and go rowing pretty soon.... Wish there was a Russian boat out there — I'd row right out and get on it. If it caught on fire, I'd row right out there and put that fire out, I would. If you want to be a sailor, the Russian boats are the only ones to sail on. The American sailors never get anything to eat and when they go to sleep they just have bunks so small that they have to hang their feet out the port holes. But the Russian sailors eat right with the captain, and they have parlors to sleep in and to read in. I'm going to be a sailor when I grow up and sail right off to Russia and work there. And you can't come."

Michael puts over his propaganda, and in little ways Teresa puts over hers. She tells Bunty not to take the Lord's name in vain, but Bunty doesn't know what she is talking about. She tries to tell her the story of the Nativity, bringing out her Christmas crèche, but to Bunty it is a Christmas story, no more.

And I am saddened as I hear the little conversations, to think of the generation of children growing up to whom religion means nothing, to whom the name of God is but an expletive, and to whom in the case of many workers' children, the social ideals of the Communists mean something definite, something to be worked for, striven for and sacrificed for, with all the budding idealism of their natures.

Teresa will stay down here on the beach for the rest of the summer with some friends who have rented the bungalow and have children of their own. They not only take care of her, but also pay rent for the place, and the money comes in very handy. I would sell the little place if I could — we need the money so badly, but it is impossible to sell property nowadays. I had paid $2,250 for the house and lot which is twenty by seventy feet, ten years ago, but it will be impossible ever to get anything like that for it.[24] However, renting it in the summer brings us money which we sorely need. Last summer we rented it for ten dollars a week. That and the twenty-five dollars a week I earned at a few odd jobs tided us over those first months when the work was being launched. I do feel strongly that we must put everything we have into the work in embracing voluntary poverty for ourselves. It is only when we do this that we can expect God to provide for us. If we do everything we can ourselves, He will supplement our efforts. This is one of the fundamental points of our work in stressing personal responsibility before state responsibility. It is only when we have used all our material resources that we feel it permissible to call upon the state for aid, that in good conscience we can demand and expect help from the state.

---

24 Day purchased her Staten Island beach house when she sold the film rights (never produced) to her autobiographical novel, *The Eleventh Virgin* (New York: Albert and Charles Boni, 1924), in 1924. She owned the house until her death in 1980.

6

A few weeks ago, I went over to St. Zita's to see a Sister there and the woman who answered the door took it for granted that I came to beg for shelter. The same morning I dropped into the armory on Fourteenth Street, where lunches are being served to unemployed women, and there they again motioned for me to go into the waiting room, thinking that I had come for food. These incidents are significant. After all, my heels are not run down — my clothes are neat — I am sure I looked averagely comfortable and well cared for — and yet it was taken for granted that because I dropped into these places, I needed help. It just shows how many girls and women, who to the average eye, look as though they came from comfortable surroundings, are really homeless and destitute.

You see them in the waiting rooms of all the department stores. To all appearances they are waiting to meet their friends, to go on a shopping tour — to a matinée, or to a nicely served lunch in the store restaurant. But in reality they are looking for work (you can see the worn newspapers they leave behind with the help wanted page well-thumbed), and they have nowhere to go, nowhere to rest but in these public places — and no good hot lunch to look forward to. The stores are thronged with women buying dainty underwear which they could easily do without — compacts for one dollar, when the cosmetics in Woolworth's are just as good — and mingling with these protected women, and often indistinguishable from them, are these sad ones, these desolate ones, with no homes, no jobs, and never enough food in their stomachs.

7

The printer called up this morning wanting to know affably when we were going to finish paying our bill (one hundred thirty dollars still to go). We told him he had better get busy and pray for it right hard.

A huckster goes by selling potatoes twenty pounds for a quarter. We stop to buy them for lunch. Margaret, whose baby is due any minute now, sits in a rocking chair in the back yard and meditates on the petunias blooming there, so the editors are cooks and the circulation manager is dishwasher.

We have often thought of the joys connected with poverty that the respectably comfortable people do not have. Living and working as we do in this store, which opens on the street in front and a back yard in the rear, we are much more in the open air than we would be if we had swanky offices somewhere. (Somebody who belonged to an anti-Jew organization came in once last year and offered us swell offices and we all but threw him out of the window.) In the morning and evening we can have meals in the yard, though of course we are in danger of having people shake their rugs or mops over us. We try to train them not to, but it is hard. In the evening after Benediction, the Italian, Polish, German and Irish neighbors gather on their front steps and chat and drink beer, homemade and not so strong as that you get in the beer gardens.

These hot nights all the fire hydrants are turned on like geysers and the street is cooled off somewhat, and not far away there is a pier down by the East River where you can sit and watch the moon come up.

Neighbors are neighborly and always ready to extend a helping hand. In fact, most of the furniture and clothing which comes into the office to be redistributed comes from the poor. They give what they can, they offer themselves and their time.

And in all these people and the things they do for us and for each other, we find the love of God working through the love of one's neighbor. "I will arise, and will go about the city. In the streets and the broad ways I will seek Him whom my soul loveth" [Song of Songs 3:2]. And, indeed, here is where you find Him, in the person of His poor.

Summer is a hard time for us, however. Priests and laymen who can afford to, write and send us their contributions to keep us going, from all over the country. But in the summer they are away on retreat, or giving retreats, or on vacations, so we are never sure of the whereabouts of our friends. We do not know whether the paper reaches them, with appeals, or whether it sits idly in its envelope waiting for the reader's return.

For the poor there are no vacations. There may be Sunday picnics, but even those mean carfare and lunches for the whole family. Labor troubles continue unabated. This afternoon in this neighborhood there is going to be an anti-war baby parade, with all the mothers decking their carriages in placards and marching down Second Avenue.

Women and children are used because it is believed that the police will hesitate to attack them as they have been attacking the unemployed demonstrators in other parts of the city. They are being used to further another kind of war — class war — but they do not recognize that. They feel they are doing right in taking their babies and demonstrating against war.

8

A heavy heat continues to hang over the city. When I hurry out at seven o'clock there is a haze over the river a few blocks down, sparkling in the sun, but no sign of the thundershowers that have been promised for the last five days.

It is pleasant before Mass to sit and meditate early in the morning in the little Italian Church down on Twelfth Street. On the left hand side the open windows look out on fire escapes and roofs, green-edged with plants. Close to the church window there is corn growing in a tub, tomato plants, basil and other pots of herbs which are fragrant if you crush them between your fingers. People are leaning out of their windows already, trying to get a breath of air.

Inside the Church of Our Lady Help of Christians, the two Italian girls sing the Mass with joyous natural voices, trilling through the Kyrie Eleison. The priest, weighed down with his heavy robes, moves with intent stillness through the sacrifice of the Mass.

I love this church of the Salesian Fathers. It is indeed what a church should be, the center of the community. Every morning at the seven and eight o'clock Masses, both of which are sung, there is a goodly gathering of people, not just devout old ladies and old men, but many young ones too.

Before and after Mass there is always a priest hearing confessions.

Every evening from five o'clock on to past nine, people dropping in, before supper, on their way home from market, from work, from play on the streets — everyone is living on the streets these hot days. There is a crowd at the recitation of the rosary and Benediction. The whole congregation sings the hymns and litanies. And even those priests who are not on duty are there somewhere in evidence. The church is their dearest home, and they evidently love to be contemplating the Humanity of Christ, present there in the Tabernacle.

Every afternoon the pastor has arranged that a shower be rigged up to the fire hydrant out in front of the church from three to six, so that the children of the neighborhood can bathe these hot summer days. When I dropped in to Benediction the other night the shower was still going, and a little baby of two was wandering up and down the gutter which had miraculously become a speeding brook, wetting her shoes and socks, and occasionally all the rest of her as she sat down now and again.

In addition to a parish school, the church cooperates with the Keating Day Nursery across the street, where the various associations have their communion breakfasts and many meetings. There is a regular settlement there and activities are always going on, winter and summer. There is also a camp, where the children are sent for a few weeks in the summer.

9

Father LaFarge paid a call on Peter Maurin at our new branch headquarters up in Harlem. There has been no money to turn on the electricity, nor yet money for candles, so Peter receives callers who come in the evening in the dark, or, rather, with just the light of the street outside. Father LaFarge said that all he could see in the encircling gloom was Peter's forefinger, motioning in the air as he was making points.

The work in Harlem continues apace. There are street meetings three times a week on different corners up and down Lenox Avenue, which go on well into the night and small hours of the morning.

Mr. Hergenhen is the commissar, and he and Peter live on soup a good deal of the time. They have to beg for their food, or for money to buy it. I picked up Peter's prayer book the other day, a little red pamphlet printed at the Monastery of the Precious Blood out in Brooklyn, and on one of the fly leaves was listed some of his needs. "Food, stencils, paper, pamphlets, etc." He didn't need to jot them down to remember them. Maybe it was a little reminder for Our Lord.

Vegetable soup — that's Peter's old standby. So yesterday, Sunday, when he came down to spend the day at the office on Fifteenth Street, we made a huge kettle of soup the like of which he had never seen before. It was a cold beet borscht (can it be that we are being influenced by Moscow, or is it just the East Side?) made from a can of beets, a chopped-up cucumber, green-topped onions, hard-boiled egg, potatoes and sour cream. All mixed together, a little dill chopped up on top, and made good and cold in the icebox (no cooking at all needed) — it was a delicious feed for a hot day. We had enough to have it for breakfast, dinner and supper.

FOUR

1

IT IS a hot, hot night. I have just been up to see Margaret at Bellevue, she has been very ill, first with a high temperature and then a subnormal temperature. She had a little baby girl three weeks ago, and after she got back here she had a relapse and Dorothy and I ran around with bottles and diapers in our hands for days. Finally, Margaret got so bad we had to call an ambulance and cart both her and the baby back. Tonight she seemed well and cheerful, but I think they will keep her another week. The baby is in a well-baby ward and gaining day by day. Dorothy and Tom are up at a Stadium concert tonight and were in for a few minutes. After I have finished writing I am going to Union Square where the first band concert and dance in the open air will be held from eight to ten. La Guardia is instituting lots of things such as taking down the railings in parks, so people can walk on the grass, opening new playgrounds and having these open-air dances and theatres.

On Wednesday ten of us distributed anti-war leaflets in Union Square and all but got mobbed by the Communists. However, a few of them came to our Wednesday night meeting afterward and continued the discussion until one o'clock. It was a very good meeting.

Teresa is still down in Staten Island. She looks wonderfully well. She instructs the other kids in seashore life and has a wonderful aquarium full of eels and killies and some lovely specimens of seaweed. I am going down tomorrow and I languish to think of it. It is so hot and stifling here…. But I seem to thrive on it. I've written four articles and have three more to write. I get about fifteen to twenty dollars each for them.

With Margaret in the hospital and Eileen gone south one would think we would be swamped with work, but so many people walk in to help get meals and do dishes and take letters that somehow things always seem to get done anyway.

Next Monday I go up to Stamford, N.Y., to speak, and back here by the fifteenth — the Feast of the Assumption. Then the new issue will be coming out and we'll be working on that. How the summer flies! We make our plans from day to day and I try not to think of the Fall, and all of Peter's plans for a school every night for ten months. The prospect of such a grind, I confess, appals me. We already work fifteen hours a day.

Just heard the César Franck Symphony which always makes me feel so happy. There is a man in Huxley's *Point Counterpoint* who realizes the existence of God when he hears a certain piece of music, and that is how I feel when I hear the triumphant third movement. My heart is lifted to God. It is a prayer of thanksgiving that God is there....

The goodness of people makes my heart expand too in happiness. Last week or so when we were closing the House of Hospitality for the summer there was an unpleasant job on hand. Most of the girls took very good care of their beds indeed. But the two old ladies, Emily and Marie, who came to us from the Municipal Lodging House, were not so clean. They were two poor old creatures, ragged and miserable, who walked in one afternoon in the midst of a raging blizzard, and they didn't complain of being wet and cold and hungry. They just said, sadly:

"We can't always be young."

They had been scrubwomen, but their days of getting work were past in these hard times. They had had no work for the last year. So they became our guests and most inoffensive, humble, retiring guests they were. They could not get out of the habit of getting up and out, as they were forced to do at the "Muni." Every morning saw them at early Mass and they were gone for the day, to sit around the armories, probably.

It took me several weeks before I got up enough courage to talk openly about how desirable it would be for them to have baths. They had such a lodging house smell about them!

But they never did take care of their beds. So when we closed the place for the summer — they had gone on Home Relief and had a little room of their own by this time — their beds had to be cleaned and all the other beds, too.

I was alone in the office that day. Dorothy and Tom had gone down to the country for a much needed rest from the city. I bought two gallons of benzine and some paint brushes and was ready for work.

And then Tina and Paula came in, hot and tired with the continued humidity. They willingly offered to help me, in spite of the fact that it was a Catholic piece of work. If it was a matter of mailing out the paper or helping distribute it, they would not have done it. After all, they are the Opposition, of the Trotskyite faith. But this was a matter of working for humanity, cleaning up after our guests of the winter.

So we went down the street carrying our pails, and we got to work. Mrs. Post had cleaned the apartment pretty well, so all was neat and tidy when we got there. There were twelve beds, four apiece, — three of them in unspeakable condition, because of the carelessness of our guests.

Tina and Paula, even when they are in house dresses, always have an air, thanks to their mother's skill as a dressmaker. Tina had on a brown linen, her coolest dress, which she wore neat and pressed for "best," and rumpled, but still stylish, for every day. Paula had on a blue blouse and a clinging gray skirt. They are both artists by trade, and it was with the touch of an artist that they set to work. It was a picture to see their graceful young bodies bent over the beds. Tina's fair hair curled around her face with the heat; Paula was flushed and dark. And as they worked, they talked: of revolutionary technique, of the Opposition and the class war tactics which were directed by the orthodox Communists against them. They talked of the street speaking that Paula had to do that night. And they worked!

What good and faithful friends they are! I was intensely grateful to them, and the work was made easier by their presence.

Margaret continues ill in the hospital, with fever every day. But her baby is thriving. We do not know when she will be able to leave. It is funny how responsibilities suddenly loom large and awful in the dead of the night.

I rush headlong on about my work during the days, but often in the dead of the night I awake terrified at the responsibilities which we assume. It was the same with the House of Hospitality when we were starting it. It seemed like such a terrific job, but it really turned out all right.

And now about Margaret's baby. It is here. It must be with us and Margaret must, too. What if it is a delicate baby? What if it cries all day about the office? What if it should get sick? What if Margaret becomes frivolous now that she is no longer in a helpless condition, starts to dye her hair again, put on lipstick and eyebrow pencil and go out of an evening, only to go through the whole sad tale again? What if she disappears and leaves us the baby? What if we cannot take care of her as we should?

But all those things are in the future. I recall St. Teresa, a headlong soul if there ever was one.

2

Peter was talking at dinner tonight:

"The NRA is pragmatism in politics.[25] Experimentation without theory is back of it. Let's try — let's try! Bump your head against the wall and then find it's hard. Try everything but the door — and only then the door. First the RFC, then the NRA, the AAA, CCC, PWA, CWA, FERA, and now it is no longer emergency administration, but rehabilitation — one foot

---

25   The NRA (National Recovery Administration) was one of many attempts by the Roosevelt administration to combat the effects of the Great Depression. As this paragraph suggests, the New Deal produced an "alphabet soup" of governmental agencies during the 1930s.

on the land — the other on industry. Attempting something without trying to get at the root of things.

"Socialism is the state doing things for people instead of people doing things for each other. It is opposed to Communism, the ideal Communism of the Church which means people doing things for each other — the corporal works of mercy.

"Socialism never implies a mode of living. Socialists believe the state will force people to be good.... Norman Thomas[26] criticized MacDonald for not having a philosophy of labor. But Socialism has no philosophy of labor. Socialism is gradualism. Gradually the state will take over everything....

"But Socialism is founded on the doctrines of Karl Marx and Engels, just as Communism is. Communism does not pretend to be Communism now. They are aiming towards Communism, they say, when the state shall have 'withered away,' to use their own phrase. Right now it is Socialism in Russia. It is the Union of Socialist Soviet Republics. It is the Dictatorship of the Proletariat. A dictatorship of a class instead of a dictatorship of an individual.

"Socialism is diametrically opposed to Catholicism because it is essentially materialist in aims and leaves entirely out of accounting our first beginning and our last end, which is God.[27]

"The problems of the day are fundamentally ethical problems. The problem which faces us is not of fighting Communists, of which so many young priests speak so enthusiastically and so ignorantly, but of changing the hearts and souls of men.

"Here is what Karl Adam[28] says:

---

26 Norman Thomas (1884-1968), six-time presidential candidate on the Socialist ticket.

27 This paragraph neatly summarizes Maurin and Day's suspicion of Socialism and of political movements in general. While often sharing particular goals with them, the Catholic Worker movement was intended as a comprehensive Christian alternative to political systems reliant upon the State for achieving their ends.

28 Rev. Karl Adam (1876-1966), prominent Catholic theologian and popular author of the influential and widely translated *The Spirit of Catholicism* (1924).

" 'Today, when poverty stalks the streets and the idol of Mammon disinherits millions and keeps them in permanent servitude, pitilessly destroying the happiness of family life, and with unparalleled levity inflaming class hatred — even today there is still room and a fertile field for the Saviour's work to be done by the Church.

" 'But it cannot be done merely by beautiful sermons.

" 'Even the great social organizations are no longer sufficient, not even the devoted labours of charitable societies.

" 'The only remedy is a new life in the Holy Ghost, a return of all of us to the paradox of the supernatural, a determined assent to the poor, crucified Jesus. That is the road to the rebirth of the West; there is no other way.

" 'The path to reform is then clear. But indeed, when describing this path, our heart fears and we would like to exclaim with the Apostles: *Lord, who then can be saved?*

" 'It is quite evident to us that we of the West will not of our own accord set foot upon this path....

" 'But are not all things possible with God? Perhaps the Lord Christ will call again from His Church apostles and saints, who, attired in the strength from on high, will bring a new spring into His Church.

" 'Perhaps He will give us a second St. Francis, a saint with a burning heart, who will seek and love poverty in human life in the brutal nakedness of its reality, in the many forms of its oppressiveness, narrowness and savagery; who will set out daily with His brethren and himself bear side by side with His children the hard yoke of dull factory-work, to share with them and lead them in to the wedding-feast.

" 'Or perhaps God will come to us in storm and tempest and we shall have to descend again into the catacombs in order to find Christ.

" 'I cannot tell, but this much I know; whether God's grace renews us in the whispering of the breeze or the roar of the storm, it will renew us only by making us small again.

" '. . . What are we to do, oh my brothers, my sisters? We are the collaborators of Christ, Christ's soldiers in the battle against anti-Christ. Perhaps Christ needs but three hundred men to overthrow the Amalekites. Perhaps only a dozen men of the people would suffice Him as they sufficed once before.' "

3

Today we are not contented with little achievements, with small beginnings. We should look to St. Teresa, the Little Flower, to walk her little way, her way of love.[29] We should look to St. Teresa of Avila who was not content to be like those people who proceeded with the pace of hens about God's business, but like those people who on their own account were greatly daring in what they wished to do for God. It is we ourselves that we have to think about, no one else. That is the way the saints worked. They paid attention to what they were doing and if others were attracted to them by their enterprise, why, well and good. But they looked to themselves first of all.

Do what comes to hand. Whatsoever thy hand finds to do, do it with all thy might. After all, God is with us. It shows too much conceit to trust to ourselves, to be discouraged at what we ourselves can accomplish. It is lacking in faith in God to be discouraged. After all, we are going to proceed with His help. We offer Him what we are going to do. If He wishes it to prosper, it will. We must depend solely on Him. Work as though everything depended on ourselves, and pray as though everything depended on God, as St. Ignatius says.

One young fellow wants to get out and demonstrate. Wants United Front with the Communists because so many of our aims of social justice are the same. Wants action, shouting, brandishing of placards, clubs, a fight, in other words.

---

29 Day's devotion to St. Thérèse of Lisieux (1873-1897) culminated in a book-length study, *Therese: A Life of Therese of Lisieux* (Notre Dame, IN: Fides, 1960).

Demands, not appeals. Class war again. Hate your enemies. Which is all wrong.

After all, we are not working for the dictatorship of the proletariat, so why work with the Communists? We believe not in acquisitive classes but functional classes. But we are not going to achieve any reform by going out and shooting all the capitalists even though we do not believe in the capitalists' system. (Personally, I'd rather shoot all the advertising men, all the moving picture men who have corrupted the minds and the desires of the youth of the country.)[30]

John Erit wishes to work through the state. To write letters to Assemblymen, Congressmen, work for better laws, minimum wage, eight-hour day, abolition of child labor. These are all palliatives. (It is interesting that the Young Communist League opposed the child labor amendment just as the reactionaries did throughout the country. And they opposed it on almost the same grounds that the Catholics did. They did not want this present state to interfere with the rights of youth. They did not wish to be limited in their desire to work. Communists are getting back to the idea that work is a noble thing — a necessity for man.)

The Catholic youth group which meets here on Wednesday nights also wants to be up and doing. They want action. They want definite things to do. They want membership.

It is all right to want definite things to do. Let them model themselves after the Communist youth groups and give out literature, speak at meetings on subjects on which they have informed themselves. To what purpose is all this speaking and distributing of literature which the Communists do?

To change the hearts and minds of men, of course, but towards Communism.

---

30 This seemingly shocking call to violence by Day is clearly intended ironically, given her absolutist demand for pacificism during the Second World War and afterwards. As she writes below (p. 177): "We oppose all use of violence as un-Christian."

Let us do the same thing. Let us canvass blocks, factories, schools, form groups to study, not Marxism, but the encyclicals of the Popes — the writings of the Church on social questions as well as on the liturgy. The two should go together. There should be daily Mass, a community act, as well as the individual work which we must each do. We believe in the Communion of Saints, we know that in the act of the Mass we are associated with a great body, the Church militant, the Church suffering, the Church triumphant.

But why should they worry about numbers? They want something to show for their efforts. Perhaps there is the desire for power, for excitement there. They want huge mass meetings, pageants, demonstrations, such as the youth movement has in Belgium and France.

Not long ago I read the life of Lenin by his widow. She wrote of a meeting which was held in Paris not so many years ago when twenty or so people attended, and she wrote glowingly of what a splendid meeting it was. Lenin was an exile and gathered his few followers around him wherever he was, and he and his wife thought their meeting of twenty — the usual number we have on these hot summer evenings — a goodly gathering.

And now, not so many years after, this man has taken possession of one hundred and sixty millions of people, one-sixth of the globe, and has established his rule, his dictatorship of the proletariat, and the people revere him as their saint.

And our youth dares to be discouraged, with Christ as its leader, with the Church at its back, — its wealth in writings, the very deeds and virtues of its saints to draw upon, — and wishes for numbers, for demonstrations, for something to do!

4

It is overcast, drizzling, warm. "The ear is not content with hearing, nor the eye with seeing." I'm thinking of this because

I'm listening to the Symphonic Hour on the radio and they are broadcasting Brahms' First Symphony.

I'm enjoying it very much, though Margaret bothers me with remarks about there being no butter; Tom asks for stencils, the baby frets, etc. Even so, I enjoy it. But we cannot depend on our senses at all for enjoyment. What gives us keen enjoyment one day we listen to with indifference the next; the beauties of the beach arouse us to thanksgiving and exultation at one time and at another leave us lonely and miserable. "It is vanity to mind this present life, and not to look forward unto those things which are to come."[31]

Hardships to offer up. Going to bed at night with the foul smell of unwashed bodies in my nostrils. Lack of privacy. But Christ was born in a stable and a stable is apt to be unclean and odorous. If the Blessed Mother could endure it, why not I? Also, Christ had no place to lay His Head in the years of His public life. "The birds of the air have their nests and the foxes their holes, but the Son of Man has no place to lay His Head" [Matthew 8:20].

Yesterday Monsignor Scanlan,[32] the Rector of the Diocesan Seminary and the Censor of the diocese, honored us with a visit to tell us about his and the Cardinal's approval of our work.[33] He says he wishes to approve a spiritual adviser for us, to be consulted on doctrinal matters only, and not on such subjects as strikes or labor in general, or legislation. Those are matters on which we are free to express our opinions.

He seemed to think we would not like this (though we are glad) and assured us it was only to facilitate our progress — that

---

31 Thomas à Kempis, *The Imitation of Christ*, Book I, Chap. 1.

32 Rev. Msgr. Arthur J. Scanlan (1881-1974), archdiocesan "adviser" to the Catholic Worker movement following Paulist Father Patrick J. McCloskey.

33 Despite occasional disagreements with the Catholic Worker (especially during the archdiocesan grave-diggers' strike of 1949, during which strikebreakers were employed by the archdiocese), Francis Cardinal Spellman (1889-1967) was a supporter and protector of Day and her work.

they would give us public approval if they thought it would not hinder us in our work.

Margaret came in with the carriage filled with the baby and vegetables. Monsignor blessed the baby and, incidentally, our food for the evening meal. Margaret would not put tomatoes on the table because they had not been blessed and she wanted this an entirely blessed meal!

Wrote an appeal and a financial report to send out.

I suppose it is a grace not to be able to have time to take or derive satisfaction in the work we are doing. In what time I have, my impulse is to self-criticism and examination of conscience, and I am constantly humiliated at my own imperfections and at my halting progress. Perhaps I deceive myself here too, and excuse my lack of recollection. But I do know how small I am and how little I can do and I beg You, Lord, to help me for I cannot help myself.

5

A quiet evening. Mr. Minas and I have just finished our usual late evening repast, cocoa, and bread and mustard or black olives. Mr. Minas sprinkles his bread with red pepper.

He is a little thin man with long white hair, a yellow face, greenish eyes with immense pupils and a predatory nose. The men who work with us get very well fitted out with suits somehow or other, but their shoes are not so good. Mr. Minas' turn up at the toes, which somehow fits in with his Oriental appearance. He is very clean always, and before he uses cups or spoons, carefully rinses them. He is always on the lookout for cockroaches and the funny little silverfish bugs which run around the kitchen drive him frantic. Always red ants are getting into the ice-box. Right now the cockroaches are under cover and not a bedbug has been seen for months. So at present he is at peace. A month ago we had fleas in my side of the house. They are gone since Tom went around with the spray gun. Now there are only centipedes on my side of the house and the funny silver bugs on Mr. Minas'.

He is very fond of our black cat which Mary Sheehan named Social Justice. He washes her face and paws carefully every day and feeds her a little bit of everything — just now, Parmesan cheese, for instance, and she is thirsty and is drinking the goldfish water, terrifying the three fish.

He writes poetry in beautiful Armenian script and carries around his notebook pinned with a safety pin to his pocket ever since he lost it this summer. That was a tragedy — we all felt that his poetry represented everything to him, all that our faith means to us. We started praying to St. Anthony that it would be returned and the next day a young Episcopalian boy came in with the manuscript. Margaret insisted he was St. Anthony in disguise.

We have been reading Dostoievsky, Mr. Minas and I, for the last few months. I've had *Crime and Punishment* and he, *The Idiot*, both of us re-reading them. I had only Sundays and late evenings, but he went around with his under his arm continually, trying to find a quiet corner, which is always difficult around here.

FIVE

1

IT IS cold and we are writing in the kitchen where there are no draughts. Barbara, Margaret's baby, sits on her mother's lap by the table and she, too, is writing an editorial, although she is only five months old. In her zeal she tries first to eat the pencil her fond mother has given her, and then the paper.

On the wall there are three pictures which attract her attention. She calls out to them, trying to crow. There is a Polish Madonna, a Negro Madonna and a picture of a Madonna and a worker by Ade Bethune.

Teresa is drawing pictures too, and when she shows them to the baby, Barbara laughs and makes bubbles. The black cat lies in restful abandon in front of the stove.

It is one of those rare evenings when there are no visitors, when the work of the day seems to be over, though it is only seven-thirty. It is a good time to sit and write editorials. An editorial, for instance, on charity. St. Saviour's High School and Cathedral High School sent down so many baskets of food, including hams and canned goods, potatoes and all the trimmings for Christmas dinners, that the office was piled high for at least three hours until they were all distributed. It is true it did not take long to distribute them, there is such need around here.

There were toys, too, dolls for the girls and other toys for the boys, all beautifully wrapped and be-ribboned.

Bundles of clothes came in, including many overcoats, and they went out as fast as they came in. They were sent in response to the story of the man who had to accept a woman's woolen sweater in lieu of underwear or overcoat. I hope they keep on coming in.

I'd like to have everyone see the poor worn feet, clad in shoes that are falling apart, which find their way to the *Catholic Worker* office. A man came in this rainy morning and when he took off one dilapidated rag of footwear, his sock had huge holes in the heel and was soaking wet at that. We made him put on a dry sock before trying on the pair of shoes we found for him, and he changed diffidently, there under the eye of the Blessed Virgin on the bookcase, looking down from her shrine of Christmas greens. But his poor, red feet were clean. Most of the men and women who come in from the lodging houses and from the streets manage cleanliness, with the help of the public baths. I heard of one man who washed his underwear in the public baths and sat there as long as he could in that steam-laden, enervating atmosphere until it was not quite too wet to put on again. For the rest, it could dry on his skin. Not a pleasant thought in bitter weather. Many of the men do this, he said.

Our prayer for the new year is that the members may be "mutually careful one for another" [Romans 13:8].

Teresa, who has been away to school this fall, was home for the holidays, perched like a little sparrow right at my elbow as I typed stories for the paper. She got a microscope set for Christmas and the best place to be engaging in scientific pursuits was usually right at the typewriter table by my side.

"Perhaps," she would murmur to herself, "there'll be bugs in the ice-box water.... Here is a slide with some of Tom's blood on it ... it's not much good.... Don't you want to look at a butterfly scale? And don't forget to write in the paper that I went picketing with you on December 31st.... That's a hot one!

"Why don't you want me to say 'That's a hot one'? I like to say it ... you won't let me say 'Come over and see me some time' — so I'm going to say 'That's a hot one.'"

Going on the ferry over to Staten Island to take Teresa back to St. Patrick's where she is going to school, the gulls stood out white against the gray sky. They swept and glided, swooping down into the water now and then after a fish. Their cries and the sound of the water as the boat churned through it were the only sounds in the winter stillness. Then there was the walk with Teresa up the country road, past a thicket of birches with the blue-green twilight sky behind them. To one side of the road was a field of yellow grass, bent by a soft wind. Alongside a path through the fields, there was a little brook gurgling cheerfully beneath the ice that caked it. There are still green things showing under the stubble, bits of wild carrot, the green of vines, even some wild geranium. And as the earth lost its color and darkened, there was still the radiance of a sunset flushing the sky.

2

The work continues back in the office until late in the evening. Visitors from Chicago, from Maryland, from New Hampshire, from Buffalo. A worker from one of the chain stores who tells us about his long day: he gets up at five-thirty to assist at early Mass, and he is never through with his work until seven-thirty in the evening. He wants to help us by distributing the papers on Sundays.... A man comes in from East Eleventh Street to tell us how the paper has reinforced his faith, and to bring us some clothes for those that are poorer than he, and he is poor enough. All day, starting at eight-thirty, there are the unemployed. They want underwear, shoes, coats, information about Home Relief. Or they just want to talk to us. There are the unemployed all day, and in the evening there are those who work and have no other time to come. So if the paper is rather disjointed and unfinished in its writing, it is because there is so much to do for twelve hours, and only a few of the left-over hours to write about the work and the thought behind the work.

As for our immediate assistants and co-workers — they continue faithfully in their voluntary co-operation. Two or three are always picketing, running errands, addressing envelopes, going to the post office, paying calls in the neighborhood, taking care of the needs of those who come in. The girls from the House of Hospitality helped us to picket the Mexican consulate on the feast of Our Lady of Guadalupe, and when they came in that morning to go with us to the high Mass which started the day's work, they told us how four of them said the rosary aloud together the night before for our persecuted fellow-workers in Mexico City.

During the month there was a call of distress from a man whose wife had just gone to the hospital to have her sixth child. His mother was to have taken care of the other five children, but the very next day she fell off a chair and broke her arm, so the little ones were left to the care of the nine-year-old eldest girl. The father found it impossible to get any help so an appeal was made to *The Catholic Worker*. One of the girls cooperating with us volunteered for the job and took charge of the little household. It meant ten days of good hard work, and one of the little ones, two years old, was ill. There was washing and ironing and cleaning to do, besides the marketing and cooking. A few of the afternoons some of the boys from the office went up to take care of the kids while she did the shopping. One of those who volunteered for this work was a seminarian on his vacation. He will make a good Franciscan, that boy. The girl had gone out on the job as an errand of mercy, not expecting any pay, but both the man and his wife insisted that she be paid and paid generously. She had been jobless for some time, so the money came in handy. The husband had been out of work for quite a time too, and money was hard earned in that big family, but it is the poor who are the most generous and the most appreciative. "I had not been able to find anyone to help us for love or money," he told us.

3

Someone wrote to us that he was always interested in hearing how the printing bill got paid — how we made out during the month. Well, this was a good month and, looking back to last Christmas when we were so poor that we had to skip our January edition, we praise the Lord and all His saints for the abundance this year. Christmas cards came to us enclosing money and little by little the bills were paid. The telephone was almost shut off but wasn't quite, the electric man came around to deprive us of light, but didn't (there had been an offering through the mail), there were a few meals of beans, and then a basket of food came in; and we were preparing to put off the January edition until late in the month when a generous check came in from a priest whom we would name except that we are afraid he would get sore, and so that bill was paid off and there was still twenty-five dollars in the bank.

This morning our dentist, who has been taking care of everybody for nothing for the last year, called up and said the marshal was on his doorstep, and miraculously enough there were twenty dollars for him. He had pulled a dozen teeth and filled another dozen and still he said his bill was only fifteen dollars. We gave him what we had, however, and we are sure that somehow or other there will be enough money to pay for the mailing of the paper. It's true that only seventy-five cents came in today, but God will supply our wants.

4

It is just after midnight and I have been sitting in the outer office alone with two mad creatures with God in their hearts. All three of us tormented in our various ways — all three of us alone, so completely alone too. They were working at putting up the long table for Frank, the circulation manager, and all his assistants to work at. They had started at seven and it was a long, but beautifully efficient job. C.'s madness consists of going in for astrology — it is his passion and it must be regarded seriously. He is anxious to help us and he worked in the Harlem office, and now this big job, even paying for the lumber, and when I keep asking for an account he keeps putting me off. He is a young German and very solitary and inarticulate, except on the question of astrology.

The other, Bernard Adelson, I met when I spoke at Father Rothlauf's last year. He came down the next night and has been with us ever since, off and on, one time speaking in an inspired fashion of the Mystical Body, of other Christs, of the Psalms, quoting them in the Hebrew, and then going off into a perfect mania of persecution talk, holding his head and speaking of madness and death.

As I sit I am weeping. I have been torn recently by people, by things that happen. Surely we are, here in our community, made up of poor lost ones, the abandoned ones, the sick, the crazed and the solitary human beings whom Christ so loved and in whom I see, with a terrible anguish, the body of this death. And out in the streets wandering somewhere is Mr. Minas, solitary among a multitude, surrounded by us all day long, but not one of us save in his humanity, denying, not knowing — yet clinging to some dream, some ideal of beauty which he tries to express in the poetry which no one but he can read.

Catherine is tossing in her bed, unable to sleep, because of the wailing of cats in the back yard who act as though all the devils were in them — Catherine, too, with the misery of her illness hanging over her — with the uncertainty, the pain and the nerve-racking treatments she undergoes.

I have seen too much suffering recently. There is the girl Father Michael sent me to visit in Woonsocket, who suffers in her skeleton body the torments Christ suffered.[34] But I cannot write about her; it is impossible to talk about these supernatural manifestations which are beyond my comprehension.

5

This morning a young Socialist came to breakfast. (Usually as I come from Mass there is somebody waiting at the door

---

34   Mary Rose Ferron (1902-1936), a Quebec-born stigmatist and subject of popular devotion among Franco-Catholic circles during this period.

to get in.) He had formerly been a Communist and now he is a Socialist. We spoke of the arguments as to the existence of God, especially the argument from conscience. The Communists have absolute standards of right or wrong, regardless of what they may say. Their practice of self-criticism proves this. From whom do those standards come? They would say from Karl Marx or Lenin, I suppose.

In the evening I attended a meeting where there was a young Catholic lawyer who had just returned from a visit to Mexico. He was enthusiastic about the public improvements in the State of Sonora, the playgrounds (there was one place just as good as Jones Beach!) and the roads, and I don't know what all, and the fact that the peons were earning two pesos a day on some of the plantations and the women could wear silk stockings!

Rodolpho Calles must have some good points, he said. This, in spite of the fact that not a church is open in the state and not a priest allowed! When I contemplate civilization which offers us silk stockings and playgrounds and electric ice boxes in return for the love of God, I begin to long for a good class war, with the civilizers lined up to be liquidated.[35]

Franciscan spirit grows hereabouts. Last night Mr. Minas, who is devoted to our black cat, was discovered washing her chest with my washrag and drying her with my towel and then anointing her with a warming unguent for a bad cough! It is good I discovered him in the act. Then big Dan, our chief-of-staff on the streets of New York (he sells the paper, either on Fourteenth Street or in front of Macy's every day) took one of my blankets to cover the old horse who helps us deliver our Manhattan bundles of papers every month. He is a truly Catholic Worker horse, Dan says, and when they go up Fifth Avenue and pass St. Patrick's Cathedral, the horse genuflects!

---

35   Another instance of ironic hyperbole by Day. See above (p. 115, note 30).

Dan delivers the papers all over New York every month when the new issue comes out, and then during the month he sells. He likes to get next to some Communist who is selling the *Daily Worker*, and as the latter shouts "Read the *Daily Worker*," Dan replies, "Read *The Catholic Worker* daily!"

Once he saw me coming and modified his shout to "*Catholic Worker* romance on every page, read *The Catholic Worker!*" He is huge and boisterous and friendly and has come to be known to everyone. We will never be able to find out how many thousands of subscriptions have come in through Big Dan and Stanley Vishnewsky, who have shared the street apostolate. Stanley writes besides, and has had articles accepted by both *America* and the *Commonweal*, and many of the little bits he has written for the CW have been reprinted in foreign papers. He has a distinct style and humor, a freshness that is rare.

Mary Sheehan has been a faithful saleswoman on Fourteenth Street too. One of her sallies was reported to me recently. A Communist passing by started cursing the Cardinal. "Why, he gets drunk every Saturday night with his housekeeper!" he said, hoping to get a rise out of Mary.

"And doesn't that just show how democratic he is," Mary retorted.

I went to the Cenacle at three this afternoon, going up on the bus through a heavy fog. The trees on the Drive were beautiful standing out so alone, the only things of beauty in a gray, dark world. I love such days; so much is hidden, and only single things like a tree or bush stand out. These are good days to walk in, not too cold, and if you go down by the docks at the foot of Twenty-third or Fourteenth or Tenth Street, the world seems to come to an end right there. There is a rare stillness only broken by the sound of the water washing against the piers. And when, as along Riverside Drive, you have the trees as well as the sense of the water (if you do not have the sight of it) there is a poignant midwinter beauty, a very restful interlude in a crowded life.

A Franciscan missionary priest from China came in last night — well after eleven — with Mr. Walsh, who is a press-man on one of the Hearst papers. Mr. Walsh has been one of our supporters for the last year and it is due to his efforts that many missionary priests in China have received copies of *The Catholic Worker*. He lived in China for some time himself and has a keen interest in the affairs over there.

There was good conversation for some hours and before Father Burtschy left he said that he would see to it that some of the writings of Peter Maurin were translated into Chinese for one of the two Catholic dailies. It was great to contemplate seeing Peter's *Easy Essays* in Chinese, but it was astounding to consider the fact that there are two Chinese Catholic dailies.

Other interesting visitors during the week were a Maltese Catholic who spoke glowingly of his devotion to St. Paul, and of the devotion of all those on the island from which he comes; and a former I.W.W. seaman who was converted to the Church some five or six years ago.

The gray heavy cold of winter has closed in. Such bitter days the streets are deserted early in the evening except for a few people who scurry along, blown by or facing the wind, seeking shelter.

Every morning from eight o'clock on, men come to the office, pinched and blue with the cold, seeking clothes. Small shoes, cut here and there to make them bigger, trousers, patched or pleated, shrunken and stained by the weather. Someone is sending us a bag of oatmeal today, which means that we can continue to feed those who come to us, warm their insides, if we cannot warm their outsides with an additional garment.

6

We have moved from Fifteenth Street, and these last weeks have been so busy I could not write. It made me miserable to leave our garden, our East side where I have lived for so long.

But one of the priests at St. Veronica's called our attention to a house in his parish which has twelve rooms so large that we can accommodate all our guests in the House of Hospitality in addition to the offices.

Dorothy and Tom will remain in their apartment on the East side, Frank and Loretta live uptown, but the rest of the crowd can live in the house, the men on the second floor and the women on the third. We will be crowded, but the rent will be cut in half. In addition to rent for the two married couples, we have been paying one hundred dollars a month for stores and the apartment for the women.

The young ones all like it, but I, who am fifteen years older and feel like the grandmother of the revolution, find it hard to be torn up by the roots like this. I lived at the place on Fifteenth Street before the paper started, I enjoyed the garden for four long summers. There I could have Teresa with me during her vacations. Now we have only a tiny hall bedroom to share with each other.

This summer, however, we are going to rent a house and garden on Staten Island, a first step towards the land, and there she can vacation with the little Negro children from our Harlem group and with the West side longshoremen's children who will visit with us. She loves the beach, and I will run back and forth as much as I can.

Christmas Day ten of us took bundles of papers down to the Municipal Lodging House at South Ferry, where 12,000 men were being fed Christmas dinner. Up at the 25th Street Lodging House 5,000 more were being provided with Christmas dinners and cigarettes. We were not given permission to give out the papers in the dining room, but we stood outside the entrance and went along South Street distributing. It was a bright sunshiny day, and very pleasant, down there by Battery Park.

The reception accorded the papers was heartening. Many of the workers knew it and had been reading it. One unemployed miner from Pennsylvania, who had come to New York to try for work along the waterfront, condemned wholeheartedly the leadership of the longshoremen's union. "I'm no Communist," he said, "I'm a Catholic, but what I say is that the unions need cleaning up."

We stood there on a cold street corner discussing the Catholic teaching on organization of workers and the friendly interview ended with his inviting me to have lunch with him.

"I'm not broke yet," he said (though he was coatless), "and I could buy my Christmas dinner myself. If you won't have a bite to eat, here, take a dime for the papers."

And I couldn't refuse him because I knew, as he did, that every little bit helps.

SIX

1

"GOD has sent the Spirit of his Son into your hearts crying: Abba, Father.

"And if it were not for this indwelling of the Holy Spirit we would never have this impulse toward the Father." — St. Augustine.

These thoughts are here because Teresa was confirmed last month, receiving the seven gifts of the Holy Spirit.

She also received a new dress, a rare thing in the life of a Catholic Worker.

We now have our Catholic Worker garden commune, and every weekend groups of young workers come down for a holiday, to study or for a retreat.

Honeysuckle is still out and the privet hedges are just beginning to blossom.

There was a thunderstorm and, as usual, after the first burst was over and it had cleared with a golden light over all the damp green, another storm rolled up, or else it was the same storm which had rolled back.

Walking through the wet, tall grass, the trees overhead showered us. The song sparrows and the catbirds sang their last songs before nightfall. In a neighbor's house, *Aïda* was on the radio. It is good to get down to the beach for a quiet breathing spell.

In the morning we had, six of us, been up to the 32nd Street courthouse to witness eviction cases.

2

Two of the girls in the House of Hospitality have been fighting constantly. Today I felt so bad about it I could have wept. I am so enraged that anyone should so consistently, month after month, act in mean, little, underhand ways that I almost wanted to beat them both. My mind was in a turmoil and yet I could not stop it. I went to church leaving word for Tina to meet me there and she came and stayed until after the rosary. (She must be getting to feel quite at home in church.) Afterwards, we went to the movies and saw a really delightfully funny film with Butterworth in it, and then we went home, both of us with raging headaches. It had been very hot all day. At the house, it was still noisy and I wept before going to sleep, and awoke with the same feeling of oppression. To Mass and Communion, still feeling oppressed, praying with distraction. And yet it rather amused me too to place the two girls together in the hands of our Blessed Mother. But it worked!

Despite my feeling of almost hopelessness and desperation, humanly speaking, I came through the day feeling singularly calm, peaceful and happy.

Three conclusions were the result of my praying: First: My getting into a temper helped nobody. But remaining loving towards all helped to calm them all. Hence a great responsibility rests on me. Second: It was cruel to be harsh to anyone so absolutely dependent, as they are, humanly, on my kindness. Third: It is a healthy sign that they are not crushed and humbled towards other human beings by their own miseries. I mean, going around meekly for fear of me, or being humble out of human respect.

One must only be humble from a divine motive, otherwise humility is a debasing and repulsive attitude. To be humble and meek for love of God — that is beautiful. But to be humble and meek because your bread and butter depends on it is awful. It is to lose one's sense of human dignity. So it is a cause for gratitude that Mr. C. and Mr. N. (it is not only women who are troublesome) and the girls should feel free to assert themselves, not worrying about the trouble they cause.

Let reform come through love of God only, and from that love of God, love of each other.

The epistle or gospel, I forget which, for St. Paulinus' day is especially beautiful:

"Out of your abundance supply their want" [2 Corinthians 8:14].

Which means charity and patience and love, as well as material goods, and abilities to help actively in the movement. It has been doing me good all week.

This morning it was the Offertory of the Sacred Heart Mass which caught my eye. Why should we expect consolations?

It is good and healthy to be oppressed, a great opportunity for growth. We are driven to prayer, we are loath and comfortless. But as Dom Chapman says, "It is the after effects which count."

And the after effects of last night's and this morning's heavy praying have been peace and joy and strength and thanksgiving, and a great deal of humility too, at being so weak that God had to send me consolation to prepare me for the next trial.

I should know by this time that just because I *feel* that everything is useless and going to pieces and badly done and futile, it is not really that way at all. Everything is all right. It is in the hands of God. Let us abandon everything to Divine Providence.

And I must remember too that often beautiful scenery or a perfect symphony leaves me cold and dreary. There is nothing the matter either with the scenery or the music — it is myself. I have endured other miseries cheerfully at times. So I must be calm, patient, enduring, and meditate on the gifts of the Holy Spirit.

I am writing this for my consolation and courage some future day when God sees fit and thinks me strong enough to bear longer-continued crosses.

It is to remind myself so that maybe I will be stronger.

3

The Epistle for St. James' Day: "We are made a spectacle to the world and to angels and to men. We are fools for Christ's sake" [1 Corinthians 4:10].

St. James is called a "Son of Thunder" for his fiery zeal.

Distribution of literature to truckmen and longshoremen.... Wrote leaflet opposing United Front on the German situation because of divergent philosophies.... Washed sheets for Mr. Breen.... The filing which we are going in for intensively.... Letters.... Reading.... Helen Crowe over and we went to see a newsreel and saw a volcano picture.... Talked of O'Leary's trial and of spies.... Mary and Big Dan, Joe and Elizabeth out selling.... Great controversy and opposition over works of mercy. No use writing about it. We talk for hours.

Yesterday one of the Educational Division of Federal Workers called about workers' groups. He wanted discussions and workers, and suggested that we recommend teachers. They want variety. It seems all they have is "modified" Marxist teaching. Strange anomaly.

4

Lord Macaulay calls Lucian of Samosata the last great master of Attic wit and eloquence. This is from *The Death of Peregrine*:

"It was now that he came across the priests and scribes of the Christians, in Palestine, and picked up their queer creed.... The Christians, you know, worship a man to this day, the distinguished personage who introduced their novel rites, and was crucified on that account."

The story goes on about the rogue Peregrine taking in the Christians so that when he went to jail for some imposture *"the Christians took it all very seriously; he was no sooner in prison than they began trying every means to get him out again, but without success. Everything else that could be done for him they most devoutly did. They thought of nothing else. Orphans and ancient widows might be seen hanging about the prison from break of day. Their officials bribed the gaolers to let them sleep inside with him. Elegant dinners were conveyed in; their sacred writings were read…. In some of the Asiatic cities, too, the Christian communities put themselves to the expense of sending deputations, with offers of sympathy, assistance and legal advice. The activity of these people in dealing with any matter that affects their community, is something extraordinary; they spare no trouble, no expense….*

"You see, these misguided creatures start with the general conviction that they are immortal for all time, which explains the contempt of death and voluntary self devotion which are so common among them; and then it was impressed on them by their original lawgiver that they are all brothers, from the moment that they are converted and deny the Gods of Greece, and worship the crucified sage, and live after his laws. All this they take quite on trust, with the result that they despise all worldly goods alike, regarding them merely as common property."

Here is another good quotation:

"All property, the more common it becomes, the more heavenly it becomes." — St. Gertrude.

"A Saint is one who has learned to spiritualize and sacramentalize and ennoble everything in the world and make of it a prayer." — Fulton Sheen.

How much time is consciously spent in prayer? Three-quarters of an hour in the morning at Mass. Rosary and visit, one half hour. Night prayers, one half hour. Say, two hours all told. Spiritual reading one or two hours. Sleep seven hours, which leaves thirteen hours of activity. Too much.

I shall add up each day and keep track.

Immediately after writing this — more activity. It was the beginning of the Campion weekend so that there were the children to be dressed and brought into town, and Teresa to be sent back to school for a midsummer retreat. Then at eleven that night up to where the *Bremen* was docked to be at the demonstration held there by the Communists.[36] We distributed the leaflet of the Friends of Catholic Germany. There was a riot on the boat, the flag was torn down, and there was some disturbance on the pier. Eight men were arrested and the demonstration proceeded up to the night court, then to the police station on 47th Street. There occurred a most vicious attack by the police on the demonstrators who were engaged in holding a meeting outside the court and singing songs. Men and women were clubbed, driven down the street and beaten. I saw two plainclothesmen beating up one of the demonstrators in a hallway. The crowd was dispersed, but at what cost of sacrifice of principle!

"To love is not to experience a particular sensation in the heart; that emotion is but a reflex phenomenon, a detail of love and the least. To love is to wish for the good, it is to give the best of one's self for the good of another; it does not mean grasping for one's self; love means giving one's self.

"As long as the understanding finds no trouble or difficulty, and is at ease, that is a sign that one's faith has not gone far enough." — Msgr. Landrieux, in *The Forgotten Paraclete*.[37]

"Every creature is a word of that divine poem, a sacred hieroglyphic, a kind of sacrament, a visible sign that contains a fragment of the idea of God."

---

36   In 1935, the German ship *Bremen* was boarded by protestors and its Nazi flag torn down while docked in New York.

37   Most Rev. Maurice Landrieux (1857-1926), bishop of Dijon and popular writer. The work referenced is *The Forgotten Paraclete* (New York: Benziger, 1924).

"When we enter upon the duties of any office, as that of regent, preacher, or superior, we ought to prepare ourselves for it by some practice of humility, mortification, or charity, such as visiting prisoners or the poor in hospitals, serving in the kitchen, etc....

"We must hope and expect great things from God, because the merits of Our Lord belong to us; and to hope much in God is to honor Him much. The more we hope, the more we honor Him." — Father Lallemant.[38]

Question: "Do you regard the Hebrew prophets and Jesus as historical figures, and if so, have they social significance?"

Answer: "They are historical figures at least in the sense that they have played quite a role in the historical development of the human mind. Whether they were the product of the human mind or whether they had some more direct material basis is not important to us. We do not enter the field of higher criticism." — Earl Browder in *Religion and Communism*.[39]

(Note: Those who asked the questions in this pamphlet came from the Union Theological Seminary. They were not representative of the religious mind. They did not uphold the supernatural, and stated that they did not believe in everlasting life.)

Finished *The Forgotten Paraclete* by Landrieux. Now reading Father Louis Lallemant's *Spiritual Teaching*, recommended by Father McSorley; *The Idiot*, Dostoievsky; Sophocles' Plays;

---

38   Charles Lallemant, S.J. (1587-1674), first Jesuit superior in New France (modern-day Quebec).

39   Earl Browder (1891-1973), president of the Communist Party of America from 1934 until his expulsion in 1945, and its presidential candidate in 1936 and 1940. The work referenced is *Religion and Communism* (New York: Workers Library, 1935).

Labor and Steel, Labor and Textiles, Personal History — Vincent Sheean's account of Rayna.[40]

5

Out on the garden commune, Edelson works in his bare feet, his trousers rolled up to his knees, his shirt off, his undershirt clinging to his back.

He works with a pick, wielding it with large, strong swings. Every now and then he pauses and crumbles the dirt beneath his feet, meditating. He will give us some weeks, he said, for the sake of comradeship, Christian Communism, co-operation, brotherhood, unity, as a member of the Mystical Body, because Christ was in his heart, in the spirit of the priesthood of the laity, and for a good many other reasons. Also because it would do him good.

Catherine Smith wanders around in a pair of baggy old trousers, muddy at the knees, and today she is carting stones and making a rock garden.

Hergenhan has been working at the vegetable garden for three weeks, bringing hundreds of boxes of topsoil from the woods to enrich the carefully prepared beds. Tomato and cabbage plants are set out, the squash and cucumbers in their neat round hills; radishes, beets, onions and lettuce — all are coming up.

Hergenhan is a German and works with order and precision.

In town, at Charles Street, there is no backyard, there are no green things to refresh the eye. I miss our petunia garden,

---

40   Vincent Sheean (1899-1975), American journalist and novelist. His *Personal History* (New York: Doubleday, 1935) detailed his relationship with Rayna Simons (1894-1927), whom Day befriended at the University of Illinois during her studies. An intellectually gifted and charismatic woman, Simons eventually moved to Moscow, where she died. Sheean attended her funeral. See Day's reminiscences of her in *The Long Loneliness*, 47-50.

the asparagus plants, the fig tree and privet hedges. It is true that across the street there is an ailanthus tree, "tree of heaven" it is called, and it arouses hunger and thirst in me for the country.

There is no other speck of green. For trees we have the masts and funnels of ships along the docks, and for grass and earth we have the uneven cobbles of sidewalks in front of warehouses and trucking stations, with bleak and ugly tenements in between.

6

Last winter Margaret became ill with arthritis and had to go to the hospital where she spent two or three months. We could not take care of the baby ourselves so it is now boarded out with another little girl of Margaret's. Now that Margaret is better she has come down to the country for a rest in the sun. She has taken to writing in order to express her happiness at being up and around once more. She writes at least a page a day, and the following is an excerpt from a month's writing:

"I dressed quickly, had my breakfast and went to the beach. I saw fish swimming as the tide was going out. I ran in with my clothes and caught one and then six more. I could not see any more. I went to the house and I looked at the calendar and it said it was a fast day, so we all had fish.

"The next day I put on a bathing suit and caught eight more fish. We all ate it and it tasted very good only it had too many bones. Bill and Rufus are digging, cutting grass and planting some kind of a climbing vine. Edelson was chopping trees and helping Hergenhan with a grape arbor. In the evening we played the piano, everyone was singing and happy.

"Tonight is Monday night. Hergenhan is watering the garden. He was half finished and it started in to rain. God saw that the garden was in need of a good watering, so he helped Hergenhan with our Catholic Workers' vegetable garden.

"All of us sat on the front porch. Teresa and I love to watch the rain fall. Then Rufus said let's put on our bathing suits and go for a walk. It was fun, rain pouring down on our heads and faces. Flashes of lightning showed us the way to the beach.

"Teresa, Bill and Rufus ran up and down on the sand trying to catch the lightning. None of us were afraid. We walked up the country road stumping our toes, Rufus stepped on a frog, — poor frog — and said, let us take it up to the house and put it in Edelson's bed. He will meditate on him. Rufus let the little frog go. We came in soaking wet. It sure was fun walking in the rain, thunder and lightning. If you have God in your heart He will protect you from all danger."

7

A day so wet and heavy that one can scarcely breathe. No sun, but the air felt hot as a blanket, hanging close over the city, and people walked around languidly, scarcely able to move with the oppression that was on them.

Down to the Houston Street Home Relief Bureau with some friends who are on Home Relief and who are registering for work relief, and there marveled at the two policemen and five husky young men hanging around the entrance. Jobholders they are, sneering at those who come for help. "A strong-arm squad," a member of the Workers' Alliance told us, "to keep delegations out of the Bureau. We were down last week, presenting a petition, and I got a black eye as a result. We come to ask for jobs and all we get is kicks and curses."

A woman with a baby in her arms, probably not more than a few weeks old, came to ask why her rent had not been paid. She was refused admittance and told to leave her baby at home next time, with her husband, perhaps.

She did not speak English very well, but she made the strong-arm squad understand that "she had no husband."

"And where did the baby come from?" they jeered as she was forced to leave.

8

Down to Staten Island in the afternoon to see how the family there were getting along. Bernard and Rudy, two little Negro boys, six and eight, from the Harlem classes, and a former Jewish rabbi, homeless because of his conversion, are our latest guests there.

There was time for a swim before supper and the water was oily calm, with the sky hanging so low over it that you could almost reach up and touch it with your hands. We all crouched in the water, digging for small hardshell clams with our hands, and found a dozen. Teresa was best at it.

After supper the atmosphere was a little brighter, with the rays of the sun stealing out from under the heavy curtain of clouds and just a suggestion of freshness in the air. So the children and Stanley and I went for a walk, arriving back in the dusk, the children stumbling not only with fatigue but because they insisted on walking with their faces uplifted to the moon.

Another morning, hot and heavy, and with the first rays of the sun the cicadas began their triumphant song. Teresa woke me to tell me they were the first of the year and it was pleasant to lie there in bed and listen to the loud crescendo rising to a climax and dying out again drowsily.

The children played out under the apple trees after breakfast, waiting for the grownups to be ready for a swim while the tide was high.

Mid-week as it was, the beach was deserted and it was refreshing to swim out into the calm bay and then float, bathed in sea, sky and sun, and silence too, save for the happy calls of the children as they played with the little waves that foamed up on the beach.

The garden progresses, and for the last few days, with the heavy rains, there had been no need to water it. We are beginning to study sprays and the labels which proclaim their efficacy for aphids, thrips and leaf hoppers, Mexican bean beetles, black fly, soft scale and midge. We have been eating lettuce, onions, radishes and a few string beans and soon the tomatoes will be ready. One of the best smells in the world is the smell of tomato plants, or perhaps the wet earth after a rain, or honeysuckle, or privet hedge in blossom. The world is full of good smells down here after the heavy smells of the city and crowded humans. Even the poison ivy we have discovered has a delicious odor when it is blossoming. So there is one good contribution from that venomous weed which has caused two of our workers to swell and burn and itch through sleepless nights.

The only trouble with the garden commune is that one cannot be there all the time. There are a dozen permanent residents and all the rest go and come to fulfill their duties in town as well as out. And it is always such a wrench to put on shoes and stockings and toil the hot long mile to the station and take the train into the city.

Bernard has just come in with another bouquet for his mother. The two children pick daily bouquets which are gathered with loving care and then forgotten: wild carrot, wild onion, bay leaves, sassafras twigs, buttercups and daisies, Queen Anne's lace, clovers and the persisting honeysuckle.

From the open window by my side as I write, the smell of new cut grass is coming in from the field by the side of the house where Stanley is cutting. He has left the city streets and his apostolate of paper selling, has Stanley, and has become the guardian of the two small colored boys for a week.

Today five little colored girls came down: Dorothy and Hattie, Louise, Bernice and Elinor. They, too, are Harlem children, and they don't need anyone to watch them, they said, because Dorothy is twelve and quite used to being guardian to three or four younger than herself.

The work in town calls, and one must go back and face evictions, court cases, hospital patients to visit, callers to see at the office and folders of letters which must be answered.

9

Christ told Peter to put aside his nets and follow Him. He told the rich young man to sell what he had and give to the poor and follow Him. He said that those who lost their lives for His sake should find them. He told people to take no thought for the morrow. He told His followers that if anyone begged for their coats to give up their cloaks too. He spoke of feeding the poor, sheltering the homeless, of visiting those in prison and the sick and also of instructing the ignorant. He said: "Inasmuch as ye have done it unto the least of these, ye have done it unto Me" [Matthew 25:40]. He said: "Be ye therefore perfect as your heavenly Father is perfect" [Matthew 5:48].

But the usual comment is: "You must distinguish between counsel and precept. You forget that He said also: 'All men take not this word, but they to whom it is given' [Matthew 19:11]. 'He that can take it, let him take it' " [Matthew 19:12].

Paul Claudel said that young people have a hunger for the heroic, and too long they have been told, "Be moderate, be prudent."

Too long have we had moderation and prudence. Today is a time of crisis and struggle. Within our generation, Russia has rejected Christianity, Germany has rejected it, Mexico fights to exterminate it, in Spain there has been a war against religion, in Italy Fascism has exalted the idea of the state and, rejecting the Kingship of Christ, has now a perverted idea of authority.

In this present situation when people are starving to death because there is an overabundance of food, when religion is being warred upon throughout the world, our Catholic young people still come from schools and colleges and talk about looking for security, a weekly wage.

They ignore the counsels of the Gospels as though they had never heard of them, and those who are troubled in conscience regarding them speak of them as being impractical.

Why they think a weekly wage is going to give them security is a mystery. Do they have security on any job nowadays? If they try to save, the bank fails; if they invest their money, the bottom of the market drops out. If they trust to worldly practicality, in other words, they are out of luck.

If they sell their labor (see Peter Maurin's essays) they are prostituting the talents God gave them. College girls who work at Macy's — is this what their expensive training was for? boys who go into business looking for profits — is this what their Catholic principles taught them? — are hovering on the brink of a precipice. They have no security and they know it. The only security comes in the following of the precepts and counsels of the Gospels.

If each unemployed nurse went to her pastor and got a list of the sick and gave up the idea of working for wages and gave her services to the poor of the parish, is there not security in the trust that God will provide? This is but one instance of using the talents and abilities that God has given to each one of us.

What right has anyone of us to have security when God's poor are suffering? What right have I to sleep in a comfortable bed when so many are sleeping in the shadows of buildings here in this neighborhood of *The Catholic Worker* office? What right have we to food when many are hungry, or to liberty when the Scottsboro boys[41] and so many labor organizers are in jail?

St. Thomas says: "The counsels of perfection are, considered in themselves, expedient for everybody," and he adds charitably, "but owing to the varying dispositions of people there

---

41   The Scottsboro Boys were a group of nine black men accused and convicted of rape in Alabama in 1931. Their trial and (almost certainly unjust) conviction highlighted the racial injustices in American society and eventually led to an end of all-white juries.

are some for whom they are not expedient because their inclinations do not tend in that direction."

But to those in whose minds these questions are stirring, there are those words directed:

"Today if you shall hear My voice, harden not your hearts [Hebrews 3:15].

"This is the true fraternity, which overcame the crimes of the world; it followed Christ, attaining the noble kingdom of Heaven." — From the Gradual for July 9th.

10

There were six of us at Mass this morning and the morning was cool, with a haze coming up from the river. Around on Washington Street, under the New York Central tracks, there is grass growing and there are crickets in that grass. A window box on the fire escape of a tenement is lush with balsam and petunia. The sun sparkles on the river and the boats plough joyously through the choppy water. These are the things that make thanksgiving easy to continue during the day.

Every good impulse, every noble deed we perform is of God, Christ in us. At the very same time there is an evil, complacent nagging going on, trying to discourage us, trying to impugn our motives, trying to spoil everything of good we do. This complacency, self-satisfaction, is to be scorned and silenced. It shows pride even to be surprised and grieved at the baseness, like sediment, at the bottom of every good deed. As long as we live there will be a war, a conflict between nature and grace, nature again and again getting the upper hand for the moment, only to be put down rigidly. If we have faith and hope, it is impossible to be discouraged.

"You never enjoy the world aright till the sea itself floweth in your veins, till you are clothed with the heavens and crowned with the stars; and perceive yourself to be sole heir of the whole world and more so because men are in it who are everyone sole heirs as well as you. Till you can sing and rejoice and delight in God, as misers do in gold, and kings in scepters — you never can enjoy the world." — From *The Meditation of Traherne.*[42]

"Many will never arrive at a high perfection, because they do not hope sufficiently. We must have a strong and solid hope, grounded on the mercy and infinite goodness of God, and on the infinite merits of Jesus Christ." — Lallemant.

"Thou, O Lord, singularly hast settled me in hope." — Ps. IV, 10.

"Grace is sometimes compared to a fountain of living water, and again to a glowing fire.... Divine grace, like water, purifies, refreshes, vivifies.... What the soul does for the body, grace does for the soul." — From *The Forgotten Paraclete* by Msgr. J. R. Maurice Landrieux.

"To him that thirsteth, I will give of the water of life freely" [Revelation 21:6].

Voluntary poverty — penance: "No efforts or expenses seem too great to purchase our escape from the afflictions which God sends us; and yet they are even more beneficial and more meritorious than voluntary penances. For God knows better than we in what regards and by what means our soul has need of being purified and regenerated. Besides, labours and penances which are taken on voluntarily and by choice leave still open, good as they are, a free field for self-love. But those which come upon us unexpectedly and undesired, even if we endure them with patience or with joy,

---

42   Thomas Traherne (1636?-1674), English theologian and writer. The work referred to is *Centuries of Meditations* (ed. Bertram Dobell; London: Dobell, 1908).

seem always impositions, not the growth of our own will and desire; and therefore they exclude pride, self-love and vanity." — St. Angela of Foligna.

Prayer: "If recollection seems difficult, at least accustom yourself to pronounce with your lips words which relate to the Passion; the habit of the lips easily becomes a habit of the heart, and within the cold heart the fire will gradually become warmer." — St. Angela of Foligna.

"O Lord, take away my heart of stone and give me a heart of flesh" [Ezekiel 11:19].

"O God, I believe. Help Thou my unbelief" [Mark 9:24].

"Lord, Thou knowest that I love Thee" [John 21:17].... "To whom shall we go? Thou hast the words of Eternal Life" [John 6:68].

11

I went back into town last Monday to find L. on hunger strike because of D.'s and J.'s tormenting. They were the workers and he was the scholar and he was not earning his salt, according to them. He nagged back, and between them life was miserable. I induced J. to take a vow of holy silence for a while, and persuaded L. not to be childish and to reconcile himself to criticism.

Transition periods are always trying. The struggle to make the scholars work and the workers study, I was thinking as I washed dishes and dish towels, and C. and D. sat upstairs reading and doing nice clean clerical work. The boys, D. and E., were cleaning beds, moving furniture, etc., and it was hard to get others to help.

The workers try to become white-collar workers and abandon working with their hands, and the scholars spend their time in work and have no time to study except by grabbing it. So much time must be given to the physical details of life, —

cleaning beds, kitchens, garbage cans, toilets. It is endless, and it seems to take such a large proportion of time. The majority of people have no machines — dishwashers, cleaners, tractors. Most of the physical work of our existence still has to be done with the hands.

12

A breathing spell in the country: A. is fixing up the tomato vines. The boys are out picking huckleberries and are going to make pie. It is very hot again and there is a sleepy sound of crickets. In spite of the eight children, the house is quiet — peaceful after the furore of town. This morning I spent hours trying to trace B., calling police, hospitals, his friends. Too many of these latter said, "He is not my responsibility. What can I do?" We have few friends in this world.

Yesterday I went to the Foundling to visit Barbara. Human distress and misery everywhere.

A social worker from Canada says that here Catholic charity is too bound up with the state, and legislation is for the individual rather than for the family, which is the true unit of society. She said too that the State Welfare Department was going to look into the matter of so many children so easily committed and so little effort to keep the family together.

They are doing it because of the expense involved, not the principle.

We had a letter this morning from the man who gave us the use of the store in Harlem. He is not in accord with our principles in regard to war, so he will not help *The Catholic Worker* any longer. Also, will we please move at once? The eighteen who frequent the center will be heartbroken.

Rumors go the rounds. Rumors that we are Communists, that I am, but not the rest, that I am arrested, or about to be.

The Civil Liberties Union called up yesterday to ask if they could defend me.

A campaign against our little brothers, the bedbugs. Sulphur candles, black flag, kerosene. Some overstuffed furniture had to be discarded. Such warm, comfortable furniture too. The little boys on the street had it torn to pieces in no time and the streets well littered. The cleaning department objects. We miss our disorderly East side where the kids make bonfires of the trash as it is set out. Our West side street cleaners say we can have bonfires in winter, but not in summer.

Last night the Liturgical group of Campions sang Vespers and Compline. They sang and sang and could not stop. The truckmen in the garage at the back of the house, the police in the station house across the street, were overwhelmed with plain chant.

Tina, our Trotskyite friend, came in to say that "yodeling is an indispensable part of every movement." Out in the Middle West and in the South the strikers sang hymns as they picketed their factories. Even while they were being clubbed, the Communists last month up in front of the 47th Street station house sang Communist songs.

It is good to see Gregorian a part of the Catholic Worker movement.

13

Rain all day long and everything damp. The woodwork in the house is sweating. Mass at eight. Drunken Michael McCarthy to breakfast with two black eyes. Read aloud to him St. Teresa's vision of hell. B., very well since his re-appearance, not so well today. Perhaps it's the weather. Margaret is better. Children came in for games and cocoa. We are picketing St. Joseph:

Stanley, Francis, me, Dan, Bill, Jim, Charlie, Mr. Hunton, Ann, so far have spent four hours.

Reading St. Teresa's *Foundations* last night gave me much courage to proceed. If our surroundings are cold, desolate and dirty with the dirt of poverty which is so hard to combat, it is the more suited to us. Our debts are now one thousand five hundred and thirty dollars. We are most completely dependent on God.

I am glad it is September and the summer is drawing to a close. I think March and August hard months to get through, winter and summer doldrums. We have never been so badly off as now. And I am beginning to feel better and better, praise God.

We can smell September, and Margaret is beginning to count the blankets. Jim is down at the fish market where there is a good Catholic whose abundance supplies our want. Bill had been to the vegetable market where he got potatoes. There will be chowder tonight. There is no money in the house, but there will be dinner, that is if the gas company does not shut off the gas for non-payment for the past two months. Too bad there isn't an onion to put in the stew.

Jim has come in with the fish in a black market bag. The friend was not there, but he got twenty pounds for fifty cents, and the man trusted him for the fifty cents. As he walks around the office displaying his catch, our black cat, Social Justice, follows him around interestedly. She has five little kittens downstairs and she is as interested as we are in the matter of meals. The kittens are satin, blue plush and brindle, Teresa says, and she wishes there were some calico ones, which means the yellow-tawny kind.

Francis comes up with the charge book for the cooperative store, and says we need bread and soap powder and scouring powder. But we remind him we ought not to charge any more with the bill already up to almost a hundred dollars. It's a job to be clean and poor at the same time. As for bread, someone will bring in some money from selling papers to buy bread.

Out in the country they are doing very well with the garden and a Catholic grocer who trusts us and trusts God. The bill out there is seventy-five dollars too, but we've put it under the statue of St. Joseph. There are plenty of tomatoes, cabbages, cucumbers and string beans, and we've even had sweet corn at half a dozen meals. There are clams in the bay, and we are on meat strike. And as for keeping clean — the difficulty there is getting into the bath tub, which is always full of baby eels and killies, the children's pets. One can bathe in the bay, after all.

This started out to be a financial account but the fresh breeze coming in from the North River and the smell of fish arising from the kitchen reminds one of the country.

We were looking over our last accounting which we sent out to our friends last September and we noted that not only has our circulation doubled, but the number of people being fed has quintupled. This means that the printing bill is $450 a month, and that the food bill for the Charles Street place and the country place combined is about fifty a week, or $200 a month. That includes fifteen quarts of milk a day, and it isn't we hale and hearty ones who drink it, but the children and invalids, of which latter there are always about four.

And lest this large grocery bill, which our readers pay after all, staggers them, let us count ourselves up.

Down in the country there are ten children right now, aged six to fourteen, and their appetites increase and multiply with the days at the seashore. (During the summer we took care of fifty children altogether.) Then there are seven adults, which makes seventeen people sitting down to a meal three times a day, or fifty-one meals served a day — 3,060 for the months of July and August. (But there are more than that, often fifty people over the weekends.) Of course, the midday meal is not rightly a meal, but just sandwiches, peanut butter or tomato, and either cocoa or milk, and you should see the bread and butter fly.

As for the Charles Street quarters, there are sixteen people living there and they've been on a long fast during the summer. Those who come back from the country tell of delicious lemon meringue pies, not to speak of ordinary food, and city workers lick their chops (especially Big Dan, whose large bulk is hard to satisfy on oatmeal in the morning, sandwiches, and not too many of them, at noon, and vegetable stew in the evening).

In addition to the sixteen living in the house, there are the two married couples living in little apartments and eating at home, whose rents and grocery bills, gas and electric, must also be paid. Also there are half a dozen coming in to eat at the office who do not live here. Rents total $150, whereas last year they were $62, and the combined gas and electricity amount to $25; laundry, $15; telephones, $18; mailing and express, $75. And as this month's paper comes out there is another printing bill of $450, and the rent goes on and so do the groceries. Disregarding the latter two items, we are faced with our large bills (there are other little ones) of $1,403 and nothing in the bank to pay them.

This, then, is the holy poverty we are always talking about. This is the insecurity which we do most firmly believe it is good for us to have.

SEVEN

1

MELANCHOLY fall days. Teresa went back to school Wednesday and I brought her to the beach Friday night for the weekend, coming into town myself Saturday to see Loretta and the new baby who was born on Wednesday. Went to tea at the de Aragons' and then to Don Bosco's Church for confession, then to the beach feeling very grateful to God for His blessings. I had been harsh and impatient interiorly with those dependent on me. I must be more kind and patient.

Then down in the country, Peter brought Carney — the mysterious, silent, nervous case — bent over with cramps and very ill indeed.

The atmosphere was anything but cheerful. Joe Bennett also very ill indeed, with his heart, flat on his back after three months on Welfare Island.

John Renaldo got me cornered to discuss his rights to have doubts, be an agnostic occasionally, how he did not see much proof of the existence of God, etc.

All in all, a sad day, aside from the relief of Mass, and I was much oppressed both by the talk and lack of talk.

Then coming in on the train, I was suddenly overwhelmed by the thought of our blessings. Are there not always direct indications of God's will as to the work we should do? Caring for the sick He sends us — that is a most necessary work. A sick person is a blessing to a house, it is said. We are greatly blessed then by these opportunities.

So today was a good day. Charlie could have written a perfect Jeremiad for it. He will not be content until he sees us "bowed in tears, with broken hearts, walking with bleeding feet." I believe in being joyful in the Lord and often argue with Charlie but I was rebuked in reading Caussade where he says: "Souls who walk in light sing canticles of joy; those who walk amid shadows sing anthems of woe. Let one and the other sing to the end, the portion and anthem God assigns them."[43]

And Tina and I have been criticizing Charlie for his Jeremiads, perhaps not so much for them as for his desire to see others wail under the blows of this life.

I must not be critical of others.

2

Here is a conversation with one of our critics:

Critical Inquirer — Are you not participating in the class war when you go out on picket lines and on the street corners? Are you not siding with the workers, one class against another class, thus taking part in class war?

Catholic Worker — No, we are trying to bring the Gospel to the man in the street, and if we find ourselves caught between two opposing forces, God help us, the police won't.

C.I. — Are you not inefficient and lax in that you are not an organization with rules and regulations?

C.W. — We are trying to work out the doctrine of gentle personalism,[44] to live a life in which people do not do things by compulsion, but of their own free will. Karl Marx said:

"From each according to his ability and to each according to his need." And St. Paul said "Let your abundance supply their want" [2 Corinthians 8:14]. Abundance we take to mean an abundance of physical, mental and spiritual energies. We try not to make rules, but look for individual initiative.

---

43 Jean Pierre de Caussade, S.J. (1675-1751), French spiritual writer and author of the classic *Abandonment to Divine Providence*.

44 Personalism here refers to the philosophical movement which makes human persons and the relationships between them irreducible features of reality (as opposed to materialist philosophies). It was a central feature of Day's worldview. See Mark and Louise Zwick, *The Catholic Worker Movement: Intellectual and Spiritual Origins* (Mahwah, NJ: Paulist, 2005), 97-115.

C.I. — While supping at the Catholic Worker office, I heard an argument as to who should do dishes, who had done dishes, who would do dishes and who ought to do dishes. Some of this was in fun but there also seemed to be animosity.

C.W. — Undoubtedly with the teasing there is also a feeling of criticism. In trying to put over this idea of the workers becoming scholars and the scholars workers, there is bound to be conflict in the transition stages. The worker will complacently watch the scholar empty the garbage cans, wash the dishes, scrub the floor, and will prefer to take the nice clean work of filing or typing cards and envelopes. Some scholars will work, and others lacking in physical co-ordination and ashamed to show their lack of ability along those lines do not co-operate in the manual labor. And the worker, showing no recognition of the work of some of the scholars, will jeer at the idle scholars. And some of the scholars will be complaining of the noise and heckling of the workers.

The same difficulties take place in regard to the lack of rules save those set forth in the Gospel (see the rule of St. Francis). Because there is no compulsion, some will refuse co-operation. Those who co-operate scorn those who do not, as well as those responsible for not making rules to force the non-cooperators to cooperate. It is a good-natured scorn, perhaps, but it is a critical attitude just the same.

C.I. — But would it not be better then to have rules in order to facilitate the work? Wouldn't it be better to kick out those who do not help?

C.W. — Things might run a little more smoothly on the surface — the office might be cleaner, for instance, and the kitchen floor washed more often, but the criticism and the lack of co-operation would go on. Let your abundance supply their want. There are always those who can do more work or who can do one thing better than they can do other things. And after all we are working with the lame, the halt, and the blind.

In the Catholic Worker Community, things do get done. People are housed and fed. More people are housed and fed because there is no red tape or so-called efficiency.

C.I. — But don't people take advantage?

C.W. — Of course. And don't we take advantage of God? Cannot we put up with others? Does not God put up with us?

C.I. — But wouldn't even more get done if each one were allotted his separate task and expected to do it?

C.W. — Some more efficiency! Some more compulsion! And after all don't we get a good deal done? Considering that we are on a voluntary basis — that no one is paid salaries — it seems that a great deal is done. Of course we do not stop to count the pieces of clothes that are distributed, the number of people fed, the quarts of milk consumed by the children. Though we may try to make a rough estimate, since people love figures and we might encourage ourselves by so doing. And after all, we do get out a newspaper, 100,000 copies, mailed to all parts of the world, which is no mean job. Most papers employ a mailing house to do the work. Volunteers do it in the office and from amongst those volunteers who come to do something simple like addressing envelopes we have gained many a friend. And after all we *do* have a division of labor, tasks divided up and voluntarily accepted.

C.I. — But to go back to the criticism at the supper table as to who does what, I thought you Christians all loved one another.

C.W. — As we indeed do. All Christians do in time of persecution. When things are going along smoothly there is bound to be friction of one personality against another. The apostles wrangled a bit in regard to who was going to sit on the right side of the Lord, and St. Paul was not accepted at first by the disciples (and who would blame them), and there was argument about bringing the light to the Gentiles, etc. And isn't there friction in religious communities? And in families? After all, there is always a war between nature and grace. I am afraid we are not always as edifying as we should be. But we don't believe that rules and regulations would help much.

After the critical inquirer had left, I began to feel guilty for justifying myself and others. After all I am a bad leader — we are all at fault — everything could be done much better. If things go wrong it is the fault of the leader.

3

Distributing papers at the power house over in Brooklyn between four and five on a hot afternoon. The Hudson Avenue plant supplies all Queens, Brooklyn and lower Manhattan. It takes 700 men to work it and 600 are organized. At the offices of the Edison Company there are 5,000 working. There are in addition, seven district offices. For the actual generating of electricity there are two hundred in the plant. The men work in three shifts and some of them work eight hours straight and have no time off for eating. They eat while working. The mechanics work from eight to five and have an hour off for lunch.

Before the men started the Brotherhood of Edison Employees, the pay was $23 to $36. Now it is $27 to $46. The men are supposed to get a pension at 65 but usually long before this the pay is lowered to $25 and the pension amounts to about $7 a week. Or perhaps they get fired for mistakes.

While we distributed there was a steady roar of the machines in our ears which filled the air unbearably. The men work in the midst of this roar all the time. We could look out over the river while we waited for the men to dribble out of the plant, over a field of weeds, burdock, dandelion and grass growing cheerfully in the shade. There is a bend in the river there and we watched the tugboats and the barges going by. The overhanging bridge was like a poem. To one side there is a gantry.

This, one of the workers said proudly, is the largest generating plant in the world.

4

Went with Margaret to the Welfare Department. The waiting room was small, and so crowded by nine-thirty in the morning that fifteen people already were standing up. The investigators came out into this crowded room to interview their "clients". It is hard to watch people trying to achieve some privacy, speaking behind cupped hands, their faces working. The investigators tell them to speak up. There were many children in the room, underweight, pale and sad. It is hard to see grown people crying and young children with set sad faces terrified at the sight of adult despair.

There is a Negro there with crucifixes in her ears. A young girl whose trembling baby has an old white face. There is a strange contrast between the impassive faces of the investigators and the twisted, anguished faces of those investigated.

5

Stanley is down for a few days to help with the wood chopping and gathering driftwood on the garden commune. Even so we have just had to buy two more tons of coal which make five for this year already. It will be good when we are on the farming commune and have our own wood. One of the best things people can do, — the very people who are with you — is to criticize the management and lack of economy though God knows what else you can do.

The difficulty to look forward to on the farm is everybody living under the same roof and getting along together, so strange a conglomeration of people as we all are.

Miss B., a former school teacher and now on PWA, is a nervous wreck, spending all her time complaining about her debts and insurance. She tries to while away the time reading voraciously and knitting, and tries to be helpful as much as possible. But recently she washed up the kitchen floor which was covered with clay which everybody has been modelling, dumping the water down the sink and stopping it up so it has not been used for the past two weeks. To get away from the contemplation of the sink, she has taken refuge with some friends in Jersey.

Francis took offense last night at sleeping in a room away from Stanley and walked out this morning without breakfast. So there are general grievances in the air. And generally grievances against me. For having such people around, for instance, and, "What's the sense of talking about a farming commune when you haven't any farmers? It'll never come to anything. There was all that talk of a summer school and nothing was done." Past failures are not forgotten or excused.

If you *are* discouraged, others will relapse into a state of discouragement and hopeless anger at circumstances and each other. And if you are not discouraged, everyone tries to make you so and is angry because you are not. It is hard to know what tack to take. The only thing is to be oblivious, as Peter is, and go right on.

6

We have meetings every Thursday night in the two big offices, but Friday night there was an impromptu meeting which lasted until twelve. Everyone seemed to drop in at once, visitors from half a dozen other cities, members of other goups, and our own crowd. We started at the dinner table, continued through the dish-washing, adjourned to the office and everyone had his say. We discussed the relationship between the corporative, the co-operative, the distributist and the communitarian movements. Some talked of the need of a positive program, others said that anyone who claimed to have a solution to world problems was a liar. Some talked of the educational approach and others the spiritual. Peter talked of the need of injecting the spiritual into the material.

The discussion was heated, as it usually is, everybody speaking with vehemence and bobbing up and down from the floor. One of the visitors, not acquainted with Peter, said he thought we were giving too much attention to the material. He criticized the disorder of our surroundings, our lack of efficiency, and advocated the liturgical life, which to him meant recitation of Prime and Vespers and Compline and a dialogue Mass every morning (the attendance of all at these hours being obligatory).

When he said that Peter paid too much attention to the economic side of things, I jumped to my feet and protested that "you can't preach the gospel to men with empty stomachs" (Abbé Lugan[45]) and that if they had been down to the Municipal Lodging House and seen 12,000 men being fed at South Ferry, they would decide that it was necessary to put some emphasis on the material. Which convinced our critics that I was an externalist, I am sure.

Most of the time when people talk of efficiency and organization, they are thinking of order, outward order. What they are really criticizing is our poverty, the fact that we spend money for food instead of for paint and linoleum. We are crowded as the poor are, with people sleeping in every available corner. We have no separate room for the clothes that come in; they are packed in boxes around the dining-room and hung in one hall closet and in another closet off the dining-room. We are often dirty because so many thousands cross our thresholds. We are dirty ourselves sometimes because we have no hot water or bath, because we have not sufficient clothes for changes, — even because we are so busy with the poor and the sick that it is hard to take time to journey to the public baths to wash.

---

45 Abbé Alphonse-Marie Lugan (1869-1931), French priest and author, whose works frequently addressed questions of Catholic social teaching.

But what am I talking about? Why am I justifying myself and my family? I am ashamed of myself for getting indignant at such criticism. It just goes to show how much pride and self-love I have. But it has been hard lately. Not only outside criticism but criticism from within, the grumbling, the complaints, the insidious discontent spread around by a few — these trials are hard to bear.

However, the thing is to bear it patiently, to take it lightly, not to let it interfere with the work. The very fact that it is hard shows how weak I am. I should be happy, however, to think that God believes me strong enough to bear these trials, otherwise I would not be having them. Father Lallemant says that we must beware when things are going too smoothly. That is the time when no progress is made.

Oh dear, I am reminded of St. Teresa who said, "The devil sends me so offensive a bad spirit of temper that at times I think I could eat people up."

I'm glad that she felt that way, too. St. Thomas said there is no sin in having a righteous wrath provided there is no undue desire for revenge.

I'm afraid I am very stiff necked. I shall read the Office and go to sleep. But first to concoct a rule for the coming year. (I read in Tanqueray that a rule of life was necessary for all, laymen as well as cleric.)

The Catholic Worker to be in the hands of St. Joseph, and Teresa and I to continue under our novice mistress, the little St. Thérèse, who alone can teach us how to do the little things and cultivate a spirit of humility. St. Joseph is also taking care of me this year.

"Can you not watch one hour with me?" [Matthew 26:40].

I shall remember this whenever I am tired and want to omit prayer, the extra prayers I shall set myself. Because after all I am going to try to pray the simplest, humblest way, with no spiritual ambition.

Morning prayers, in my room before going to Mass. I always omit them, rushing out of the house just in time as I do. If I were less slothful it would be better. Remember what Léon Bloy[46] said about health. Not try too hard to catch up on sleep but to be sensible about sleep nevertheless.

Around the middle of the day to take, even though it be to snatch, fifteen minutes of absolute quiet, thinking about God and talking to God.

Read the Office as much as I can, if only Prime and Compline, but more whenever possible.

One visit during the day, always without fail.

The rosary daily.

I do plenty of spiritual reading to refresh myself and to encourage myself so I do not have to remind myself of that.

The thing to remember is not to read so much or talk so much about God, but to talk to God.

To practice the presence of God.[47]

To be gentle and charitable in thought, word and deed. (Most important of all.)

7

These last fall months have been hard ones, but hardest of all for Mr. and Mrs. J. who have had charge of the garden commune all summer and will be there all winter.

When the summer months were passed with their hosts of children, scores of young workers and students and all the visitors, over-running the place for weekends, and the quiet fall days came, even heavier responsibilities came. The summer was hard but the past few months have been harder. In the

---

46   Léon Bloy (1846-1917), prolific and widely read French Catholic author.

47   Reference to the spiritual classic *The Practice of the Presence of God* by Brother Lawrence of the Resurrection (1614-1691). Day later wrote the introduction for a popular edition of this work (*The Practice of the Presence of God* [trans. Donald Attwater; Springfield, IL: Templegate, 1974]).

summer we were dealing with healthy, normal young people. In the fall there was not only one but half a dozen sick, mentally and physically, suddenly on hand to be cared for.

Father Coady, one of the heads of the Antigonish movement,[48] said one time that we could all do ten times as much as we think we can do. It was certainly true in this case. I'm sure Mr. and Mrs. J. felt that they had all they could possibly handle during the summer. If anyone had asked them to take charge of a group of sick ones such as suddenly congregated with us, they would have felt utterly incapable of doing the work. As it was, it just drifted up on them. Adelson decided he would move in. Then another, then Carney. Peter brought Carney down, the others came by themselves. And since our policy is never to turn anyone away, there they were. They had to be accepted. But surely it was too much for one couple to bear. A household of sad afflicted creatures.

And then Joe Bennett came down to die. He had worked for the last year or so in the South, and when he became critically ill, the priest with whom he was working brought him north and put him on Welfare Island. Joe got in touch with us and begged to be allowed to go down to the country.

He was fatally ill, and felt that he was not going to recover, but he fought bitterly against death. He did not want to die and he knew that only a miracle could save him. He prayed frantically, almost rebelliously, for a miracle.

"How can God be good," he moaned every time he saw me, "to let me suffer like this. He must heal me. I don't want to die."

It was heartbreaking. Mrs. J. nursed him tenderly, brought him delicacies to tempt his appetite. He read, he had a little radio by his bedside. Outside the trees were turning red and gold. There was the sound of the waves crashing on the beach in the

---

48   Rev. Moses Coady (1882-1959), one of the founders of the Antigonish Movement, a cooperative movement in Nova Scotia in the mid-twentieth century aimed at economic and spiritual improvement of the working class.

fall storms. It was too unbearably beautiful, he cried, and he did not want to die.

We took turns going down to see him to keep him company and to try to ease the strain in the house. But it was one day when no one was there but Mrs. J. that Joe took a turn for the worse, became delirious and began beating his head up against a radiator in bitter rebellion. Mrs. J. tried to hold him. Adelson ran to a neighbor's to phone for Father McKenna, the nearest priest. He was so unmanageable that the priest advised he be taken to a little private hospital down the bay about a mile and there he died a few days later. I had been to see him the morning before as he lay there semi-conscious, no longer suffering, no longer rebellious. He had received the last rites and once when he opened his eyes clearly for a moment, he said good-bye. I kissed him as I left. The next morning he died. And for months now I have felt guilty, because I was not there with him, because he was alone in the hospital, and not with his friends those last terrible moments when the soul is leaving the body. We must be alone when we die, that I know, but I do know too that I would like to have friends beside me to hold my hand, to make me feel the strength of their prayers, their strong, happy prayers that would see where I could not see, the peace and light of the world to come. But I was not there — Joe died alone, and he was the first one to help me that May Day we started *The Catholic Worker*. There will never a day pass but that I remember him in my prayers, and I pray he remembers us now. And I ask you who read this to pray that he has found refreshment, joy and peace.

8

"The good of the soul does not exist in its thinking much but in loving much. And if you were to ask how is this love to be had, my answer is, by a good resolution to do and suffer for

God, and by carrying out that resolution into act whenever opportunity occurs." — *St. Teresa's Foundations, Chapter V. 2.*

Let people "not lay the blame on the times, for all times are times in which God will give His graces to those who serve Him in earnest." — St. Teresa.

"It is so easy to pray … Prayer is the heart's desire, and the heart always knows how to desire….

"Prayer is the great channel of grace. The two movements of prayer, to feel my misery and to feel the goodness of Jesus, are the two movements of aspiration and respiration. Set forms are sometimes needful to maintain the respiration and keep distractions away.

"O! my Jesus, give me all the graces that I should ask of you, if I knew their importance — give them to me just as if I prayed for them, for my intention is to ask You for them with love and reverence." — *A young Trappist who died not long ago.*

I must recall the words again of St. Teresa — that the only way we can show our love for God is by our love for our fellows. And not an abstract love either. If I cannot remember and contemplate my own worse sins, hidden, and more subtle, then God help me! And if I cannot be patient under trials which the Lord compliments me by sending me, then all my other work is vain. It is not by editing a paper or by writing and speaking that I am going to do penance and achieve sanctity. But by being truly loving and gentle and peaceful in the midst of trouble. Lallemant says that when we are comfortable, beware. It is only when things are hard that we are making progress. God is good to send trials. They are a special mark of love.

Caussade says that those circumstances which surround us are the very ones God wills for us.

Dear Lord, keep us from pride and self will! Help us to love one another. It is easy to love saints. What do we know about each other's inward struggles.

"Love in action is a harsh and dreadful thing compared with love in dreams." — Fr. Zossima in *The Brothers Karamazov.*

EIGHT

1

IF IT were not for the generosity of a subscriber who loaned us the use of his car for the search we might still be looking and our readers might still be looking for news of the farming commune we have been talking about starting all winter. The search was begun really a year ago and continued sporadically through the year. By Christmas we began to look more intensively.

Every time a group ventured out, the rain began to pour, turned to sleet, caked the pavements and hindered our advance. The elements themselves seemed to conspire against our hunt. Every time we went out we skidded into snow banks, went off the road, narrowly escaped collisions and barely saved the borrowed car from wreck.

But our farm was finally found on top of a mountain where level fields stretched out for twenty-eight acres and overlooked a magnificent scene on all sides. There are peach trees, some apple and cherry trees, raspberry bushes, half an acre of asparagus. The house has three bedrooms, each roomy enough for three beds and an attic big enough for eight. There is a large dining-room and good sized kitchen. The outbuildings are falling apart. The road to the place will always need mending. There are eight acres of woodland. The price of the farm is twelve hundred and fifty dollars, and we are able through the generosity of a friend to pay a thousand in cash and we can make up the rest immediately. In return for the use of this money, we are to build her a house and give her an acre of land. We have a good builder and the debt will be repaid or begin to be repaid at once.

We are beginning the farm as humbly as we began *The Catholic Worker* which started with no staff, no headquarters, no mailing list and no money. But this small beginning is part of our propaganda. St. Francis says you cannot know what you have not practiced. From now on when we write about the land movement as a cure for unemployment we will be writing about a small group of people who are on the land and who, without funds and by making real sacrifices, are trying to build another way of life for themselves.

We have the land, the truck to do the moving and on April 15th a group will go to take possession. This experiment, written about from month to month, should be of interest to groups of families, to the unemployed, to the college graduate who comes out of school and does not know which way to turn. [49]

2

When Communists and Socialists laughingly accuse us of wasting too much energy on temporal matters and remind us "Seek ye first the Kingdom of Heaven" [Matthew 6:33]. I think the words of the Pater Noster: "Thy Kingdom come *on earth* as it is in heaven." [Matthew 6:10] We must make it possible for people to fulfill the new commandment Jesus gave — that we love all men. Communists like to say that it is only charity (in its present ugly sense of a dole) that is enjoined, and they make charity seem ugly, and try to persuade men only to work for justice, when charity is highest of all and includes all.

We must never forget that works of mercy include enlightening the ignorant and rebuking the sinner. St. Paul was advocating a boycott when he said: "And if any man obey not our word by this epistle, note that man, and do not keep company with him, that he may be ashamed. Yet do not esteem him as an enemy, but admonish him as a brother" (II *Thessalonians*, 3[:14-15]).

---

49   The first Catholic Worker farm in Easton, PA, continued from 1935 until 1947, when internal conflicts led to its dissolution and sale. See Forest, *All Is Grace*, 144-149.

Thomas á Kempis says when we are feeling dry as dust, sad and unhappy, to employ ourselves in exterior works of mercy.[50] I know by experience how some good brisk house-cleaning can revive one's spirits. Manual labor, bringing order out of chaos, also brings serenity to the soul and we have been having a good deal of that lately, as we have moved from Charles Street.

3

Little Felicia stood on the sidewalk as we moved into the Mott Street house last week and surveyed us with a pleasant smile.

"Can we come into your office and to your meetings?" she wanted to know. Some young high school students stood around and read copies of the paper aloud and a group gathered and listened.

"Are the meetings free?" they asked.

Dominick who is eight and several of his black-eyed friends were the active ones, insisting on helping us to move in, helping to store things in the cellar down under the store where the office of the paper will be from now on.

Charlie O'Rourke and Frank O'Donnell stood down below while we passed them planks, small tables, sections of book cases and stored them away in corners for future moving to the farm.

"There's a big rat like a kitten running around down here," called Charlie O'Rourke calmly.

"We have lots of rats," said Felicia. "When they come out in the room we jump up on the bed while my father chases them with the broom."

"It's funny when he catches them by the tail," said her friend Susie gayly.

---

50 *The Imitation of Christ*, Book III, Chap. 51.

Our new home on Mott Street is a rear tenement of twenty rooms and an apartment in the front building and store in front, the use of all of which is given us by one of our readers. It is a good solid old house, the banisters like iron, the walls of brick and built to stay. There are plenty of windows and in the morning the sun comes in. We brought some plants in from Staten Island and hope eventually to have a little grotto out in the yard with St. Joseph in it, to oversee the house. The day-lilies and daisy plants will last for awhile and then can be replaced by other flowers from the farm.

We are overwhelmed with the space of our new home and so far as we ourselves are concerned, the rats do not bother us at all.

The moving day, Saturday, April 18th, was a happy one. There must have been twelve loads of furniture coming down from Charles Street on the old truck we bought last month. Hard as the work was, it meant that those able bodied ones who were working and who are looking forward to working on the farming commune, were that much nearer to the country. One of the movers, with a gigantic ice box on his shoulders, grinned at me as he passed.

"I'm a longshoreman and I'm used to heavy work," he said, stretching himself as he set down his load. "*The Catholic Worker* has been a good friend of ours and when I and my friends came in to get some of your breakfast this morning and found you moving, we were glad we could help you."

The work of painting and cleaning is still going on, but we are at home in that we feel settled and happy in our new abode, at home in that we are welcoming guests as usual, who we are sure will excuse the present disorder. There is love and devotion going into the decorating of the house. Our benefactor is donating linoleum for the kitchen and dining room and curtains for the entire house and it will be a clean cheerful place. We cannot promise always to be orderly when there are so many guests that the walls bulge with them. But the disorder that will be present will be a comfortable disorder.

The Lord sends us more rooms to accommodate guests and at once there *are* more guests, fellow workers who have no other place to go. There is a seamen's strike going on and many of the men have been sleeping on the floor of the strike headquarters for weeks. Down in the country too, the house is crammed, and with this large community numbering about fifty who need to be fed three meals a day, we are faced with the fact that there is $6.80 on hand and a grocery bill of two hundred, and a printing bill of four hundred. Rosemary, who leads the kitchen police, now says she can feed an able-bodied man for two dollars a week, but that is without meat.

4

It was after this early spring seamen's strike that I made the following speech and rewrote it as an article afterwards, to try to clarify our stand in regard to conflicts such as the present one we were engaged in:

"Let us be honest, let us say that fundamentally, the stand we are taking is not on the ground of wages and hours and conditions of labor, but on the fundamental truth that men should be treated not as chattels, but as human beings, as 'temples of the Holy Ghost.' When Christ took on our human nature, when He became Man, He dignified and ennobled human nature. He said, 'The Kingdom of Heaven is within you.' When men are striking, they are following an impulse, often blind, often uninformed, but a good impulse — one could even say an inspiration of the Holy Spirit. They are trying to uphold their rights to be treated not as slaves, but as men. They are fighting for a share in the management, for their right to be considered partners in the enterprise in which they are engaged. They are fighting against the idea of their labor as a commodity, to be bought and sold.

"Let us concede that the conditions at the Victor RCA plant down in Camden, where a strike started last month, which is said to involve 13,000 men, are not bad conditions, and that wages and hours are not bad. There probably is a company union which is supposed to take care of such conditions and complaints, but it perpetuates the enslavement of the worker.

"Let us concede that the conditions of the seamen are not so atrocious as the *Daily Worker* contends. (It is no use talking about the steward's department on passenger ships which has had, and in some cases still has, unbearable hours and conditions of labor.) Let us get down to the fundamental point that the seamen are striking for — the right to be considered partners, sharers in responsibility, the right to be treated as men and not as chattels.

"Is it not a cause worth fighting for? Is it not a cause which demands all the courage, and all the integrity, of the men involved? *Let us be frank and make this our issue.*

"Let us be honest and confess that it is the social order which we wish to change. The workers are never going to be satisfied, no matter how much pay they get, no matter what their hours are.

"This, of course, is the contention of the ship owners, of employers and industrialists the world over. They know that strikes are going to go on, no matter what concessions are made along these lines. They too will not face the fundamental issues involved.

"During the seamen's strike in the spring and the months after when the men were staying at the Catholic Worker House on Mott Street — there were about fifty who came and found jobs and went away to have their places taken by others — we had an opportunity to talk to many of them. There was many a round table discussion over the preparation of vegetables and the washing of dishes and the mailing out of the paper (for the men joined in our work while they were with us). They have written to us since they left, and they return to see us when they come back into port.

"One night we were talking with a Communist, a young fellow from Iowa, born of a Catholic father and a Methodist mother. It was hard to talk to him — we were both convinced we were right, we were both animated by the truth — but he refused to concede the spiritual. Philosophically we differed. But a great many truths came out in these arguments.

"He used to stand in the middle of the kitchen floor, a dish towel in his hands, and suspend all operations while he talked. Tennessee, Yank, Ryan and the others went on working, laughing at his earnestness and his inability to co-ordinate work and discussion.

"He used to take refuge in anti-clericalism, in attacks on our refusal to face facts, in what he liked to label our 'sentimentality.' Often he would be driven to name-calling because he felt himself defeated in argument and there was no other refuge for him.

"But there were many things we agreed on.

"He was telling us one night how he caused a disturbance on board ship over the constant mess of stew they had been served. Overtime work, crowded quarters, uncomfortable mattresses, the menu, all these were the issues seized upon as a chance for a disturbance, a miniature strike. He had been spending his days at sea figuring out ways to forward the revolution, and on this occasion it was stew.

"We asked him whether he really thought that a cause worth fighting for to the shedding of blood. We asked him whether the other seamen, who were fundamentally sane, did not object to these obstructionist tactics of the Communist. If they did not hinder their own cause by this tactic?

"He maintained that if they would not join in it was because they were cowardly and selfish.

"We maintained that it was because they knew it was not the cause for which they were fighting.

"We pointed out that there on Mott Street they were sleeping six in an apartment, between blankets, no sheets, that the food was insufficient, and the washing facilities most primitive. They had no showers, no hot water to wash out their clothes. (And they were always washing out their clothes. A cleaner lot of men would be hard to find.) They had to walk ten blocks to get to a public bath.

"We pointed out that if the men were running the ship themselves, they would put up with any sacrifice, go without food, submit to crowded quarters, take a minimum of pay, if only they were recognized as masters of their own destinies. 'And that is why we are working towards a workers' republic,' he said triumphantly.

"We made him admit that some men were capable of leadership and others weren't, that some men were trained to hold certain positions and had to hold them. We brought out Tawney's ideas of functional classes as opposed to acquisitive classes.[51]

"But the worker had no chance to improve himself so he could become an officer, he claimed. Or if he had, he was still in the position of being a flunkey, or a hireling of the masters. There was always the profit system, the idea of labor being sold as a commodity, whether it was the labor of the captain or the crew.

"It was, we conceded, the whole social system that was out of joint. And it was to reconstruct the social order, that we were throwing ourselves in with the workers, whether in factories or shipyards or on the sea.

"The co-operative movement is a good one because it offers an opportunity to rebuild within the shell of the old with a new philosophy, which is a philosophy so old that it seems like new. And in the co-operative movement there is a chance for a

---

51   R. H. Tawney (1880-1962), British economic historian and social critic. His *Religion and the Rise of Capitalism: A Historical Study* (New York: Harcourt Brace and Co., 1926) was considered by Peter Maurin an essential text for the Catholic Worker movement.

real united front and for a peaceful and ethical accomplishment of our aims. But where there is no chance at co-operative enterprise right now, in factories and on ships, what then?

"The Popes have hit the nail on the head. 'No man may outrage with impunity that human dignity which God Himself treats with reverence … Religion teaches the rich man and employer that their work people are not their slaves; that they must respect in every man his dignity as a man and as a Christian; that labor is an honorable employment: and that it is shameful and inhuman to treat men like chattels to make money by, or to look upon them merely as so much muscle or physical power.'[52]

"These are fundamental principles which the A. F. of L. has neglected to bring out. They have based their appeal on enlightened self-interest, a phrase reeking with selfishness and containing a warning and a threat. A warning to the workers of the world that they are working for themselves alone, and not as 'members one of another.' One can see how it has worked out in this country. What percentage of the workers are organized? A fraction only of the laboring men of the country. And how has the highly organized workman cared for his poorer brother? There has grown up an aristocracy of labor, so that it is an irksome fact that bricklayers and printers receive more than farmers or editors in the necessary goods of this world — in goods which we should strive for in order that we may have those God-given means to develop to the full and achieve the Kingdom of Heaven.

"We are not losing sight of the fact that our end is spiritual. We are not losing sight of the fact that these better conditions of labor are means to an end. But the labor movement has lost sight of this fact. The leaders have forgotten such a thing as a philosophy of labor. They have not given to the worker the philosophy of labor, and they have betrayed him.

---

52   Leo XIII, *Rerum Novarum*, para. 40, 20.

"And the inarticulate rank and file throughout the world is rising up in rebellion, and are being labelled Communists for so doing, for refusing to accept the authority of such leaders, which they very rightly do not consider just authority. They intuitively know better than their leaders what they are looking for. But they allow themselves to be misled and deceived.

"We have so positive a program that we need all our energy, we have to bend all our forces, material and spiritual, to this end, to promulgate it. Let us uphold our positive program of changing the social order.

"But let us too examine the Communist means to the end which they claim they are working for, a true brotherhood of man. We do not talk about a classless society, because we acknowledge functional classes as opposed to acquisitive classes.

"We agree with this end, but we do not agree on the means to attain it.

"The Communists say: 'All men are our brothers except the capitalists, so we will kill them off.' They do not actually believe in the dignity of man as a human being, because they try to set off one or another class of men and say 'they are not our brothers and never will be. So let us liquidate them,' and then to point their argument they say with scorn, 'Do you ever think to convert J. P. Morgan, or Rockefeller, or Charlie Schwab?'

"They are protesting against man's brutality to man, and at the same time they perpetuate it. It is like having one more war to end all wars. We disagree with this technique of class war, without which the Communist says the brotherhood of man can never be achieved.

" 'Nothing will be achieved until the worker rises up in arms and forcibly takes the position that is his,' the Communist says. 'Your movement, which trusts to peaceful means, radical though it may seem, is doomed to failure.'

"We admit that we may seem to fail, but we recall to our readers the ostensible failure of Christ when he died on the Cross, forsaken by all His followers. Out of this failure a new world sprang up. We recall to our readers the folly of the Cross which St. Paul talks about. "When we participate in strikes, when we go out on picket lines and distribute leaflets, when we speak at strike meetings, we are there because we are reaching the workers when they are massed together for action. We are taking advantage of a situation. We may not agree that to strike was the wise thing to do in that particular case. We believe that the work of organization must be thorough before any strike action occurs, unless indeed the strike is a spontaneous one which is the outcome of unbearable conditions.

"We oppose all use of violence as un-Christian. We do not believe in persuading scabs with clubs. They are workers, too, and the reason they are scabs is because the work of organization has been neglected.

"We oppose the misuse of private property while we uphold the right of private property. The Holy Father says that 'as many as possible of the workers should become owners,' and how else in many cases except by developing the co-operative ideal?

"While we are upholding co-operatives as a part of the Christian social order, we are upholding at the same time unions, as organizations of workers wherein they can be indoctrinated and taught to rebuild the social order. While we stress the back-to-the-land movement so that the worker may be 'deproletarianized,' we are not going to leave the city to the Communist.

"Month by month, in every struggle, in every strike, on every picket line, we shall do our best to join with the worker in his struggle for recognition as a man and not as a chattel. We reiterate the slogan of the old I.W.W.'s: 'An injury to one is an injury to all.' St. Paul says 'When the health of one member of the Mystical Body suffers, the health of the whole body is lowered' [paraphrasing 1 Corinthians 12:26].

"We are all members, one of another, in the Mystical Body of Christ, so let us work together for Christian solidarity."

NINE

1

IN THE country. My job is being cowherd. I can sit under a tree with pen and paper and write to the readers of *The Catholic Worker* and all I have to do is to see that Rosie, the Holstein, does not stray from the southeast pasture where the fences are being repaired by Francis and Eddie.

It is an irregular pasture, roughly shaped like the letter K, one end shut in by woods, the other by apple trees. It is up on a hillside and down on my left is the asparagus bed in the field below and then more sloping fields, some very steep, to the river road and the Delaware. Beyond that are more sloping fields, and hills, green and brown like a patchwork quilt. Immediately by the side of me is a hedge of raspberry bushes and a sparse clump of sumach.

There is hot sunlight after a day and night of rain which replenished the cisterns; there are sounds of woodchopping, a train in the distance, a bumble bee, the sound of the cow munching and cropping the grass.

There is also the sound of the old Ford truck operated by Jim Montague, drawing a two-horse plough guided by Cyril Echele.

We want to get the kitchen garden planted, and there is no horse nor money to buy one. Someone suggested we get one on the installment plan from a neighboring farmer, but with three dollars in the bank we would be violating principles in making so large a purchase with no money in sight. We know St. Joseph will take care of the printing bill (four hundred dollars to be paid), and the groceries which are paid for from week to week. We are frugal enough, God knows, though we have plenty on the table.

The horse and equipment will come — we will pay for it. The truck method of ploughing was recommended to us by

Louis, former occupant of the farm, who now lives down the road.

We went in to see a Polish neighbor yesterday and she was just coming in from the woods with an apronful of coral mushrooms to cook up with butter gravy for supper. Here it is only May and already we have all the asparagus and rhubarb we can eat, dandelion and dockweed, mushrooms and milk. As yet we have no chickens and are buying eggs for 25 cents a dozen down the road.

To many throughout the country our farm will seem sadly inadequate as to size. In writing to correspondents in Kansas, we have to explain about intensive cultivation and producing for use. In writing to a correspondent in Belgium the other day, this was not necessary as they are limited as to space over there and understand the intensive cultivation of small parcels of land.

If we were financed our readers could say:

"Oh, it is all very well for you — you've got money in back of you. But what about us? How are we to start out, without stock, without funds, without hands."

That is where the farming commune idea comes in. People can work together, can pool their resources, can think in terms of mutual aid.

2

But this account started to be a day at the farm. We are cooking on an old wood range collapsed in the middle. K. prepared vegetables, weeded, washed dishes and washed up the sloping kitchen. Bill Callahan in high boots shovelled manure into an old wagon to be towed out into the north field and scattered.

For a few early hours in the morning I had planted onion seeds, six long rows of them, and as I crouched and bent and planted, I thought of the three million children and women working in the cotton fields, from dawn to dark. I thought of the women and children in the beet fields and onion fields in the middle and far west and I thought how even the six-year-olds were pressed into the gruelling service until they were deadened and worn and a deep smouldering resentment grew and grew within them, shaping them for revolution or for the flight from the soil to the cities.

After supper the boys all went out to mend a portion of the road where it comes up the hill, slanting perilously between fields. With the truck and plough they ploughed up one side, Eddie using a pick as supplementary help and Bill at work with the shovel.

But Cy had the idea of chaining a wide board behind the truck and all of them standing on it, balancing themselves with ropes, the truck pulling them along to level out the ploughed-up portion.

Washing up the supper things in the house, we didn't know what was going on until we heard loud yells of joy and triumph and went out to see the fun. The stunt worked pretty well, but in the course of the levelling one or more of the workers was always flung off into the field.

Every night, for the last week, the cow got lost, until the pasture was staked in, and wandered half a mile across fields to her former home. Margaret, in the city, told me she dreamt the cow had run away, but returned, bringing three more with her. No such luck! She wandered away all right, and Francis, Paul and Eddie had the job of pursuing her. On that evening, she was found in the pasture with six other cows, cropping peaceably away, and it wasn't until they had separated her from the rest, that they noticed the bull coming after them.

Francis didn't say how he felt, but Eddie confessed his terror. They couldn't get around to the stile but had to lift up a barbed wire fence and push the cow through. It was a moment!

Before bedtime, around nine, we all gather together, for the rosary and litany. Tonight there was a little breeze outside in the apple trees sighing around the house. The moon shone down on the hill top, washing the fields in a soft glow. There was quiet and perfect peace and a happiness so deep and strong and thankful, that even our words of prayer seemed inadequate to express our joy. May St. Isidore, patron of farm workers, pray for us and praise God for us!

3

Mott Street. Outside in the street the sun pours down but it is not too hot for the little girls to be skipping rope. St. Joseph stands in the window of *The Catholic Worker* store, surrounded by green plants, and looks out at the children.

A little while ago a funeral passed by. We were just coming from Mass and heard the band playing. On all sides of the white hearse were little girls dressed in their First Communion dresses, carrying flowers. Two men carried a mounted picture of the dead child, dressed in white surrounded with more flowers.

The sun was shining, and a little girl was dead, a little girl from one of these crowded tenements hereabouts where six children and more are crowded in three and four rooms — where the rats, as little Felicia said, are chased by her father with a broomstick.

There is sun in the street, but from the cellars and areaways a dank musty smell redolent of death rises. There is sun and gayety in the streets, and the little girls skip rope around the pushcart of pineapples, but one little girl was carried in a coffin down the street, while the band played its slow, mournful and yet triumphant dirge. She was through with this short and dangerous life which is yet so dear to us all. There is one less to skip from beneath the wheels of trucks and gather around the crowded kitchen table in the tenement. There is one less mouth to feed, one less pair of shoes for the father (who supports eight on fifteen dollars a week) to buy.

One less little girl.

The day after tomorrow we are bringing the first batch of children down to the farm. They will be loaded on the truck with baskets of mason jars which kind friends sent in, with the blankets other poor families contributed for them, with the cots the seamen have been sleeping on in our hospice.

It is our readers who are making this possible, who have sent us in seventy-five dollars all told to pay for the food for these young ones. There are about fifty children we have promised to bring down to the country, and there is seventy-five dollars to feed them with.

If it seems too brutal to tell of the funeral which we saw this morning, we can only say that life down here is filled with these contrasts of brutal facts, and self-sacrifice and patience. Our lives are checkered in this way with violence and death, sunlight and joy.

Some of those very seamen who were clubbed on the picket line are down in the country right now fixing up the place for the children who are coming on Saturday. And one of our readers who is on relief sent in a dollar to help feed our charges.

4

We are developing the idea we have long had of the lay apostolate, and there are now amongst us enough fellow workers to send out into the fields and factories to work and attract new followers of *The Catholic Worker* movement. This last month four young fellows hitch-hiked from the farm down to southern New Jersey to work on the commercial farms. One of them is going to enter the seminary, and the work he has been doing this summer only adds to his preparedness for the life that is before him. Another one of the Catholic Workers has gone down to work in the steel mills, and yet another has gone up to New England to get a job in any factory that suits his fancy. Two others are going out this month to yet another factory in the New York district.

During this last month there have been about fourteen children at the farm all told. A few of them went back to the city because they were homesick, but two of the boys were so delighted with farm life that they have learned to milk the cow, hoe the corn and raid the grapevine of one of our neighbors. Fortunately, it is a friendly neighbor, a Communitarian himself.

The four police dog puppies presented to us by this same neighbor are about as uproarious as the children. Three of them are black and tan, but one, Teresa says, is peach colored. Little Annie is probably the most vociferous of the children. Coming down to the farm in the truck, she surveyed the wide fields and woods and exclaimed on the size of the park we were passing through. Eleanor can tap dance like a professional, and her neatest trick is to tie tin cans to her feet and dance on them. The noise is very satisfying. Bernice is her big sister. She is ten and Eleanor is eight, and it was a great sight to see the motherly little girl scrubbing down her dusky sister Saturday night so that her delicious brown skin was all but veiled in soapsuds. Mary Giogas, who is Greek, did a lot of sewing out under the apple trees for her little sister Annie, who had a new dress to wear practically every day. She needed lots of clothes, so the rag bag was raided often for pieces. Her face looked tattooed after the many slices of bread and elderberry jam which she consumed, and, as for her dresses, she looked good in what she ate, Loretta said.

5

During the month there was a grand festa in town which extended all around Mott Street, but we were at the center of the whirlpool, inasmuch as one of our neighbors in the front house is president of the association which runs the festa for the Feast of the Assumption and the Feast of St. Roche. The noise was tremendous. It began with a band of fifty coming into our backyard and sitting on planks for their concert practice which lasted two hours and ended in quite a bit of wine drinking and a fight.

Outside the streets were aglow with color and light and booths were set up to sell all kinds of fruit and nuts. Charcoal stoves were working overtime preparing sweet corn and broiled sausages and liver. There was a bandstand and free-lance orchestras and dancing up and down the street. All day, every day, there were processions and banners, and Saturday night with lightning adding fireworks to the show, the statue of the Blessed Virgin was escorted with many maids of honor and children in white, carrying lighted candles and bouquets of flowers up and down the winding streets, Mott Street and Mulberry Street, Hester and Canal, blessing them all.

Our latest guest at St. Joseph's house is a Russian boy who was injured in the Gastonia textile strike in 1931 in a clash with a picket. Boris was a national guardsman and received a clout over the head which landed him in the hospital for eight months. Our opponents, the upholders of violent revolution as a means to achieving peace, would consider him a class enemy inasmuch as he was on the opposite side in a strike. But realizing that our conflict is with principalities and powers rather than with human beings, we see in Boris a fellow member of the Mystical Body, badly in need of indoctrination.

Eddie Priest came in this evening begrimed by toil and much in need of a shave. He's taking a turn at the lay apostolate in industry (and working for much needed cash!) and his job is spot welding, assembling, working a drill press, a punch press, and a hand metal brake in a sheet metal works in Brooklyn. His job is from eight to five-thirty, with forty-five minutes for lunch, and there are fourteen fellow-workers, all youths.

6

The way the priest at the Church of the Transfiguration goes up to the altar with out-stretched arms in the morning, the humble reverence of the Franciscan at the Church of the Precious Blood on Baxter Street as he kneels at "The Word was made Flesh and dwelt amongst us,"[53] the gallant and tender figure of St. Joseph clasping the Christ Child at that same church, the willing co-operation of all the workers around Mott Street this turbulent month when there was so much moving to be done, and all the work of the paper had to go on — these were some of the things which put us in mind of the love of God this past few days.

We picketed St. Joseph this past month, when we were sending out an appeal — asking him to take care of our temporal necessities, as he had to take care of the temporal necessities of the Blessed Mother and the Infant Jesus during those long hidden years at Nazareth. It was a peaceful and loving picketing, the crowd of us taking turns to go to the church and there in the presence of Christ our Leader, contemplate St. Joseph, that great friend of God, and Protector of His Church. One of the girls in St. Joseph's house, when we announced the picketing at the breakfast table, wanted to know, very startled, whether she would have to carry a sign.

"Be faithful to our time of prayer rather than to our words. For instance fifteen minutes before and after Communion. In the middle of the day as well at night. And ejaculatory prayers as often as possible." — Archbishop Goodier, S.J.[54]

7

In the country the material and the spiritual have their proper relationship. There one can wholeheartedly say that the material is good; that it is good to enjoy the material things of

---

53   John 1:14, from the Final Gospel which concludes the Extraordinary Form of the Mass.

54   Most Rev. Alban Goodier, S.J. (1869-1939), archbishop of Bombay (Mumbai) and prolific spiritual writer.

this world; that one can love the world and God Who made it, and not be a materialist and separated from Him.

Teresa is following the ploughman and gathering worms for the three ducks and the chickens. The pastor of our church in Easton came up to see us and was introduced to the fourteen or so at the Catholic Worker farm. He has impressed us all, because on meeting us he maintained a proper reserve which was without suspicion. There are several ways of being catechized in regard to the paper, its project and aims. Very often we are questioned with suspicion with the attitude, "You're guilty until I know you are innocent."

Yesterday I went down to see Sister Edith who is the principal of the Catholic High School here in Easton. She is going to co-operate with us and already is arranging for us to speak, both before the students and the parent-teacher groups. Also, groups of high school students are going to come up to the farm during the summer.

Most of the Catholics in Easton are industrial workers and it is very hard to keep the church and school going. The high school building is not large, but every inch of it is utilized for class rooms and library, and during the vacation months, Sister Edith allows the unemployed young men who are graduates of the school to hang around the building, use the library and have a special room for themselves to congregate and smoke in.

While I was talking to her, I heard children's voices around the convent and she told me how she took in some of the children of employed mothers to care for them during the day. She certainly seems to be one of these people who does with all her might whatsoever her hand findeth to do [Ecclesiastes 9:10].

8

6:00 A.M. "This," says John Griffin, working over his flower bed where he is doing some early transplanting, "is rather a masculine bed, strong in line and color — but this one — ah, that will be a tender little one." And he hovered over the portulaca, spotting weeds.

The sun came up over the mist in the valley at five-thirty this morning, and the rooster perched on the water barrel under the apple tree and crowed; the hens clucked, the ducks quacked and the hound dog raced a few last times around the lower meadow, barking hoarsely. He had made a night of it.

John has done all the work beautifying the house on the outside. Flower beds enclosed by rustic fences, terraces, rock walk, a flight of steps leading down into the asparagus bed at the head of which I am now sitting.

Already the sun is beginning to get hot. Paul, the earliest riser, is taking the cow up the hill. She is his special care; and under his ministrations she has become an affectionate pet. The other evening while we sat out under the trees, she went from one to the other of us, licking our hands and breathing her strong herbish breath into our faces.

John Cort[55] has gone out to harrow the west field with a rake, preparatory to our last planting. Victor is going on with the cultivating of the sweet potatoes. Julia has wandered on down to Easton to the seven o'clock Mass, leaving all her charges, the five Giogas children, sound asleep in bed.

They say they like the farm "more better" than the Huguenot place. "Are we coming to a different place every year?" they want to know, thinking of the ground the C. W. has already covered. They are working right along with us, the children are, picking gooseberries and weeding the asparagus bed where there is no danger of mistaking vegetables for weeds.

This morning the work includes jam making and delousing the children and writing an article. And then I'll crawl

---

55   John Cort (1913-2006), Catholic convert and early follower of the Catholic Worker movement. In his long life, he later became involved in the labor movement, served on the editorial staff of *Commonweal* magazine, and eventually served as an assistant director of the Peace Corps.

along the row of two-inch high beets for an hour and do some weeding.

I had intended to do some reading this early morning, and I have beside me a treatise on prayer, and *Labor and Steel*.[56] But this spot where I am sitting is no place for reading. For praying, yes, but every spot around here says to us "Sursum Corda" ["Lift up your hearts" — *ed.*].

On the hillside writing letters. Hot, but with a breeze. We all went to 8 o'clock Mass; Carney, Michael Flynn, Francis, Paul, Griffin, Gibson, Jim, Eddie, Pat, Kate, Mary, Steve and I. Last Sunday Carney got the Professor to go for the first time in years. Gibson is going to Confession this Saturday for the first time in seventeen years. The boys don't know how much good they can do by translating the spiritual into the material as they are doing.

Awoke at five, as the sun came up. Five men already up. Gibson had coffee ready and a roaring fire in the stove, although already, early as it was, it promised to be a very hot day. I started reading Lauds, but more got up. At 7:30 Mass, five of us; and then over to Dr. Koiransky's to get a setting hen and rooster. A mile from the place we heard a steady ringing noise filling the air, the kind of noise you hear going under ether. It persisted over the noise of the rattling truck (and a bad road at that) and we could not imagine what it was. When we got to Dr. Koiransky's, his farmer told us it was the seven year locust which, for the last few days, had descended upon them. The sound of the insects is ominous.

About chickens. The doctor's housekeeper was telling us many things. A special box the chickens like so that they wait in line to lay in it. About cycles — the eggs get smaller and smaller during the month and then reach normal size again. First they lay early in the day, then later and later; the afternoon eggs be-

---

56   Horace Bancroft Davis, *Labor and Steel* (New York: International Publishers, 1933). Davis (1898-1998) was a prominent Marxist economist of the period.

ing the small ones. It must be the moon. While you are saving eggs for a setting hen, you must turn them every two days. If she wishes to set she will collect the eggs from the other hens herself, rolling them to her nest.

The doctor's cow is a pet. She is red-brown, wears a Swiss bell, and loves to put her head in the back door.

Last night we said the rosary out under the trees, praying for rain. The moon was coming up. There was a smell of sweet clover in the air and it was very quiet. Carney led. Now there are nineteen of us.

It is still very dry and a lot of planting and transplanting to do yet. Seed potatoes have gone up to five dollars a bushel. The work is coming along fine and the place is beginning to look as though people lived there who loved it. John Griffin with his flower garden and his statue of the Blessed Virgin, put up as a prayer for water. The wall which Flynn built, the weeding out of the gooseberry bushes and rhubarb, by Steve; Mr. O'Connell's screen door; the gardening by Paul, Ordway, etc., the harrowing by Hughes and D'Orsay — all these things have been going on last week.

9

Sunday. Mott Street again. For the last four days an awful spell of heat, the worst in forty years they say. All night people sit out in the streets, mothers holding their heavy sleeping babies. Sprinkling trucks spray the garbage up from the gutters on to the sidewalks and steamy fetid odors rise and choke one. The heat does not bother me as the smell does.

We have a houseful of invalids. Charlie Rich is sick with the heat. Never well at any time because of his stomach ulcers, he goes around reading the Office of the Dead, his eyes heavy and his face drawn.

L. has been out on a drunk and is lying trembling in his room while he is here. He has just stolen five dollars from me, the money we had to send the sharecroppers package of clothes, and he must be tormented in soul as well as in body.

Harold Medonet, in the same room with them is well; working now and paying off his debts. He has just finished a milk driver's job which almost finished him. He was working eighteen hours a day. Also on the top floor are Rush, left over from the elevator strike, an elderly man; Joe from Arizona, a tramp boy; Ordway, an ex-seminarian, formerly with a Trappist monastery in Kentucky.

Mr. Breen has also been sick this week. He has delusions constantly.

"They are making fun of the Church," he screamed suddenly yesterday. "They are pretending to perform a baptism in the speakeasy in the front." (The speakeasy where they sell wine night and day to singing, roistering laborers who all but murder each other when they are bawling out Sardinian songs, adds to the general unrest.)

Katherine is lamenting my ultimatum about her cat which has gone about soiling the house. Beatrice, Celia and Ruth are well and happy. But Kate Smith who is sharing my room is just back from the hospital. Her tumor on the brain is irremovable.

Rosemary is in the country. Frank and Loretta are in town. A new woman from Kentucky, Caroline they call her, is staying with us. Carney came in from the farm today also suffering from aberrations. It is not the time of the full moon, but he says July is always a bad month for him. He accuses everyone of racketeering, of talking about him, of wanting to put him away, and threatens violence. He says also he was warned to lay low until the Triborough bridge was completed, that he was not a member of the religious community and that he had been followed down to the Philadelphia convention by someone who said in his ear, "So Dorothy Day only gave you a dollar." He is definitely in a bad way.

10

At the Farm. Fish soup is cooking, also beet greens for one o'clock lunch. I've been canning tomatoes all morning — 12 quarts — and my hands are so tired I can scarcely write. A perfect day for working, good breeze. I'm sitting out under the old apple tree, on a very good but not very handsome bench that John Griffin made out of an unused shutter. The three ducks are trying to take a bath in front of me. The drake is constantly biting at the neck of one of the ducks and she turns and returns the caress. Then they both lift themselves preeningly and raise their wings and flutter. The rooster and one hen are sharing a worm and murmuring together.

John Griffin has gone into town to see about collecting some money owing to him and on his return we'll probably go out and buy two pigs. John Curran drove him and five homesick kids to town in the morning, which leaves two. Griffin would have hitch-hiked, only Curran had to call for some pitchforks and shovels at Mrs. Williams in Short Hills. Mary is also away, visiting her friend in the Oranges. Jim, Bill and the kids are down getting Frank and Loretta and the baby. And now there is a lunch to get on the table. Everything is very peaceful, but there has been some controversy as to whether Carney should be down.

11

Mott Street again.

One P.M., and I am most comfortably settled in the extra apartment in the front house which Miss Burke turned over to us. It will be good to be able to sit up and work in the evening and not worry about waking Kate up.

Today was very full. I arrived in New York at 9:30 and little Dan met me, thinking I was carrying a suitcase of tomatoes, but

Rufus, Sylvia, Margaret Bigham and Tom set out with them by car yesterday. (They have not yet arrived here.)

First of all a long discussion with John about personalism, hospitality, state responsibility and organized charity. (He was objecting to caring for such people as A.,B.,C.,D.,E., etc.). It was a long one. He is very conscientious and sticks to the job of being in the office, seeing people, indoctrinating, spiritual reading at the table, etc. I am very critical with him, but I do think he is a good worker.

Then Carney — I told him he could not go down to Easton now, and I think it came as a great shock to him. He told John later, very threateningly, that he was going to write letters to certain people about us, that we are racketeers and not doing our duty by him. (Some of the duties are to provide him with clothes, a commutation ticket to Easton which costs eighty dollars, better food, and security from persecution.)

Mr. M. came next, telling me of his hunger and suffering, his quarrel with Rosemary over taking stuff from the kitchen. I must give Knut Hamsun's *Hunger*[57] to Rosemary to read. She manages beautifully usually but sometimes there is a conflict.

Then came Ed. He was to have sailed Saturday, but before sailing the entire ship got drunk and he fell off the wagon, too, and was fired. He was feeling like hell about it and swears he won't go to sea any more; it will be the same thing over again. He was too confident, after going to daily Mass and Communion. It's always the way. Thank God he came back at once. I would have felt badly if he had not. He's all right now, is going down to the farm tomorrow to help with the barn and road-mending, and thence to Bethlehem to try for a job as a steel worker.

---

57   Knut Hamsun (1859-1952), distinguished Norwegian novelist and winner of the Nobel Prize for Literature in 1920. Curiously, during the Second World War he was a Nazi sympathizer and was tried for treason afterwards. The work referenced is *Hunger* (trans. George Egerton; New York: Knopf, 1921).

Talked to Julia about the children who are next going down, then about the Legion of Mary which she's working with in Father Rothlauf's Parish.

Father Eustace from Dunwoodie in for an hour and we talked about the Fascists in Spain, the rural workers in New Jersey. While he was here, Father O'Loughlin from Turin, newly ordained, came in and gave us his blessing. He was only here a moment. He has been getting the paper since the seventh issue.

Texas, Clark, Arizona, were the next on the program and I suggested they go down to the bean and tomato farms in southern New Jersey (which are beginning to assume the aspect of the salt mines of Siberia) and join Eddie Priest, Ordway, Bergen and the other seminarian, for a month. Our funds are so low (the electric and telephone are being shut off Wednesday, but we were able to send the co-op $35 today, thank God). Just now Texas, Clark and Arizona are singing in the yard, "It don't mean a thing if you wake up and sing in the morning," and various other songs. The Italian girls from the neighborhood join them, leaning out of their windows. Now it has started to rain and they have had to go inside, but they are still strumming on an old ukelele of Stanley's. It scandalizes people that they all have such a good time; but where should they go — to pool rooms, down along the waterfront? Why shouldn't they make a hangout of the place? They get a good deal of serious conversation with people like John Cort, the reading at the table; Rosemary does her share, trying to get them back to Mass, etc. They can't be serious all the time. Arizona has worked at restaurant jobs, Clark on pleasure yachts as a seaman, and Tex also was a seaman.

Late in the evening, a Dutchman, Jocham, came in telling us of the work of a great priest in Holland. Jocham was a seaman, a steward for fifteen years on the Mallory Line, and now is on home relief. He is sixty years old.

12

Downstairs in the yard there are a dozen men sitting at long tables, drinking wine. The yard is decorated with benches and electric lights, as is all the street in front for blocks around.

Today is the last day of the festa celebrating the Assumption.

I went to the farm Wednesday night, and came in to town yesterday morning after five-thirty Mass. A fearfully close day, hard to breathe.

This feast day is a happy one for me, and filled with resolutions. First to pay every possible attention to my own soul as Father Lallemant stresses. Again a rule of life to be determined on; more time spent in prayer. I shall start again trying to make that six A.M. Mass, so that I can have time for thanksgiving, meditation and reading early in the morning. There is so much to do; people require so much of one; there are always callers and letters, and, in this neighborhood constant noise. And in the country the same demands made upon me, work to participate in, etc. So I must do more to guard every moment and keep recollected. I can help people far more then, anyway.

"And he that ministereth seed to the sower, will both give you bread to eat, and increase the growth of the fruits of your justice." 2 *Corinthians*, 9:10.

13

Low in mind all day, full of tears. Got up at six to wash leftover milk pails and get breakfast, talked to Bill about the *Newman News* and Ordway about marriage, and jobs, Mass at 7:40.

Bill and John Curran, Bergen and Ordway went in to New York to distribute papers at a Communist rally at Madison Square Garden. Mary got fifty dollars from her sister and contributed it to the grocery fund.

What with the Easton, New York, Boston, Ottawa, Toronto, and Missouri groups, all discouraged, all looking for organization instead of self-organization, all of them weary of the idea of freedom and personal responsibility — I feel bitterly oppressed, yet confirmed in the conviction that we have to emphasize personal responsibility at all costs. It is most certainly at the price of bitter suffering for myself. For I am just in the position of a dictator trying to legislate himself out of existence. They accept my regime which emphasizes freedom and personal responsibility, but under protest. They all complain at the idea of there being this freedom in town and here, that there is no boss.

Today I just happened to light on Dostoievsky's *Grand Inquisitor* which was most apropos. Freedom — how men hate it and chafe under it, how unhappy they are with it.

On Sunday night in town I read Maritain's *Freedom and The Modern World*.[58] I read while the Italians outside sang and shouted their allegiance to Mussolini. It was hard concentrating then just as it is hard now with all the gnat-like disturbances incidental to life in a community.

This week, Eleanor and Bernice, two colored children, and Mary and Annie Giogas are down and they are singing and dancing all the day. I should be happy to see them, products of Harlem, and Ed Keohane and Charlie Keefe, lower west side, enjoying the country so much. John Griffin with his beautiful flower garden; Dave after two years in jail; these children, invalids and unemployed ones; but I have satisfaction in nothing.

"Are we trying to make a farm here or aren't we?"

A statement of that kind, an attitude of criticism of all that Peter and I stand for, has the power to down me completely, so that I feel utterly incapable of going to Boston and meeting all

---

58   Jacques Maritain, *Freedom in the Modern World* (New York: Gordian, 1936). Also see above, p. 45, note 13.

their trials and discouragements. Nothing but the grace of God can help me, but I feel utterly lacking, ineffective.

In town the usual crosses; Carney calling us all racketeers, calling the spiritual reading pious twaddle. E. with his vile accusations; the misery of M. and P.; Kate's illness; the threatened suit against us; the bills piling up — these things to be topped by such a lack of understanding of the personalist idea from those you expect the most from, lays me low. Since I got back from Pittsburgh, I have this completely alone feeling. A temptation of the devil, doubtless, and to succumb to it is a lack of faith and hope. There is nothing to do but bear it, but my heart is as heavy as lead, and my mind dull and uninspired. A time when the memory and understanding fail one completely, and only the will remains, so that I feel hard and rigid, and at the same time ready to sit like a soft fool and weep.

Tonight Teresa had a nose bleed, a head-ache and a stomach-ache, and although the latter probably came from eating green pears, as she confessed, still to think of the little time I have with her, being constantly on the go, having to leave her to the care of others, sending her away to school so that she can lead a regular life and not be subject to the moods and vagaries of the crowd of us! This is probably the cruellest hardship of all. She is happy, she does not feel torn constantly as I do. And then the doubt arises, probably she too feels that I am failing her, just as the crowd in Mott Street and the crowd here feel it.

"You are always away."

And then when I get to Boston —

"This is your work, why are you not up here more often?"

Never before have I had such a complete sense of failure, of utter misery.

"O spiritual soul, when thou seest thy desire obscured, thy will arid and constrained, and thy faculties incapable of any interior act, be not grieved at this, but look upon it rather as a great good, for God is delivering thee from thyself, taking the matter out of thy hands.... The way of suffering is safer, and also more profitable, than that of rejoicing and of action. In suffering, God gives strength, but in action and in joy the soul does but show its own weakness and imperfections." — St. John of the Cross.

"Personality is compounded of the body with its appetites and the soul with its rational will; concupiscence springs from original sin and leads to actual sin; it often anticipates reason and is thus a hindrance to the good a man really wants to do: unwished for uprising of temper is a good instance." — St. Thomas.

At the Farm. Rain and cool weather. Everything is soaked from a steady downpour. Mary and Kate are doing up tomatoes. John F. is pruning the tree. Joe has to take it easy because of a cracked rib. Frank Mammano has a festered finger. Steve is sick in bed. Jim has gone to see about fencing for the pigs with Teresa, Eddie and Charlie and the other kids. Carney is working on the Studebaker. Bill is preparing to go to town.

14

In Boston for three days. Spoke to large outside group, and they collected forty dollars. Nothing in the bank and two checks bouncing. Father Sullivan here with Doctor O'Brien from Fordham, and friends. Free-for-all fight on personalism and Fascism. At Mary McSweeny's for the night. Summer school Friday, and met Father Lord, D. Willman, etc. Went to one of McDonald's classes on co-ops. Met Doctor Sullivan at three. Meeting at Lowell at eight. Stayed at Mary Ryan's. Left for summer school where I did not have to speak. Father S. till two. So did not see much of our C. W. crowd and will have to go back September 9th. Took boat at five for New York. Still low and dragged out. Feeling nothing accomplished.

During this week, August 24-28. Saw Mr. Sheed for lunch, Father Reinhold from Germany, McDonough, the organizer of the fishermen of Boston, Mr. Moody, and any number of people from summer school, where I spoke Thursday, ineffectively, breaking down as to voice right on the platform. Mr. Schwartz drove me down here where the atmosphere is morose and the weather does not help. Reading Caussade and New Testament and hiding my sadness from others does help.

TEN

1

THE trees are getting bare, but still it stays warm. Coming down at night from the city, the warm, sweet smell of the good earth enwraps one like a garment. There is the smell of rotting apples; of alfalfa in the barn; burning leaves; of wood fires in the house; of pickled green tomatoes and baked beans, than which there is no better smell, not even apple pies.

Now there is a warm feeling of contentment about the farm these days — the first summer is over, many people have been cared for here already — and we started out with capital of a thousand dollars to pay for the farm and nothing else at all. From day to day we did not know during the course of the summer where the next money to pay bills was coming from, but trusting to our co-operators, our readers throughout the country, we went on with the work. In spite of our collective faith, there could not help but be a feeling of strain at times when there was so much to be done and no money for tools or equipment, not even enough to pay for food. But now all our bills are paid, and there is a renewed feeling of courage on the part of all those who are doing the work, a sense of confidence that the work is progressing.

This month of thanksgiving will indeed be one of gratitude to God. For health, for work to do, for the opportunities He has given us of service; we are deeply grateful, and it is a feeling that makes the heart swell with joy.

During the summer when things were going especially hard in more ways than one, I grimly modified grace before meals: "We give Thee thanks, O Lord, for these Thy gifts, and for all our tribulations, from Thy bounty, through Christ our Lord, Amen." One could know of certain knowledge that tribulations were matters of thanksgiving; that we were indeed privileged to share in the sufferings of Our Lord. So in this month of thanksgiving, we can be thankful for the trials of the past, the blessings of the present, and be heartily ready at the same time to embrace with joy any troubles the future may bring us.

The backyard between the front house where we have two apartments and two stores, and the rear house which is St. Joseph's House proper, has been filled with huge barrels and from early morning until late at night there has been what should be a rustic job going on. Barrels are washed out, grapes come in by the truckload, the cellars are open to the warm fall air, the work of making wine for the whole neighborhood is under way. Some of the Italians in the front house are making barrels for this family or that in the neighborhood. And this is not a matter of scandal or extravagance. The Italians with their spaghetti and wine dine frugally and healthily, and there are few real drinkers amongst them.

Some day we will bring Teresa's camera, which she won at a school raffle, into town and take pictures of pushcart-lined Mott Street, St. Joseph's House and the wine keg-lined yard between the houses and publish them in the paper. Until we can afford a picture page, however, our readers must be content with word pictures.

2

Tonight ten of us went up to Madison Square Garden to distribute a few thousand papers before and after one of the Communist meetings which are held there every week. The Garden holds twenty thousand and is always packed to the doors. There is always a crowd who cannot get in.

"What's the idea of distributing literature to that gang of reds?" one of our friends wanted to know.

And we reply, that if one person of all those twenty thousand who throng the Garden is to the slightest degree moved by anything he finds in *The Catholic Worker*, we will have considered it a good night's work. We heard of one man who was brought back to the faith last month through *The Catholic Worker*, and that one bit of news was enough to make us intensify our efforts.

It is a little recognized fact that revolutions are started by just such seemingly insignificant acts as distributing literature. The first time Leon Trotsky was sent to jail it was because of printed leaflets urging the workers in Odessa to organize.[59] In the history of the working class movement men have gone to jail, been put to death, have been sent into exile for running a newspaper and printing literature which the government considered subversive.

If the forces of the enemy set such store by the distribution of literature to acquaint the working masses with their theory of revolution (and Lenin said that there could be no revolution without a theory of revolution) then most assuredly we are doing the right thing by distributing *The Catholic Worker* on every possible occasion.

There are forty thousand members of the Communist party in the United States. There are twenty thousand people in the Garden at the Communist meetings. Not by any means a majority of them are Communists. Many are sympathizers. Many are good trade unionists. Certainly the great mass of workers, convinced though they may be that better conditions can only come about through violence, do not want class war. Surely the great majority if faced with the choice between good and evil, God or the devil, would not choose evil. It is on this assumption that we are working. It is for this reason that we go out into the highways and byways, out on the street corner and the picket line with our paper.

This is being written down at the County Court where I am waiting for the commitment clerk to come down from the Bellevue psychopathic ward. The paper must go to press today,

---

59   Leon Trotsky (1879-1940), one of the founders of the Soviet Union and first commander of the Red Army. Day interviewed him for the radical newspaper *The Call* during his visit to New York City in 1917.

but there is a work of mercy to be done. One of our women has fallen into the hands of the state (and the state is becoming an inexorable guardian) and they have decided she is psychopathic and needs to be committed to the Manhattan Hospital. It is to rescue her that I am here — to plead to the judge to release her in our care. She had been with us six months and we had known her and helped her for some two years before that. What peculiarities she has we can cope with, but aside from any mental disorder, perhaps the result of cruel hardship and loneliness and insecurity, we are convinced that a most grave injustice is being done which we must prevent.

Right now I should be down at the printer's overseeing the makeup of the paper, because Bill Callahan, our managing editor, who of all the crowd is best at makeup, is away, and John Cort and Eddie Priest, though they can get a story and write one — though they fit in every other way into the scheme of life of *The Catholic Worker* — are not as yet at ease in writing heads and balancing the front page. Not that I am so hot myself. But I should be there, I think fretfully.

However, I shall sit and wait, and as to how things are going in the crowded print shop where three other papers are going to press at the same time — I shall just have to leave that to the Lord, and our inexperienced fellow workers. When it comes to choosing which is the most important work this morning — one human being is of greater importance than all the papers ever published — I am sure our readers agree. So when they find errors in the proof-reading or in the heads, an unbalanced job in the putting together of the paper, they will excuse us.

3

As I waited for the traffic light to change on my way to the Seamen's Defense Committee headquarters, I was idly saying my rosary which was handy in my pocket. The recitation was more or less automatic, when suddenly like a bright light, like a joyful thought, the words Our Father pierced my heart. To all those who were about me, to all the passersby, to the longshoremen idling about the corner, black and white, to the striking seamen I was going to see, I was akin, for we were all children of a common Father, all creatures of one Creator, and Catholic or Protestant, Jew or Christian, Communist or non-Communist, were bound together by this tie. We cannot escape the recognition of the fact that we are all brothers. Whether or not a man believes in Jesus Christ. His incarnation, His life here with us, His crucifixion and resurrection; whether or not a man believes in God, the fact remains that we are all the children of one Father.

Meditation on this fact makes hatred and strife between brothers the more to be opposed. The work we must do is strive for peace and concordance rather than hatred and strife.

We have opened a relief kitchen over on the water front for the striking seamen and a good part of my time I spend over there. It is a big store, and the men from strike headquarters sent over some ship's carpenters today to make benches and tables and stands for literature. The place is full from seven in the morning until midnight. Always there are two of us here from *The Catholic Worker* to keep the coffee going. We have three five-gallon coffee pots and at that we can't keep up with the consumption. Hundreds of loaves of bread a day are consumed, and the peanut butter, which we buy in 25-pound cans, disappears so that there are periods of famine. The radio goes all day and there is conversation and much reading. If the men can concentrate on reading, I guess I can concentrate on writing. I have to jump up to start more coffee, swab off the tables outside, wash out cups, answer questions, etc.

Talk about reading. You'd think that seamen, used to the quiet of the seven seas, would not be able to stand the constant coming and going around here. But they do not seem to mind it, those who want to read. Glancing around the other day at what they were reading I noticed the *Preservation of the Faith*, the *Sign*, the *Commonweal*, *The Catholic Worker* pamphlets, *The Catholic Worker*, the *Wanderer*, in various hands. One fellow sat and read Conway's *Question Box* all evening. We have many copies of the Holy Father's Encyclical on labor, many books on labor, Monsignor Ryan's, Monsignor Haas', Father Husslein's and many others. Every four hours when the pickets are coming off watch, there is a larger rush of business. Then there are lulls when it is possible to sit at the typewriter some more.

There are about twelve thousand men on strike around the New York and Jersey waterfronts. We are on the west side of Manhattan, just around the corner from strike headquarters.

The strike has been going on for the last two months and during that time the Communists have been helping the strikers constantly. The Young Socialist League goes around from midnight on with a truck carrying hot coffee, though it isn't very hot when they reach the last piers. The Young Communist League also keeps a headquarters open where they serve coffee and have literature. They also run innumerable dances, plays, socials and meetings.

At the Christmas midnight Mass, the church down on the corner which is for all waterfront workers, was filled with both longshoremen and seamen. Joseph P. Ryan, the president of the longshoremen, who pulls down a salary of $15,000 a year, and against whom there is a strong rank and file movement, was present at the altar rail. He has been keeping the longshoremen from helping the seamen with their strike, and when he went to a waterfront meeting in Baltimore last week the enraged members of his union tried to assault him and it is said they succeeded in pulling a leg off his trousers.

He is bitterly opposed to Joe Curran, the leader of the striking seamen, but the two of them were present at midnight Mass. Another instance of religion drawing people peaceably together.

Just now there does not seem to be any possibility of the strike ending. It has been a long struggle already, and the men revolting against their corrupt union officials at the same time that they are carrying on a strike against the shipowners for union hiring halls and better pay and conditions, have had no funds to work with. They picket through rain and sleet and cold. They do with skimpy meals served at the strike kitchen. They sleep wherever they can get a bed. And they continue to hold on. They are grimly enduring, fighting for principle, for the right to be treated as men, not as chattels.

Thanks to the generous subsidies provided by the government to the merchant marine, those shipowners can afford to sail their ships without freight or without passengers. They have everything on their side. And the money provided them comes from the pockets of the American taxpayers. There has been some talk of the government taking from them the privilege of carrying the mail, and withdrawing from them the tremendously generous subsidies, but that has not been done yet.

Goodness knows how the strike will turn out. It is one of the most orderly strikes I have ever seen though so far about eight of the strikers have died, either from pneumonia or from knife or gunshot wounds from the enemy. But aside from occasional small skirmishes the strike proceeds quietly, determinedly. According to *Time*, the news weekly, this has been the costliest strike in maritime history. But the shipowners are determined to win, and the corrupt, old union officials are helping them along with it.

4

I just sent someone out to see how much it would cost to rent chairs from an undertaking parlor for a meeting this evening at which we will discuss Christian associations of working men, such as the Holy Father advised — the long-range program trade unions ought to have.

… Another intermission to talk to a member of the cooperative society who is trying to keep up with our orders and help us collect food. They sent down apples and oranges, prunes and sweet rolls the other day.

… Another intermission, a drunken engineer, the first one under the influence of liquor that I've seen so far, comes up to the desk to tell me how much all the sailors appreciate the moral and physical support to thc "guys on the firing line" … A sudden rush and another five gallon pot empty and needing to be replenished … A truck driver comes in to give us three dollars to help out in the expenses. The bill from the cooperative for the past week is ninety-eight dollars. That's from Monday to Saturday, not a full week. They are wondering where we are going to get the money. But that's for St. Joseph to worry about.

An hour later. This month I've been reading the Encyclicals of the Holy Father as I've gone about town on the subway and elevated. They are the best kind of spiritual reading because they are directed to us now, at the present time, for our present needs. The Encyclical on labor is perhaps the best known, but they are all pertinent, deep and searching in their analysis of the present day and our conduct at this time.

Peter Maurin likes Leo XIII's on St. Francis of Assisi best of all.[60] It calls all the faithful to the practice of voluntary poverty during this materialistic age when Catholics are tainted as well as everyone else. I like the one on St. Francis de Sales, telling how he preached against heresy even when his whole congregation walked out on him; how he distributed literature, tramping through the fields and mountains in his search for souls, sleeping in the snow and the cold, the love of God warming him all the time.

5

Frank Jones is the member of the Strike Strategy Committee in charge of finance, and he came over to our branch on

---

60   Leo XIII, *Auspicato Concessum* (1882).

Tenth Avenue to be interviewed on how the strike is financed and how much it costs. He is a young fellow, very serious and burdened with the care of the thousands of seamen who need to be housed and fed.

"During November it cost $550 a day, and I hate to tell you our deficit. We don't like to make it public because it disheartens the men. The other night at the Madison Square Garden meeting the ticket sales amounted to $1,200 and the collection $2,200. Only a third of those attending paid admissions. The unemployed and strikers got in free. There was about $600 in pledges, and we don't count those until we've collected them.

"We make some money on the sale of the *Pilot*, the men who are out on the streets bringing in from sixty cents to six dollars a day.

"I don't know what the food costs, or how they get it. Somebody else has charge of that. We put up about two hundred men down in the neighborhood at South Street at twenty cents a night, four hundred up around headquarters here, one hundred in Harlem and two hundred in Greenpoint. A lot of the men are staying with friends, or have some money left from their pay, although they donated to the strike fund as they came off the ship."

Since the strikers are in revolt against the corrupt union leaders who hold the money the men have been paying in for dues for years, the Strike Strategy Committee is always faced by a money shortage.

The rent of the headquarters on Eleventh Avenue, near 23rd Street, comes to $85 a month, although they used to pay $50. Dominick Curzio is the agent for the building and just last month he served a dispossess notice on the strategy committee. They had to pay $300 down and sign a lease agreeing to pay $85 a month hereafter, making all repairs themselves. When they were arranging the details of the lease, Dominick remarked that his lawyer was also Joseph P. Ryan's lawyer.

6

The days continue warm, flu weather, everybody calls it, and our doors at Tenth Avenue stand open a good part of the day. The hall is crowded all the time, all the benches occupied and many standing.

One fellow I noticed sleeping with his head on the long table in the middle of the room most of the afternoon. Later he came up to get a cup of coffee at the stand by the kitchen door and said he had a chill. I noticed that his eyes were bleary and that he looked feverish, and recommended that he sleep on one of the two beds in the back room where Bill and Joe are sleeping now (their beds are already taken at Mott Street).

One of the seamen recommended eucalyptus oil on sugar and went out to get some and we dosed him with that, but he continued to lie there shivering under heavy quilts and coughing rackingly.

I got a thermometer later and took his temperature and it was one hundred and three. The only place he had to stay was a twenty-cent lodging house in the neighborhood, so thinking a hospital the best place for him, I called a taxi and took him down to St. Vincent's. But it was filled and I had to take him to Bellevue.

All day the place is packed, the men coming and going, on and off watch, and they sit around for hours at a time too, reading the Catholic magazines, papers and pamphlets that we have around the place. Many of the books we have on hand have been borrowed. All the copies of the Pope's Encyclicals which we had have been taken and tomorrow we'll have to order a hundred more. Groups get together to discuss not only the strike and the probabilities of winning it, but the questions of nationalism, war, pacifism, economics, the machine and unem-

---

61   Section mistakenly numbered as "4" (and the subsequent section as "6") in the original edition.

ployment, and again and again the question of Faith is brought up, and how, without a supernatural outlook, unions cannot help but fail, how without a Fatherhood of God, there can be no brotherhood of man....

News was just brought in of a young fellow on the picket line, ailing for days, who collapsed on the line and had to be taken over to Bellevue, where they found he had pneumonia. It is eleven o'clock at night as I write this, and there are still about a score hanging around the hall, which Bill is trying to sweep up. Word has just been brought in that a squad of terrorists patrolling the waterfront is on the loose in the neighborhood. They are the same as those who, with the assistance of guns, leaped on the running boards of trucks this morning and forced the truck drivers to drive through the picket lines to the piers. Six of the strikers were beaten up tonight with clubs. One of them has a broken shoulder. Warning was brought from headquarters that they were liable to come in and break our place up. Such are the usual tactics in labor warfare. The testimony of the LaFollette Committee[62] has brought this out plainly. And yet, whenever there is violence, it is usually laid at the workers' door.

7

Every morning about four hundred men come to Mott Street to be fed. The radio is cheerful, the smell of coffee is a good smell, the air of the morning is fresh and not too cold, but my heart bleeds as I pass the lines of men in front of the store which is our headquarters. The place is packed — not another man can get in — so they have to form in line. Always we have hated lines and now the breakfast which we serve, of

---

62   The Senate Committee on Education and Labor, Subcommittee Investigating Violations of Free Speech and the Rights of Labor (1936-1941), chaired by Wisconsin Senator Robert LaFollette, Jr., investigated the frequently illegal practices used by employers to prevent unionization of the workplace.

cottage cheese and rye bread and coffee has brought about a line. It is an eyesore to the community. This little Italian village which is Mott Street and Hester Street, this little community within the great city, has been invaded by the Bowery, by the hosts of unemployed men, by no means derelicts, who are trying to keep body and soul together, while they look for work. It is hard to say, matter-of-factly and cheerfully, "Good morning" as we pass on our way to Mass. It was the hardest to say "Merry Christmas", or "Happy New Year" during the holiday time, to these men with despair and patient misery written on many of their faces.

One felt more like taking their hands and saying, "Forgive us — let us forgive each other! All of us who are more comfortable, who have a place to sleep, three meals a day, work to do — we are responsible for your condition. We are guilty of each other's sins. We must bear each other's burdens. Forgive us and may God forgive us all!"

Every day at 181 Tenth Avenue there is that other host of men to be fed — over a thousand a day. Even though the strike is over, the men must be cared for until they get back on the ships again. They are hungry and must be fed. They are still sleeping three in a bed, or lying in rows up in the union hall, fifty or a hundred stretched on newspapers. These are not despairing men like the others. These are men who have been fighting for better conditions for themselves and for others, for their union, for safety for those who go to sea and for those passengers who venture abroad on business or on vacation. These are men who are used to danger and imminent death and hard work, and their unemployment is because of a labor dispute and has only lasted two or three months. To them we have brought not only food for the body, but food for the soul in the shape of Catholic literature, the Catholic teachings on all those problems which affect their day-to-day existence. The work there is a hopeful work.

But the work at Mott Street must go on. We must continue to feed our guests and we must appeal to our readers for help. We spent $1,500 last month just for food, but it would be impossible to say how many thousand meals were served. There is no way of counting the men (ours is not turnstile charity) and we have not yet estimated the thousands of pounds of coffee, sugar and milk and bread and cheese we use. We only know that right now we have a debt of $1,200, not to speak of four hundred dollars for the last month's printing bill and the same for this.

The help our friends have given us moves us almost as much as the poor we serve. In addition to the help we have received in the way of money to cover the cooperative bill there has been such help as that given by one housewife from Rockville Center. Every morning she drives her husband in to work and stops at Mott Street with loaves of bread and pieces of clothing. One seaman sent us two Christians checks he received, one for $2 and one for $5. Frank, one of our own group, has been handing us $2 every week or so out of his $10-a-week salary. Pat, another of our gang, who earns $15 a week at the Commodore, gives us $3 a week. Two of the girls in the House of Hospitality got temporary odd jobs and gave us $5 and $3. In these little ways, from the poorest, money has come in to keep the work going.

We have placed our troubles, of course, in the hands of St. Joseph. I burned a candle before his altar yesterday morning and contemplated the gallant figure of the workman saint as he stood there, his head flung back, his strong arm embracing the Child, a smile on his face as he looked down at the congregation of kneeling workers at Mass. We told him frankly:

"You must help us. The Holy Father says that the masses are lost to the Church. We must reach them, we must speak to them and bring them to the love of God. The disciples didn't know our Lord on that weary walk to Emmaus until He sat down and ate with them. 'They knew Him in the breaking of bread': And how many loaves of bread are we breaking with our hungry fellows these days — 13,500 or so this last month. Help us to do this work, help us to know each other in the breaking of bread! In knowing each other, in knowing the least of His children, we are knowing Him."

This would be a hopeless work if it were not for the fact that we are aiming at starting these same "works of mercy stations" in other parishes throughout the country. We are breaking the trail.

We were saying last night that if we could have foreseen the hordes that were to come to us the past two months, we never would have had the courage to begin. But we can only work from day to day. We can only beg from issue to issue of the paper.

ELEVEN

1

NOW that the strike is over, there is a lull in the work and a good opportunity for a few days at the farm.

The February sun is pouring into the kitchen and dining-room of the farm. The temperature is thirty — yesterday it was twelve at this time in the morning, and the house is perfectly comfortable with wood fires going in the two rooms. The rest of the house is, of course, like an ice box. We take hot bricks to bed at night. It is one of the thrills of a lifetime to feel one's warmth gradually permeating the icy sheets and one's breath making a corner warm for one's nose. A pleasure the inhabitants of steam-heated apartments can never know. A cup of hot coffee never tastes so good as when coming out of an ice cold room into a warm kitchen.

An interruption to go out in the kitchen and admire the butter. Rosie is giving about nineteen quarts of milk a day now and there is butter-making every other day. This morning it took only twenty minutes to churn and I have just finished sampling the bits off the wooden paddles of the churn. There are two quarts of buttermilk which will be used for pudding and biscuits today.

Bessie, the calf, will be three months old the 10th of February and she is still the most beautiful thing on the farm. She must weigh about 150 pounds by now, and it is the most graceful 150 pounds you ever saw. John Filliger and I took her out for a walk this morning and her walks are adventures. First you have to see that Rosie is properly secured in her stall. Once when her offspring was out she broke the rope that secured her, knocked down the barn door and with cries of anguish rushed up the hill after John and the calf. She leaped and kicked and tossed her head, expressing her fears as to her young one's safety. She doesn't want to lose this, her latest born.

This morning she mooed like a fog horn a few minutes as we took Bessie out with a chain about her neck, but otherwise she was quiet. Bessie has sprouting horns now and a set of teeth, and she is weaned, but passing through Rosie's stall, she made a dive for her. A little more breakfast wouldn't come amiss, she indicated. But she's off milk altogether now, so we heartlessly dragged her away and out into the fields around the house.

It was a good thing it was not icy out. Snorting with enjoyment she leaped and then started to run, pulling at the chain which John had wrapped around his hand. They raced down the hill together almost to the kitchen door, and then she pulled up prancing. Her small hoofs sounded hollow on the frozen ground and she danced a few steps gracefully, tossing her head. The dogs, Paprika and Kaiser, barked with excitement, not wanting to be out of anything that goes on.

Bessie likes the small world she has come into and went around sniffing appreciatively at the wood-pile and the table under the trees where the washing is done, and she left the print of her wet nose on every rock and log. The ax and saw she smelt and tossed her head at them. Then she was off again, this time up the hill, bounding madly in the cold sweet air. She is just as clean and white as when she was born.

The four black pigs are growing stout and lusty. When John goes out to pour the skim milk into their trough they dive madly into it, feet and all. One of them is Teresa's, a present from Mr. Breen, purchased with a check from a *Commonweal* review. She can't tell the pigs apart, however, and each time she comes to the farm on a holiday she has to pick one out all over again. "It's the one with the straight tail", she will say, and then the unaccommodating pig curls his tail up scornfully.

2

Part of the House of Hospitality has moved down to Easton. As we keep explaining, our idea of hospitality means that everyone with a home should have a guest room. Two women who help us with the paper and who are interested in our ideals, have moved into tenement apartments on Mott Street and use their spare rooms for those in need of hospitality. One of the striking stewardesses is staying in one apartment, and another woman temporarily out of employment is staying with our friend in the other.

Loretta O'Donnell has two of the girls from the House of Hospitality with her; during the day they work over in the Easton office on South Fourth Street, where the business office is now. There are two babies, and two guests whom we cannot really consider guests, since they have become part of our community during these past two years.

Lying on the couch while the chestnut logs snapped warmly in the big stove, I read Kagawa's *Brotherhood Economics*,[63] which is one of the best and simplest accounts of the co-operative movement I have come across. Peter says he links up the idea of communitarianism and co-operatives very well, and I enjoyed reading his brief account of the mutual aid movement among the early Christians and communities of monks. It is a short book, and a simple book, surveying economics from an entirely fresh angle.

3

In Flint, Michigan.[64] St. Antonino, who was Archbishop of Florence in the fourteenth century, anticipated Marx when he said that all value depends upon labor, whether of hand or

---

63   Toyohiko Kagawa (1888-1960), Japanese peace activist and Christian social reformer, advocate of cooperative associations as the basis for social change. His *Brotherhood Economics* (New York: Harper Bros., 1936) has strong affinities with the Catholic Worker philosophy.

64   Day covered the famous "sit-down strike" at the General Motors assembly plants in Flint, Michigan, in 1936-1937, which resulted in the company's signing its first agreement with the United Auto Workers.

head. He was a man who was called upon to pass judgment on many of the vexed economic problems of his day.

I was thinking of St. Antonino and labor's place in the scheme of things as I came up from Cincinnati, where I had been invited to visit Archbishop McNicholas. I was thinking that, now again, industrialists, bankers, merchants and labor leaders were looking to churchmen to make pronouncements on the moral aspects of our economic problems.

It was the moral aspect of the sit-down strike that was bothering the general public and since the general public gets only what the newspapers and radio present to them, and since neither churchmen, nor the general public can climb in windows of barricaded struck plants to talk to strikers and get a picture of the situation, I had to try to get that picture.

At present writing there are thirty major strikes going on all over the country. Last month, the General Motors strike and the sit-down tactics used at Flint were headline news. A picture of one sit-down strike will be more or less representative.

Flint, Michigan, is a small town about an hour and a half north of Detroit by bus. The main streets are paved, but most of the side streets are dirt roads. The houses are, for the most part, small and poor.

The two Fisher Body plants stretch for blocks and blocks. I could not get near the Chevrolet plant, which was held by the strikers, because the National Guard, 4,000 of them, guarded the entrances of all the streets that led to that plant. At some streets machine guns were set up. At all the streets the guardsmen came at you with shining bayonets if you approached. Most of the boys were young, school boys or factory workers, many of them unorganized workers themselves.

George Torr, who had been an auto worker for ten years, was driving me around. He was a paint sprayer, and went to work at seven every morning and worked until four or five in the afternoon. He felt the effects of the paint, he said. He and his fellow workers had to stand with arms uplifted, spraying headlights on cars, and when he asked the boss to get the workers a platform so that they would not have to stand in a torturing position all day, his request was disregarded. Six weeks passed and they asked again. A third request would have cost them their jobs.

It was the speedup which bothered the men most. The workers packed tightly around the cars, with not a second off to get a drink of water or go to the toilet. It was only recently that they got five minutes off, morning and afternoon. The more money men made on the piecework plan, the more the speedup, in order to cut down the wages.

"When I get home nights, I can only eat and fall into bed," Torr said. "Eight o'clock was my usual bedtime. Eat, sleep and work that's all my life is."

Torr is a young man — his mother is only 45 — and he has two children, eight years old and twenty months. His job during the strike was on transportation duty, driving organizers and strikers around.

It was around 11 o'clock when we drove up to Fisher Body No. 1, where the strike started. Only one end of the long plant was occupied by the four or five hundred men. The plant stretches a long way down the street and the front is faced with a strip of lawn, but no riot fences. The whole length of the building is open, so there were strikers standing guard at every window. A wooden box had been built up as a platform at one window so that it was possible to clamber up to the window and climb in more or less as one would straddle a fence. Half a dozen guards were here to examine the visitors' credentials. Only those newspaper reporters were allowed in who possessed Newspaper Guild cards (a new tactic with strikers who are not afraid to antagonize the press since they believe it is on the side of capital anyway).

The Catholic Worker is generally recognized as a labor paper, as well as a religious one. Many of the men were familiar with the paper, so it was easy to get permission to go into the plant.

Inasmuch as the sit-down strike has been used as a non-violent tactic to prevent scabs from taking the jobs of the workers, and to prevent the employer from removing the machinery and thus depriving the worker of his right to work and earn a living, we of *The Catholic Worker* have upheld it. Objection has been made that the men wreck the plants they occupy, but I went all over the Fisher Body plant and saw no evidence of deliberate injury.

Of course the men slept on piles of upholstery and seat cushions which they made into beds, and so without doubt some materials were damaged. But the law against smoking on the main floors of the plant was upheld and the men smoked only in the cafeteria in the basement.

Another small depredation was the use the men made of a bolt of unbleached muslin from which they tore hundreds of strips to use as scarfs.

"That's in case of tear gas attack," Henry Van Nocker, secretary of Local 156 of the union told me. "The gas is soluble in water and the men wet the scarfs and use them so they can keep up the fight."

The men were divided into shifts and there were hundreds of them sleeping in different parts of the plant. The building being open to the street, and a warrant out for the arrest of the sit-downers, the men expected an attack at any time, and they were ready for it.

Though the sit-down strike is a non-violent tactic, the men were ready to repel efforts to evict them, and during the forty-one days of their siege, they had fashioned themselves clubs which hung at their belts, and there were boxes of heavy hinges and bolts ready to be used as missiles.

These were their arms, and their preparations seemed pitifully inadequate to me in view of the machine guns and riot guns of the militia and the guards of the companies.

I talked with many of the men in the plant and their determination to hold out for recognition of their union and mitigation of the speedup was unanimous. Most of them were Americans, many of them Southerners. I was interested to hear of the square dances they went in for, introduced from the South. There were not a great many Catholics among them. There were some Hungarians, and Poles, however, and these were Catholics.

That night I attended a strike meeting in the hall of the Pengelly Building, a rickety old two-story frame block which the strikers had rented. Downstairs there was a restaurant, upstairs union offices, and above that the hall which held about a thousand workers.

The meeting had been going on from seven-thirty and now it was almost eleven. There were young and old men, women and children. There were babies in arms and little ones sitting around the edge of the platform, thrilled at being out so late. They crowded the chairs, sat on the window sills and packed the doors.

Josephine Herbst was one of the speakers, a pro-communist writer, who came to report the strike; there was Adolph Germer, organizer and officer of the United Mine Workers' Union, of which John L. Lewis is president in addition to being leader of the Committee on Industrial Organization. After the meeting broke up, small groups remained in different parts of the hall talking and one group stayed to sing.

These were the people, these family groups, against whom the National Guard was called. I stopped in the publicity department downstairs and found Carl Haessler, one of the editors of the Federated Press in charge of the department. I had known him as a Socialist years ago and knew him to be thoroughly Marxist now in his philosophy. Students from the universities at Lansing, Michigan, and Madison, Wisconsin, were there assisting him, getting their first taste of actual strike work.

One young fellow, blond, wide-eyed, said that he majored in philosophy. "A good foundation," I commented, "for labor work."

"Oh, do you think so?" he said eagerly. "But I didn't get any Marx and Engels in college," he added regretfully, "no real modern philosophers except the aesthetes." I asked him if he had ever heard of Gilson[65] and Maritain, but they were only names to him. He was interested that they were teaching scholastic philosophy in Chicago University and at Harvard.

These college students regard Marxism as a philosophy of life. Haessler also taught philosophy at the University of Illinois where I had gone years ago.

My reflections as I came away from Flint had to do with the future of labor in the United States. Not only the necessity for organization but the necessity for a long range program of action, for an educational program which would deal not only with co-operatives and credit unions but also a philosophy of labor. The C.I.O. is a trade union movement, and nobody wastes any time wondering whether John L. Lewis or John Brophy are Reds. The public in general knows that they are not. They are working to organize the industrial workers, those hitherto unorganized ones who make up the great masses of workers in this country. But what of the college students, the editors, the writers, the propagandists who take advantage of every labor struggle to get into it, inject the Marxist philosophy of life, and seek to sway the workers, and prepare them for the "final class struggle"?

Communism is a way of life and it is as a philosophy of life that it must be met. There was plenty of Communist literature, such as the *Daily Worker* and the *New Masses*, sold not only at the union headquarters, but also sent into the struck plants for the sit-downers to read and ponder over during the forty-one days they had interned themselves.

We point the need to Catholic students, not only of philosophy, but of journalism and of history, and of going to vol-

---

65 Étienne Gilson (1884-1978), Catholic philosopher and scholar of St. Thomas Aquinas.

unteer as apostles of labor and taking advantage as the Communist does of the opportunities each strike offers to reach the masses, to learn from them and to teach them.

4

Mott Street. There's no time now to have conversation with the men who come in for coffee and bread and cheese with us in the morning from six to nine. The store is packed full, the line extends down the block almost to Canal Street. They stand there in the rain and cold sometimes for half an hour before they reach the store.

This month there was a mission over on Baxter Street and we closed the store from nine to nine forty-five so that those who wished to, could go to Mass. Sometimes there were seventy-five who went and sometimes only twenty. "You can't preach the Gospel to men with empty stomachs," Abbé Lugan said.

We put out a little leaflet to distribute to the men. We said:

"We are not running this coffee line like a mission. We have no religious services. We are just trying to give you hot coffee and something to eat every morning. We hope you all will take copies of *The Catholic Worker* and read it and find out what we are trying to do here and in other cities where we have groups working.

"Naturally, we would like to have you get to Mass and make the Mission, those of you who are Catholics, and who might like to get to church for half an hour or so every morning this week. We'd like to urge those who are not Catholics to go, too.

"We want you to go because Christ, our Brother, is present there in the Blessed Sacrament. Christ Himself was a Worker, while He lived here on earth. St. Joseph, to whose care He was confided while on this earth, was a poor carpenter. They always lived in poverty, and Our Lord said of Himself:

" 'The foxes have holes, and the birds of the air their nests, but The Son of Man has no place to lay his head' [Matthew 8:20].

"Our Lord has a special love for each one of you, and they say that He is always more ready to give than we are to receive. So we do feel that we should urge you to go over to the church on Baxter Street, just to be in His Presence for a little while each morning.

"We want to ask you, too, to please pray for us all, and ask St. Joseph to continue his help, which makes our coffee line possible."

Back around the first of December when the line was just beginning, I remember one conversation a group of us had while we were having breakfast. It was a Sunday morning after Mass and the line had thinned down. There were a steeplejack, a sand-hog, a carpenter, a restaurant worker, and a mechanic talking and the subject was our industrial civilization, the machine and unemployment, the land and co-operatives. The wage system can be discussed thus with the unemployed, although you get only a half dozen or so at a time. Still, those you do reach, go out and talk to others. One of them spoke of large scale farming. He had picked cotton in the southwest at one cent a pound. You had to feed yourself, too. In the wheat fields it used to be seven dollars a day and board and now it is two dollars a day and feed yourself. Jobs are hard to get in the southwest now because of Japanese and Mexican labor, and the labor of all those migrating from the dust-bowl area.

5

I find a little paragraph in my note book, "Michael Martin, porter, idle for five years, brought in $2."

It was a thanksgiving offering, he explained, and he wanted to give it to some of our children in honor of his daughter in Ireland.

And I remembered how I spoke down in Palm Beach last month before the Four Arts Club, on the invitation of a convert. They told me, when I had finished, "You know we never pay speakers," and another woman said, with a tremor, "Miss Day, I hope you can convey to your readers and listeners, that we would give our very souls to help the poor, if we saw any constructive way of doing it," and still another told me, "The workers come to my husband's mill and beg him with tears in their eyes to save them from unions. I hope you don't mind my saying so, but I think you are all wrong when it comes to unions."

They all were deeply moved, they told me, by the picture of conditions in Arkansas and the steel districts and the coal mining districts, but, "You can't do anything with them, you know, these poor people. It seems to me the best remedy is birth control and sterilization."

We are told always to keep a just attitude toward the rich, and we try. But as I thought of our breakfast line, our crowded house with people sleeping on the floor, when I thought of cold tenement apartments around us, and the lean gaunt faces of the men who come to us for help, desperation in their eyes, it was impossible not to hate, with a hearty hatred and with a strong anger, the injustices of this world.

St. Thomas says that anger is not a sin, provided there is no undue desire for revenge. We want no revolution, we want the brotherhood of men. We want men to love one another. We want all men to have sufficient for their needs. But when we meet people who deny Christ in His poor, we feel, "Here are atheists indeed."

At the same time that I put down these melancholy thoughts, I am thinking of Michael Martin, porter, and the hosts of readers and friends *The Catholic Worker* has who have spread the work far and wide, who not only help us to keep the coffee line going, but who on their own account are performing countless works of mercy. And my heart swells with love and gratitude to the great mass of human beings who are one with their fellows, who love Our Lord and try to serve Him and show their love to His poor.

Our pastor said recently that sixty million of our one hundred and thirty million here in the United States professed no religion, and I thought with grief that it was the fault of those professing Christians who repelled the others. They turned first from Christ crucified because He was a poor worker, buffeted and spat upon and beaten. And now — strange thought — the devil has so maneuvered that the people turn from Him because those who profess Him are clothed in soft raiment and sit at well-spread tables and deny the poor.

TWELVE

1

HAVE you ever heard a man scream as he was beaten over the head by two or three policemen with clubs and cudgels? Have you ever heard the sickening sounds of blows and seen people with their arms upraised, trying to protect their faces, stumbling blindly to get away, falling and rising again to be beaten down? Did you ever see a man shot in the back, being dragged to his feet by policemen who tried to force him to stand, while his poor body crumpled, paralyzed by a bullet in the spine?

We are sickened by stories of brutality in Germany and Russia and Italy. A priest from Germany told me of one man who came to him whose back was ridged "like a washboard", by the horrible beatings he had received at the hands of the German police in concentration camps. I shudder with horror at the thought of the tortures inflicted on Catholics, Protestants, Jews and Communists in Germany today.

And here in America last month there was a public exhibition of such brutality, that the motion picture film, taken by a Paramount photographer in a sound truck, was suppressed by the company for fear that it would cause riots and mass hysteria, it was so unutterably horrible.

I am trying to paint a picture of it for our readers because so many did not read the story of the Memorial Day "riot" in Chicago in front of the Republic Steel Mills.[66]

Try to imagine this mass of people — men, women and children — picketing, as they have a right to do, coming up to the police line and being suddenly shot into, not by one hysterical policeman, but by many. Ten were killed and one hundred

---

66 In the "Memorial Day Massacre" at the Republic Steel Mill in Chicago on May 30, 1937, police fired into a retreating crowd of protestors, killing ten and injuring many more.

were taken to the hospital wounded. Tear gas and clubs supplied by the Republic Steel Company were used.

I am trying to picture this scene to our readers because I have witnessed these things first hand, and I know the horror of them. I was on a picket line when the "radical" squad shot into the line and pursued the fleeing picketers down the streets knocking them down, and kicking and beating them. I, too, have fled down streets to escape the brutality and vicious hatred of the "law" for those whom they consider "radical". And by the police anyone who protests injustice, who participates in labor struggles, is considered a radical.

Two years ago I wrote an account in *The Catholic Worker* of two plain-clothesmen beating up a demonstrator. I told of the screams and the crumpling body of the man as two men who had dragged him into a hallway, beat him up against the wall aiming well directed blows at his face, smashing it to a pulp.

We protested this to the Police Commissioner and our protest was respected and acted upon.

We are repeating the protest against the Chicago massacre because the only way to stop such brutality is to arouse a storm of protest against it.

On whom shall the blame be laid for such a horrible spectacle of violence? Of course, the police and the press in many cases lay the blame on the strikers. But I have lived with these people, I have eaten with them and talked to them day after day. Many of them have never been in a strike before, many of them were marching in the picket line as in a supplicatory procession, for the first time in their lives. They even brought children on that line in Chicago.

Shall we blame only the police? Or shall we blame just Tom Girdler of the Republic Steel Company? God knows how he can sleep comfortably in his bed at night with the cries of those strikers, of their wives and children, in his ears. He may not hear them now in the heat of battle, but he will hear them, as there is a just God.

Or shall we blame the press, the pulpit and all those agencies who form public opinion, who have neglected to raise up their voices in protest at injustice and so have permitted it? In some cases the press have even instigated it so that it would come to pass. Inflammatory, hysterical headlines about mobs, about expected riots, do much to arouse the temper of the police to prepare them for just what occurred. The calm, seemingly reasonable stories of such papers as the *Herald-Tribune* and the *Times*, emphasizing the violence and the expectation of violence, do much to prepare the public to accept such violence when it comes to pass.

In that case we all are guilty inasmuch as we have not "gone to the workingman" as the Holy Father pleads and repeats. Inasmuch as we have not inclined our hearts to him, and sought to incline his to us, so that we could work together for peace instead of war, inasmuch as we have not protested such murder as was committed in Chicago — then we are guilty.

One more sin, suffering Christ, worker Yourself, for You to bear. In the garden of Gethsemane You bore the sins of all the world — You took them on Yourself, the sins of those police, the sins of the Girdlers, and the Schwabs,[67] of the Graces[68] of this world. In committing them, whether ignorantly or of their own free will, they piled them on Your shoulders, bowed to the ground with the weight of the guilt of the world, which You assumed because You loved each of us so much. You took them on Yourself, and You died to save us all. Your Precious Blood was shed even for that policeman whose cudgel smashed again and again the skull of that poor striker, whose brains lay splattered on the undertaker's slab.

And the sufferings of those strikers' wives and children are completing Your suffering today [reference to Colossians 1:24].

---

67   Charles M. Schwab (1862-1939), president of Bethlehem Steel from 1904 to 1916 and leading manufacturer of munitions and ships during World War One.

68   Eugene Grace (1876-1960), president of Bethlehem Steel from 1916 to 1945.

Have pity on us all, Jesus of Gethsemane — on Tom Girdler, those police, the souls of the strikers, as well as on all of us who have not worked enough for "a new heaven and a new earth wherein justice dwelleth" [2 Peter 3:13].

2

Last week I went down to Johnstown for the special purpose of meeting Michael Sewak, Burgess of Franklin, a town which borders Johnstown and in which are four of the most important gates of the Cambria Steel plant. In Johnstown there are three. The sheriff of Cambria county is Michael Boyle, the brother of Bishop Boyle of Pittsburgh, in whose diocese the priests in the Catholic Radical Alliance are doing such good work on the labor front, in speaking, writing and aiding strikers.

Sheriff Boyle is opposed to the use of force. He does not want tear gas and guns used against the workingmen of his county. But Mayor Shields of Johnstown, a heavy-jowled, sleek politician, is all for strong-arm stuff. He glories in the praise he is getting from industrialists all over the country, and he shamelessly accepts the aid of the Bethlehem Steel Company in the way of guards, police and guns, "to keep order" at the Cambria gates in Johnstown.

Sheriff Boyle and his friend Burgess Sewak were in agreement. Burgess Sewak had nine policemen, none of them armed and at their gates there was no trouble, nor any rioting. Shields has 1,400 men sworn in and they have plenty of rioting. Taxis cruised the streets with armed men. He refuses to give "protection" to C.I.O. organizers, which is one way of telling them to get out of town. An *unlawful* way.

Sheriff Boyle was the one who telegraphed Governor Earle of Pennsylvania to declare martial law in Johnstown in order to curb the activities of Shields. It was the first time that I ever saw the state troops and the strikers cheer each other, and behave like brothers. There is not much chance of rioting when men act like that towards each other. There is a much better chance that there will be a peaceful waiting and negotiating for an agreement.

It was good to talk to Burgess Sewak. He lives in a little house up on the side of a steep hill in one of the worst slums I have ever visited. Those who talk of the high wages of steel workers should visit Franklin and see the homes of the workers.

Down in the municipal building he told me about himself. He's been in office for eight years. He's worked in the steel mills for fourteen. He is married to a Catholic — he is a Greek Orthodox, and all his children are being raised Catholics. All his brothers and sisters have married Catholics and become Catholics.

"In my household we have two sets of feast days, those of the Greek church and those of the Catholic. My wife never forgets. It sure gives a holiday aspect to our home."

Burgess Sewak as well as Sheriff Boyle are the kind of men we need in public life in this country. We don't hear much about them in the papers, because they see that law and order is maintained, because they are maintaining human rights as above property rights, because they are trying to prevent bloodshed instead of provoking it as Mayor Shields and the newspapers which feature him are doing. They are the unsung heroes.

But labor does not forget, and the community does not forget. Theirs is an example which other officials might well follow. Sheriff Boyle is a Catholic. Mayor Shields also calls himself one. You can choose between them.

3

I am writing this from the farming commune down in Easton, and outside my windows seven children are sliding down the hill and leaving a long streak in the yellow grass. The hill rises up over the back of the house and the old road winds around up to the farm which we own. This one at the foot of the hill we rent.

Mary, Helena, Catherine, Christina, Annie, Eleanor and Teresa are the seven children, and the first five of them are some of Julia Porcell's charges from Harlem. They don't live there any more, their new home is on Forty-third Street, we believe, but Julia follows them around through the years. They have been her special friends for three years now, ever since we had quarters up in Harlem. The family have been on relief for some years, and the mother has been in the hospital for a good part of the past year. So they need lots of milk and sunlight and fresh air. The mother and the other four children are coming down later, and probably the father too.

This farm is ideal for us with its big barns, where the children are camping out. The boys have one barn — Ray, Bill, Mike, Donald and any other company who comes along. There are five more of us besides the children sleeping in the other barn. And the two bedrooms at the farmhouse are filled too. Altogether there are about thirty-eight people down here this week-end and about thirty are here for some weeks.

Every morning a crowd of us go down to Mass in Easton and after Mass I stay in the Easton office for letters and writing until noon. The afternoon is spent in more reading and writing and looking after the children.

It is a happy place, this farm, with its bright sunny days, the heavy odor of milkweed blossoms coming in through the windows and the daisies studding the fields. Every night we have black raspberry shortcake, and there is all the cherry jam you can eat. Rosie doesn't give quite enough milk to go around — she's down to twelve quarts a day now. Mollie will soon be giving us more.

(Annie, the little monkey, is climbing on a ladder from the barn, so I'll cut this short and take the children up the hill to hunt for salamanders in the spring. In spite of strikes and brutality, controversy and war, this world is filled with joy and beauty and the children bring it to us anew and help us to enjoy it through their eyes.)

4

While I am trying to write this on a hot August day, the Mott Street house is being torn down around us, and put together again. The story which began last January, telling of the threat of eviction because ours is an old style tenement, conflicting with fire laws, has now reached a climax. It is not the unhappy climax of an eviction. The house is being made over to conform with the law. Which means that partitions are being torn down, some doors blocked up, walls knocked out and all sorts of strange asbestos block and sheets of wire lath are being put up. As we go up and downstairs the banisters are being taken down and steel railings put up. The air is filled with the dust of plaster and old wood and the women go about with their heads covered to protect them from the dirt. The din, which begins at eight, is terrific. The entire backyard is filled with sandpiles and heaps of refuse. There is only a footpath through. The families in the front house go about their business of eating, sleeping, cleaning, and so do we. It looks as though the house were being bombarded, and sounds like it too. It is hard to think.

The dining room and kitchen are being enlarged, and the upper floors made into dormitories so there will be no longer four rooms on a floor. There will be less privacy than ever.

We love our neighborhood. There is not a beauty parlor in it and not a news stand for blocks. Each street is like a little Italian village, and on these hot nights there is music and dancing in the street and everybody stays up until after twelve, because the houses are so hot and airless. The babies are sleeping in their carriages and two-year-olds toddle around the curbstones; the playgrounds keep open till late. It's a good walk to the river, North River, or East River, and sometimes we walk down to the

Battery to rest our eyes, short-sighted with living in canyons of tenements, by the long fresh view over the Bay.

In the daytime, markets are the most beautiful places in the world. Glorious color strikes the eye and the appeal to sight and taste makes one forget the offense to smell. There are fish markets with their eels, snails, blue-black mussels with the sea-weed clinging to them, little clams and octopuses and all kinds of fish.

There are fresh figs, fresh almonds, melons, peaches and plums — every kind of fruit is heaped on the push carts, even Concord grapes with their first hint of the autumn to come.

Housewives go by with their shopping bags, hucksters sing their wares, music stores blare with song, children dodge to and fro between the stands, beggars edge through the crowd with hat outstretched, and leisurely storekeepers sit by their wares enjoying the sun. There are even some good smells in the air — smells of spaghetti, ravioli, olive oil and roasts, coming from the little restaurants on all sides.

And two streets away is the Bowery with its stark hunger and colorless misery.

5

"You be the father and your name is Patrick, and I'm the mother."

"And we have so many children!"

"Yes, six have to sleep in this bed, and we'll let two come into bed with us. Then it won't be so crowded."

"Come on, children, you can't play any more, it's time for bed. And don't take so long about undressing. Father, are you going to bed?"

"No, I been sleeping all day."

"Well, you better sit up all night than come to bed after and wake the children up. Then they'd all start crying."

"Come on, time to get up and have breakfast, lazy. My, what a crowded house."

The days rush by, breakfast, supper, and bed. Tragedies, accidents, sickness, all greeted with equanimity. For it is the children, playing dolls outside the door while I write. Teresa, Eleanor and little Dorothy, the latter two from Harlem, one a Catholic and the other not. They are about the same size and age, the three of them, and there is never a dull moment. There are dolls and puppies and cats and books, and to see the three of them sitting in a row on the couch reading is a sweet sight. This is the first summer with us for these little colored girls, but we hope they come every summer and grow up with us as some of the boys from Charles Street have for the past three summers.

During the summer we have had about fifty children with us for longer or shorter periods. A few got homesick and had to be taken back to the city. Many of them stayed for two weeks or a month. We never had less than ten at a time and most of the time there were fifteen. And when I think of the catastrophes that happen to Teresa's families of dolls, I thank the Blessed Mother for her care of all these children during the summer. Eddie got sick once from eating green apples; Charlie, an eighteen-year-old, cut his head diving, there were a few cases of poison ivy and a few cut fingers. The worst was that of little Mickie, the bad boy of the crowd, who sliced his own hand good and plenty while he was trying to put his bedmate's Sunday clothes through the corn chopper.

Oh, the happiness of having space this year on the farm! The rented farm which adjoins the thirty acre farm we own, has a four room house and two barns and a chicken coop. The little boys with one of the men to watch after them, have had one of the barns, and plenty of floor space for extra guests who didn't mind doing without beds. The women's barn (which is also big enough to hold a kitchen and dining room), had the disadvantage that it leaks like a sieve, and during a week of rain such as this last, beds have been shifted to every position till we felt we were on rafts in mid-ocean. Usually we woke up with our feet in a puddle of water. In the house, the kitchen and the three bedrooms were always filled. All summer we had two invalids with us and the vitality of the children seemed to bring health to them too.

We can do without beds and sleep on the floor, we can sleep in wet beds; we can do with most primitive washing and toilet facilities; but with space there is a sense of luxury.

We are all praying to St. Joseph to get this farm for us in some way. It costs four thousand dollars, a huge sum, but it is certainly worth it. And what to us is an unbelievably large sum, should seem like nothing to our patron. Surely you can see, St. Joseph, that we need this place, so can't you remind somebody who has an abundance to buy it for us?

During these two months, Mary Johnson has made 1,500 beds, let us figure, and served 4,500 meals. She gives this service to us — the family she has adopted out of the loving kindness of her heart. Donald has washed dishes after 4,500 servings, Stephen Johnson working in town during the summer has contributed four-fifths of his salary; a deaf girl working at housework for five dollars a week, leaves us a dollar every week to help out; seamen from the seven seas whom we fed last winter, have contributed from twelve ships to help out; one seaman turned over $150 on his return from a voyage; one young fellow supporting a family contributed his lunch money for a good part of the summer.

All these workers giving abundantly of their talents, energies and earnings, and giving at such a sacrifice, surely will bring the graces of God down on the work. We are sure that if it is His good pleasure, we are going to get this farm. We certainly need it, and He has not failed us yet. There were plenty of rosaries said with that intention and the prayers of little children are most potent of all.

All during the summer there were priest visitors at the farm. Father Joseph Woods from Portsmouth Priory was with us for two weeks, and Father Palmer from Long Island was with us still another two weeks. We certainly wouldn't be without priests to offer up Mass if we had a chapel. We had to spend the money we had set aside for a chapel this year, realizing that Temples of the Holy Ghost were more important than temples made with hands. So this is another thing we need. And while we are about it, there is money for building. Two married couples on the farm now and little houses (two rooms would be sufficient) needed for them by spring. Father Lallemant says we compliment God by expecting great things from Him, so we're listing these wants. And there's the printing bill, over a thousand dollars by now; and the grocery bills, about five hundred.

At the present moment we feel like the Israelites, crying out to the Lord in the Wilderness. And we are sure that He will hear us.

We've been reading the Old Testament a great deal this summer; and when we pray importunately for these material needs, because we have a very large and hungry family of about a hundred, we are reminded of the words of Moses. When Pharaoh, tired of the disasters which were overtaking him, and yet greedy, told Moses to take his people and get out, only leaving the herds behind him, Moses refused. "There shall not a hoof remain of them," he said, "for they are necessary for the service of the Lord Our God" [Exodus 10:26].

And I do indeed feel that all these things I have been mentioning "are necessary for the service of the Lord Our God", so we shall continue to pray for them.

6

Chicago — *Fall 1937*. I must keep a more careful record of places and persons even if it means sitting up in bed writing after an 18-hour day.

For instance, there is this place, so many details of which I do not want to forget but will unless I write them down.

It is the first rectory I've ever stayed at and it is a great privilege to be here. The door bell rings day and night, its parlors are cluttered up with people, everyone works from dawn till way after dark, and everyone is very happy.

We are on the South Side in an uneven neighborhood which has good and bad houses, but mostly slums. Around on Michigan Avenue, the houses are beautiful, but, across the street, are some little houses so awful that it is hard to believe temples of the Holy Ghost are housed there.

The pastor pointed out one house which some children had pushed over on themselves, and he had waited hours while the fire department extricated them, to baptise them. Neither child was hurt badly, strangely enough.

Father and I were walking around the neighborhood looking for a little house for another House of Hospitality for his side of town.

"I cried when I got home that day," he said. "I don't know what was the matter with me. I never do that."

It is a joy to be with such priests as these. They are all so gay and the pastor is like an older brother.

He used to be a missionary in the Philippines and as we sit over a good breakfast of liver sausage and toast and fruit and coffee he tells me of living conditions there.

"At first we were allowed three dollars a month to live on. All we had was rice and leaves most of the time.

"Later when I had three sisters come out for teaching, we were allowed ten dollars. You couldn't buy anything. Money wasn't much good. When some of our kind friends sent us clothes, we could exchange them for food, fish and chickens. Sometimes we had grasshoppers, locusts, they were cooked first in salt and water and then served with a little vinegar and lard. They were delicious. We liked it. They eat dogs there, too, and they say that they are very good but I never ate any. We never had any bread until I began to bake some. We just had rice, and to keep our teeth in chewing habit, we had water buffalo meat. Fresh it was tough, but dried it was worse. And sugar cane to chew on too. Between the meat and the grasshoppers, I preferred the grasshoppers.

"My bread was very good. We used a five gallon can as the oven, putting the coals and charcoal in the bottom and making an oven on top. We put the bread in an empty sardine tin. I sent some to the sisters and they said it was better than theirs. But I didn't have much time for gardening or baking. I had to go on horseback, and on rafts, in all directions, to reach my people.

"During the war about twenty-eight of us Germans were arrested and shipped back to the United States — I don't know what for. All of us were confined to a fo'castle (there were six priests among us) and it was terribly hot. When they shut off the ventilating system to rest the machinery, some of them fainted. There we were for weeks. We had beans seventy-eight times. Yes, it was a hard life."

The house here is big and the pastor gave me his room because it is the only one with a private bath. The windows look out on a gnarled ailanthus tree, which grows so well in city back yards. There are some shrubs in the tiny back yard, but the grass is trampled down by the police dog and the puppy, a mongrel called Valentine, whom Father says Martin de Porres sent him for a pet. The police dog is a watch dog, not a pet, but the little cur wags his whole hind end and is a friend of all. I can see why Father never ate dog meat.

The rooms are large, but the furniture is very poor and the rugs worn down to the nap. When they need any "new" furniture they go buy it at the Catholic Salvage Bureau around the corner. Fortunately for them there are no ill-advised though loving parishioners to smother them in gifts such as oriental rugs.

While we were looking for a place this afternoon we passed little ramshackle frame houses all bent and reeling, and the front yards were planted with lettuce, radishes, golden glow and iris, and even some rows of corn. On one street, here in the heart of the slums, there was an apple tree in bloom and a parrot out in a bush in the front yard. Wish we could find a place on that street, but there is great difficulty in finding any place around here, it is so congested. There are often several families, and sometimes dozens of families living in one house. Many of the worst buildings have been torn down and there is no new housing to take their place.

7

At St. Louis. Three of us from the St. Louis group started out before five one morning (it was the octave of the Ascension) to go to the Convent of the Precious Blood at O'Fallon, Missouri, for High Mass at six. We had time to recite Lauds as we sped along at sixty miles an hour, and the nuns, novices, postulants and aspirants were just starting Prime when we arrived.

In the chapel, surrounded by noble trees and lawns, were the robed women, and the beauty within completed the beauty without. I never heard Mass sung so, with such clear, pure and hearty singing, not the thin, attenuated singing one is accustomed to associate with women's voices and Gregorian chant.

Purity was a positive virtue there in that chapel. There was strength, joy and love strong as death there.

I thought too, how there at this liturgical center, they had most truly made the Mass the crown of the day. The morning took its rightful place, its emphasis. Matins, Lauds, Prime, led up to the Mass, followed by Terce and Sext and then the great work of the day was done — surely as perfectly as it is ever done in this imperfect world. The rest of the day is relatively unimportant and declines to nightfall when God's creatures sleep.

8

While I was at the convent I thought of how we said Compline at Mott Street.

When Margaret beats on a pan lid at 6 p.m. that means supper and the redoubled beating means that Peter Maurin is downstairs holding up the eating by a discussion. He is probably in the middle of making a point.

When the pot lid resounds at seven, that means Compline and we are sorry to say that the gong has to be supplemented by one of the dish washers poking his head in various rooms where more discussions are going on to shout, "All set!"

We are always trying to explain why we say Compline instead of the rosary.[69]

The two great commandments are to love God and to love our brothers. When we are praying the official prayers of the Church, uniting in praise, we are loving God. And because we are praying together, we are loving each other. Some may say this doesn't follow. Margaret may have just had an argument with John about money for carrots; Joe Smolko may have just accused Texas of getting out of washing the dishes; John Cort and Bill Callahan may have been combatting each other over what is a just war. But just the same, we know that when we are united together in the community room in this evening prayer, we are conscious of a Christian solidarity. As members of the Church, we are united to the whole Church. We are united with Christ Himself who is head of the Mystical Body. We may not do it very well, our poor efforts may be feeble, our hearts may not be right, but the will is there, and united with Him we partake of His merits. He is the only one who can pray right, and we are praying with Him so our prayer is effective. Then too, we are united with each other, and we benefit by all the merits and graces of our brethren. We lift each other up. "Two are bet-

---

69 For Day's early embrace of the Liturgical Movement, see p. 45, note 12.

ter than one, for if one falls the other lifts him up" [Ecclesiastes 4:10]. "A brother who is helped by his brother is like a strong city." [Proverbs 18:19]

The great cry of Peguy's life was a cry for solidarity. "We must be saved together," he said. "We must come to God together. Together we must all return to our Father's house. What would God say to us if some of us came to Him without the others?"[70]

9

After the long services at the convent Father Hellriegel was our host at breakfast and it was a hearty meal, as it should be after such hearty singing. We sat long at the table.

Father Hellriegel, the chaplain of the Convent, is a mountain of strength and energy and has that happiness of one who does well what God wants him to do.

After being up since four-thirty, we ate heartily of bacon and eggs, home-made bread and butter, and there were sausages, cheese and green topped onions on the table, of which Father ate ten before I could get the plate and take half a dozen myself.

Speaking to the nuns was a great pleasure and they are all going to pray for *The Catholic Worker*. Such a power house supplies us with the energy we need for our work.

The students at the high school were farmers' sons and daughters and it was good to talk to them too. We will have there one more C.W. group, I hope.

So many places covered this trip and so many different audiences. In St. Louis I spoke before our own group twice, before several high schools; before one group of workers in an enameling plant and before six hundred steel workers.

---

70   Charles Péguy (1873-1914), French poet and essayist.

The last crowd were just organized by the C.I.O. in Granite City, Illinois, and, though the town allows no Negroes after dark, white and colored were in the same hall, in the same union; this is something which the C.I.O. has achieved which the A.F. of L. failed to do.

THIRTEEN

1

YESTERDAY on the bus to San Diego two older men were talking about the President, and loud enough for everyone in the bus to hear. They called him a yellow coward, with the heart of a louse, a maniac on the verge of total insanity. They talked of their investments and losses. They talked of public utilities. And every other minute they cursed him. Each mention of wages, public works, unions, led to increased bitterness.

"There'll be bloodshed yet," they concluded, and grimly added that they'd like to take part in it. Hate was etched into the bitter lines of their faces and into their voices.

I could not help comparing their attitude with that of the two hundred or so unemployed I had talked to the day before in Los Angeles at an open Forum of the Workers' Alliance. I talked of Christ the Worker, of a philosophy of labor, of the farming commune as a solution of unemployment. I told them of Peter, and his social program for the lay apostolate.

The men I talked to wanted work, not a dole. They wanted private property (the idea of homesteads and community farm combined appealed to them). They wanted peace and brotherhood. They were interested in government help but would rather have work, provided it meant something to them — was building for their security and future. They were interested in a constructive program, not in fighting a class war. And when I thought how betrayed they are by their intellectual leadership, my heart wept.

It was enough to make one weep just to hear those two men talking on the bus. I thought of Peter Maurin and how he loves to indoctrinate wherever he goes, talking on street corners and buses and restaurants, wherever he happens to be. But his is a conservative indoctrination, and not a message of hate.

I spent a few days in San Diego, and a full month in Los Angeles, speaking at schools and colleges and at the open forum which Dr. Julia Metcalfe holds every Monday night in her circulating library at Gramercy Place.

In San Francisco I was invited to speak before the Maritime Council of the Pacific, before the Marine Cooks and Stewards and before the Firemen's Union and the Machinists' Union, in addition to the seminary, St. Mary's College, San Francisco University, St. Boniface Hall, and many other groups, so numerous that I could not cover them all. I shall have to return next winter in order to fill some of the engagements I rashly made so far ahead.

It is good to speak to labor groups on the philosophy of labor which Peter Maurin is always talking about. Most union leaders throughout the country, A.F. of L., C.I.O., whatever they are, tend toward Marxism in their philosophy.

They have thought of labor as a commodity, in spite of the Magna Charta of labor, the Clayton laws of 1914, which stated that labor was not a commodity to be bought and sold. But they have treated their labor as a commodity to be bought and sold over a counter.[71] They have not thought of labor as a discipline imposed upon us all (thanks to the Fall), and also as a vocation. They have not thought of the worker as a co-creator with God. (God gave us the materials and by developing these materials we also share in creation.)

One of the cheering notes of the trip was meeting priests who had been appointed for labor work in their dioceses. There was Monsignor Keating and Father O'Dwyer in Los Angeles, who had given a Mission (also many blankets) to the seamen during the 1936-1937 strike. Father Keating has an open Forum every Sunday night at the Labor Temple under the aus-

---

71 The Clayton Antitrust Act of 1915 (not 1914) was the first federal legislation to explicitly exempt organized labor from antitrust regulation, on the grounds that human labor is not a product.

pices of the St. Robert Bellarmine Guild for Labor and Industry of which Father Keating and Father O'Dwyer are the directors, although Archbishop Cantwell is the president. Both the directors are fraternal members of the Central Trades and Labor Council, and both C.I.O. and A.F. of L. members attend the meetings of the Guild.

In San Francisco, Father Donahue, who also teaches at the St. Patrick's Seminary at Menlo Park has been appointed to study the problems of labor. I met Father Donahue the day I arrived and he drove me down to see Father O'Kelly, the seamen's priest, who has headquarters for seamen at old St. Brendan's Church. Thereafter Father O'Kelly (who always insisted upon calling me Miss O'Day) drove me about himself, giving me several days of his time to see San Francisco and to drive out to see Tom Mooney.

One of my pleasantest memories of San Francisco was the dinner I had with Father O'Kelly, Father Donahue and Father Phillips who had been in a rural parish north of San Francisco for fifteen years and who had organized the apple growers into a cooperative. Both priests spoke at the social action conference held for priests in the Archdiocese during the summer.

Father Paul of St. Boniface's parish is a friend of *The Catholic Worker* at a big down town church which reminds me of St. Francis of Assisi on 32nd Street, New York. One of the features of the church are communal breakfasts after the Tuesday novena Masses and after first Fridays, held in a big hall where I spoke on several Thursday nights. I spoke in St. Elizabeth's Parish in Oakland, also a Franciscan church, to three groups in the morning, afternoon and evening.

Father Paul had visited us this summer at Mott Street, and our *Catholic Worker* friends in San Francisco keep in touch with each other through him.

I visited also the Berkeley Book Guild which is right at the gates of the university, handy for the thousands of passersby. Meetings are held and Father Phillips is giving a course in co-operatives. Mrs. P. W. Alston loaned her library to the store and when she moves to New Orleans as she intends next summer, she wants to loan it to a store down town in order to encourage the starting of a Catholic Book Store in that very Catholic city. Dr. Ann Nicholson and Mrs. Alston are the spirits behind the work.

The very best library I have ever seen about the country is the Paulist library next door to St. Mary's where there is an immense reading room with tables filled with magazines and comfortable chairs and very good lighting. Employed and unemployed frequent the place and spend hours in reading. There wasn't a day passed that I did not drop in while I was in San Francisco. For Minna Berger, who runs the library, through Father Gillis, was our first *Catholic Worker* in that city, and every month she displays the paper in the window.

It is scarcely necessary to start a hospice for men, for the St. Vincent de Paul Shelter has housed 78,652 men in the last year. There are three hundred and twenty beds, and breakfast is also served. Bed and breakfast cost fifteen cents, and if men have not the money, some agency supplies it. There is a day shelter next door, with an open fire place and tables and benches. Next door there is a handball court and there is a gym downstairs. In the basement of the night shelter there are showers and wash tubs and a barber shop, in addition to storage room for baggage.

Altogether I lost count of the number of times I spoke or the number of miles I traveled.

During the trip I spoke at two seminaries in addition to many colleges and Church groups, also to auto workers, steel workers, agricultural workers and unemployed.

I talked at length with Archbishop Mooney, Bishop Schrembs and Archbishop Cantwell who have all been very helpful and encouraging in the work we are doing in their diocese.[72]

---

72   (Arch)bishops Mooney, Schrembs, and Cantwell were the ordinaries of Detroit, Toledo, and Los Angeles, respectively.

2

I am staying for the day and night at the distractingly beautiful home of one of our readers up in New London right on the Long Island Sound. I woke up this morning feeling as though I were in a lighthouse. The house hangs right out over the water, and the soft gray waves played gently against the rocks below my window. The sky was overcast, the water gray, the sky blue and there were lavender tones on the horizon. The rocks stood out, yellow and brown. Such beauty makes me very happy. It is something you can store away in yourself to think about and refresh yourself with during times of stress and turmoil.

I have been travelling incessantly for the past month and will not be back at *The Catholic Worker* office until tomorrow. I have been down to West Palm Beach where I spoke to different groups, poor ones and rich ones. After a week there I proceeded to a little farm upstate where some of our readers are trying to build up a co-operative farm, and after a night and day there, I took the bus to Birmingham, Alabama. In Birmingham, I was the guest of Sister Peter Claver, a member of the Missionary Servants of the Most Blessed Trinity, who is an old friend. It was Sister Peter Claver who gave the first dollar to *The Catholic Worker* almost five years ago when she was engaged in colored mission work in Newark, N. J. and the Oranges. Now she is stationed in Birmingham where the Missionary Servants have charge of the Catholic Charities. She and her Sisters, seven of them, were staying in a little house built right on the back of a church in the outskirts of Birmingham, near the steel plant. The parishioners, most of them Italian, work in the plant.

The priest there is an Italian who knew Don Luigi Sturzo, former head of the Popular Party of Italy, now an exile in England, writing for English periodicals. Father Donazann, I was happy to find, recognized the fact that Father Sturzo did far more to combat Communism in Italy (by doing away with the reasons for it) than Mussolini, who later reaped the credit where Father Sturzo had sown. Father Donazann told us how workers in his American parish were dropped from the steel mills when they joined a union years ago, and had never been rehired from that day to this.

Sister Peter Claver's office, and the headquarters of the Catholic Charity Bureau in Birmingham, is on a poor street, in a poor little house of four or five rooms. The house is unpainted, but "very nice inside", said Teresa, who was going around with me. She stayed there with one of the other Sisters while Sister Peter Claver and I travelled about.

I love to see Catholic Charity workers living among the poor in small places, in places so humble that the poor do not fear to come. If we only had small centers like that through all the cities, in many parishes, instead of one large central bureau, charity would mean love.

I had interviews with the vice-presidents of the United States Steel Company and the Gulf States Steel Company. The latter is a Catholic who did not agree with "either Pope Leo XIII or Pope Pius XI, in their encyclicals on labor," he said very frankly.

Mr. Geohegan, of the Gulf States Steel, invited us out to see his plant at Gadsden, a town fifty miles away where the Sisters conduct the Holy Name of Jesus Hospital, the only institution the community has. So that afternoon, two of the Sisters, and Teresa and I, drove on to the hospital where we stayed overnight. It was Teresa's eleventh birthday the next day, and while the Sisters arranged a little party for her and escorted her around the hospital, Sister Peter Claver and I went to Alabama City, a part of Gadsden, where the steel plant is located. Sister Peter Claver is a good companion — I wish she were working with us. I always have the feeling about both her and Father Joachim, that they fit in everywhere. Just as Father Joachim, a few years ago before he was ordained, came and encouraged us, in our picket line in front of a New York City department store, so Sister Peter Claver was perfectly at home in the noise and confusion of a steel mill. I can imagine either of them going anywhere in their quest for souls.

We spent hours at the plant, walking what seemed miles while we covered the whole production, from the making of steel to the making of nails and barbed wire. We watched them pour out the molten metal into huge cauldrons (they have six open hearth furnaces) and then into forms. We watched the re-heating and the rolling mills where they pressed out the blocks of metal into thin plates. We watched them corrugate the plates. We watched the men work with long coils of the flaming metal, whirl them like lassoes as they were made into cables and wire.

Much of the work was dangerous and laborious. The men took pride in it, calling us to their different machines, which they slowed up in order that we might watch the processes which turned out our nails and chicken fencing.

They wear shoes the toes of which withstand 2500 pounds pressure (when working around the furnaces) and all the men wear glasses to protect their eyes. And in spite of the terrific heat (the metal reaches 2900 degrees, I believe), they must wear reasonably heavy clothes to guard them from sparks and bits of molten steel and slag.

There are three thousand workers in this plant, and the president has declared that never will he permit a union. Wages have been increased and hours shortened, but that these gains have been brought about by the pressure of workers attempting to organize throughout the industry, is a fact that Mr. Geohegan disputes.[73]

---

73 While the workers eventually unionized with the United Steel Workers, the Gadsden (Alabama) plant of Gulf States Steel (which went bankrupt in 2006) remains a major source of litigation by former employees over its use of cancer- and mesothelioma-causing asbestos.

3

Fred Brown is no longer unemployed. He no longer goes to the union hall on Eleventh Avenue every day to see whether his number is called. Fred Brown, seaman, twenty-four years old, shipped out on his last voyage a few weeks ago. He had been staying with us on Mott Street for four months, and we had known him for the past year or so. He was taken sick on the Monday following the feast of the Immaculate Conception and by Thursday night he was dead.

He had gone to Communion along with the rest of us on the feast day and on the Tuesday night before he lapsed into unconsciousness and was taken to the hospital, he had said to one of his former shipmates, sitting by his bedside, "While I'm ashore, I'm going to get to daily Mass after this when I get better."

We went to see him at Columbus Hospital Wednesday and Thursday but he was unconscious while we were there, and Thursday evening at five o'clock he died. It was a bitter shock; not just his death (it had been a good death after all) but because the tragedy of his passing was made bitter by a theft in the house, the theft of his one suit of clothes.

He had nothing, as most seamen have nothing, and just before his death, his one suit had been taken. (There are, of course, those among us of the lame, the halt and the blind, who commit these despicable acts driven by God knows what necessity, but who must be forgiven as we need to be forgiven our own mean sins.) Fred would have forgiven them; wryly, perhaps, and with a shrug, but far more readily than we did on this occasion.

But the misery that this poor dead boy had nothing to be buried in remained a tragic incident connected with his death. Jim Schneid, a recent Catholic Worker recruit and so still possessed of two suits, gave him one of his, his Sunday one. They were the same height, over six feet and about the same age.

The body was brought to Graciano's funeral parlor around the corner on Mulberry Street and laid out there on Saturday. The delay occurred because Fred's only relative, his brother, could not be found. Then, until Monday evening, his friends stood watch at the bier, hour by hour.

On Monday morning, the hours from four to six fell to me, and I read a meditation on Purgatory which was healing for my sadness.

"The soul in Purgatory feels the irresistible attraction of that Beauty of which he has a glimpse at Judgment. He is drawn to it with a vehemence which carries with it his whole being, and flings him upon God as the wave upon the shore. And he is driven back incessantly, for he is not yet ready for the embrace of the all-Holy."

Father O'Donnell, Apostolate of the Sea Chaplain, sang the solemn high Mass at the Shrine Church, at Twenty-first Street and Tenth Avenue, a few doors away from where our strike kitchen was last year at this same time. In his generosity it was not just a low Mass, but the most solemn, the most glorious the Church could offer.

As we sped up the Hudson River viaduct from Canal Street to reach the Church, we could see smoke coming from the stacks of the *Leviathan*. "She too is preparing for her last voyage," one of Fred's shipmates said. When we crossed the East River an hour later to reach Calvary Cemetery, a freighter passed beneath the bridge, on its way out to sea, the sea that Fred would never travel again. It was a beautiful sunny day, soft and mild, and out at Calvary the bare trees stood out blue black against a sky bright as the Virgin's robe.

Father O'Donnell, Father Dugan and Father Quinn accompanied Fred's body to the grave and blessed it. As we knelt about the open grave, the ground beneath our knees felt damp and springy. All around us was the death of winter, the life of tree, bush and vine imprisoned in the ground.

But that good earth beneath my knees, that earth which was accepting Fred into her embrace, that very earth echoed the promise of the Resurrection and reminded us of the words of Job:

"I firmly believe that my Redeemer liveth, and that I shall rise again from the earth on the last day and that in my own flesh I shall see my God" [Job 19:25].

4

Outside the rain pours down in sheets but it is warm. Men stood on our coffee line this morning like dripping pedestals, but at least they were not shuddering with the cold as they have been so many mornings lately. I was looking over our last February issue this morning and note that we were feeding about four hundred men a morning then. Now the line has doubled and still we go on. God alone knows how, because these last two weeks there has been nothing in the bank. Just what came in every few days went to the grocer, and the printer waits patiently. Half a dozen speaking engagements brought in some money which went right to the wholesalers for coffee, sugar, milk and bread.

We spoke last year too, of the necessity of starting this work in other centers throughout the country, and we write with joy that Pittsburgh, Detroit, Milwaukee, Boston, Houma and many other places have started and are feeding the Ambassadors of God who come to them.

Already over in England, the staff of the English Catholic Worker has opened a House. We know the difficulties of these undertakings, so it is in place to reiterate some of the principles by which we began our work.

We emphasize always the necessity of smallness. The ideal, of course, would be that each Christian, conscious of his duty in the lay apostolate, should take in one of the homeless as an honored guest, remembering Christ's words:

"Inasmuch as ye have done it unto the least of these, ye have done it unto me" [Matthew 25:40].

The poor are more conscious of this obligation than those who are comfortably off. I know of any number of cases where families already overburdened and crowded, have taken in orphaned children, homeless aged, poor who were not members of their families but who were akin to them because they were fellow sufferers in this disordered world.

But if family complications make this impossible, then let our friends keep in mind the small beginnings. I might almost say that it is impossible to do this work unless they themselves are ready to live there with their guests, who soon cease to be guests and become fellow workers. It is necessary, because those who have the ideal in mind, who have the will to make the beginnings, must be the ones who are on hand to guide the work. Otherwise it is just another charity organization, and the homeless might as well go to the missions or municipal lodging houses or breadlines which throughout the depression have become well-organized and accepted as a permanent part of our civilization. And that we certainly do not want to perpetuate.

We began with a store, expanded on to an apartment rented in the neighborhood, from thence we moved to a twelve-room house and now we have twenty-four rooms here in Mott Street.

It is not enough to feed and shelter those who come. The work of indoctrination must go on. There must be time for conversations, and what better place than over the supper table? There must be meetings, discussion groups, the distribution of literature. There must be some one always on hand to do whatever comes up, whether that emergency is to go out on a picket line, attend a Communist meeting for the purpose of distributing literature, care for the sick or settle disputes. And there are always arguments and differences of opinion in work of this kind, and it is good that it should be so because it makes for clarification of thought, as Peter says, and cultivates the art of human contacts.

We call attention again to the fact that the Communists have set themselves to do four things, according to the reports of the last meeting of the Third International: to build up anti-war and anti-fascist groups in the colleges; to organize the industrial workers; to start a farm-labor party and to organize the unemployed.

Houses of Hospitality will bring workers and scholars together. They will provide a place for industrial workers to discuss Christian principles of organization as set forth in the Encyclicals. They will emphasize personal action, personal responsibility in addition to political action and state responsibility. They will care for the unemployed and teach principles of co-operation and mutual aid. They will be a half-way house towards farming communes and homesteads.

We have a big program but we warn our fellow workers to keep in mind small beginnings. The smaller the group, the more work is done.

And let us remember, "Unless the Lord build the house, they labor in vain that build it" [Psalm 127:1].

In the editorial of this issue of *The Catholic Worker*, we speak of plans to form unemployed groups with the end in view of getting them on the land, of starting a movement in that direction all over the country. We do this with the full recognition that these bread lines, this work of feeding the hungry, must always go on. "For the poor we have always with us." That is a saying which has irked many for nineteen hundred years. They have not been able to take it. The Marxists use it with sneers, saying that Christianity preaches "pie in the sky", and the rich use it to excuse themselves from aiding those same poor. But we must recognize the hard fact, that no matter how good a social order, there will always be the lame, the halt and the blind who must be helped, those poor of Christ, the least of His children, whom He loved, and through whom there is a swift and easy road to find Him.

I came across the most profound expression of this last month in Bernanos' *Diary of a Country Priest*,[74] a tremendously moving book which has become a best seller in France. Poverty and suffering, and the joy of Christ found through them! The book is overwhelming on first reading, and one feels the necessity of going over passages again and again to get their full meanings. All of us who are engaged in trying to build a new social order, who consider ourselves revolutionaries, need this book for a fuller understanding of the place our work takes in the temporal scheme. It helps us to preserve a balance.

Peter is always making lists of books for people to read so I shall give my own list herewith:

Diary of a Country Priest; Mauriac's *Life of Christ*;[75] Dostoievsky's *Legend of the Grand Inquisitor* in the *Brothers Karamazov*; Chautard's *Soul of the Apostolate*;[76] Father Knox's *Abridged Bible*; Maritain's *Freedom in the Modern World*, and *True Humanism*.

That is plenty for several years' reading.

5

We are always having fresh occasion to make the point of personal responsibility, much to the amazement of our hearers

---

74 Georges Bernanos (1888-1948), French novelist, whose 1936 novel *The Diary of a Country Priest* (London: The Bodley Head, 1938) ends with the famous line "All is grace," which Day would repeat throughout her writings over the years. It was also adopted as the title for William Miller's edition of her notes from the Lacouture Retreat (*All is Grace: The Spirituality of Dorothy Day* [New York: Doubleday, 1987]).

75 François Mauriac (1885-1970), French novelist, winner of the Nobel Prize for Literature in 1952. The work referenced is his novelistic *Life of Jesus* (trans. Julie Kernan; London: Hodder & Stoughton, 1937).

76 Dom Jean-Baptiste Chautard, O.C.S.O. (1858-1935), Trappist abbot and spiritual writer. His *The Soul of the Apostolate* (trans. Rev. J. A. Moran; London: Burns and Oates, 1926) is considered a classic of Catholic spirituality.

who often doubt our sanity when we start expounding. It was the Health Department last month. We protested their right to come into our home at 115 Matt Street and snoop around our kitchen. We were not running a restaurant or a lodging house, we explained. We were a group of individuals exercising personal responsibility in caring for those who came to us. They were not strangers, we pointed out, since we regarded them as brothers in Christ. We were not an institution, or a Home with a capital letter, but a home, a private home. We were protesting in general against the tendency of the day to emphasize state responsibility, and we considered ourselves good Americans as well as Christians in working as individuals. We were protesting against organized charity which made so many hate the beautiful word charity.

We were able to convince the supervisor and the office man as to our principles and motives, but not so the inspector, who surveyed us with a stony glare and a great contempt. We did finally concede that we do come under the law which held that we were feeding the public, when it came to the coffee line, and that we would have to comply with their regulations there. So now the work is going on, with no money in sight to pay the plumber. St. Joseph, the good workman, will have to take care of this for us.

When we succeed in persuading our readers to take the homeless into their homes; having a Christ room in the house as St. Jerome said, then we will be known as Christians because of the way we love one another. We should have hospices in all the poor parishes. We should have coffee lines to take care of the transients; we should have this help we give sweetened by mutual forbearance and Christian Charity. But we need more Christian homes where the poor are sheltered and cared for.

Last winter, the Communist readers of the *Daily Worker* fed a few thousand seamen on Thanksgiving and Christmas Day. When they gave a banquet they did not invite their rich neighbor, but the men who were in need. And what an indoctrination this was! They were knowing Marxist teaching through the breaking of bread, instead of Christian.

So we do not cease to urge more personal responsibility on the part of those readers who can help in this way. Too often we are afraid of the poor, of the worker. We do not realize that we know him, and Christ through him, in the breaking of bread.

It saddens us to have *The Catholic Worker* come down again to four pages, but it is better than skipping a number. We are so broke that we dare not run up a printer's bill. We are most daring in regard to groceries, feeling confident that our Lord will not let us down. He is too grateful to St. Joseph for the care He got on this earth to disregard his requests, and St. Joseph is our special protector in this work. And the one thing we are sure of in feeding the unemployed is that our Lord wants us to do this work, so we must do it. We are liable to make mistakes in the paper, not being theologians or philosophers, nor experts in the line of economics and sociology; but we can make no mistake in feeding God's hungry ones.

FOURTEEN

1

IT WAS nineteen above zero and Herbert Joyce had just hitch-hiked from West Virginia. Herbert is two and a half years old. With him was his father, twenty-five, a glass-blower. His mother had deserted Herbert when he was six months old.

Herbert was looking for a bed for the night. He had a woolen overall suit on, and no sweater underneath, and tiny galoshes on his tired feet. When he arrived at *The Catholic Worker* office at supper time he was very hungry indeed.

Nobody knew what to do about the baby, and I was out at a meeting and didn't get back until after eight. By the time I came home he was fast asleep on his father's shoulder. They were just waiting.

The top floor front at 115 Mott Street was full to the doors. Ten men slept there and there was no room for a father and child. The rear house was full, every bed taken and every room as full as could be. There was the dining room table, of course, but he might roll off that. There were the offices, but one office already had a bed put up in it and there were no other beds to put up in the other offices nor any blankets. And it was nineteen above. Not as cold as it was to get, but still cold enough.

Crowded or not crowded, Mott Street is scarcely a place for a baby two and a half years old. Unheated at night, oil stoves during the day, no hot water, no extra bath, no privacy. The two top floors were occupied by women, some of them nervously incapable of work, physically shattered by hardship and insecurity. Not fit company for a baby. And one certainly didn't want to put him in with a lot of men, unemployed, of all ages.

So first we tried the McMahon Temporary Shelter for Children. No, that was filled up and besides it was quarantined for scarlet fever. There was the St. Barnabas Shelter over on Mulberry Street, also temporary, so we tried them, and the matron there told us there was a bed. We walked the ten or twelve blocks to get there and found that there had been a mistake. They were quarantined there too, with dysentery. We should try the Foundling, they said.

During this time there had been a policeman who had been assisting us in our search, very friendly and sympathetic, anxious to help us though he assured us that New York wanted no transients, least of all transients with babies.

Once before the Foundling Hospital had helped when Margaret had gone to the hospital with arthritis. The hospital had taken in her baby and afterwards had boarded it out. So we went with confidence to the Foundling Hospital. There was a subway right at the door of St. Barnabas which let us out practically at the door of the Foundling, so the journey was not so bad. But once there we had to wait and be questioned. By this time it was after nine.

The nurse in charge took our names, the details in regard to the baby, the father, the mother, our interest in the case.

"How long would we wish the baby kept?" she asked.

"A few weeks, until we could find a place to board the baby so the father could find work," we told her. *The Catholic Worker* could put up the father, but it was the baby that needed special care.

The nurse left to speak to the sister in charge and came back with word that we were to go around the corner to the police station on Sixty-seventh Street. I don't remember what she said, but my understanding was that this was a formality to be gone through and being quite used to the ways of charity organizations and the efficiency that demanded that the recipient of charity be made to go through as many inquiries and as much red tape as possible, regardless of the immediate need, we remained patient. After all the baby was asleep. The father might be tired of carrying the sleeping young one — all the way from West Virginia where he should have remained, of course, and lived on the ten dollars a month the relief allowed him — but he had to put up with it. Every one was only too happy the baby was not awake and crying.

So we went to the station house, bare, drab and inhospitable. It was some time before the desk sergeant could give us any attention. He had to talk to a landlord who was having trouble with drain pipes or something. A man of property, worthy of attention. He had to talk to another policeman about getting a woman drug addict over to Bellevue. He seemed to be stalling, meditating over our case for a while when he had finished these two cases. Finally he called the Foundling. We heard his end of the conversation, but not the other.

"What do you want me to do about it?" he wanted to know.

"O, you want me to investigate! Well, I don't blame you, they look fishy to me."

This was hard to understand. Mr. Joyce might have looked fishy, and so might I, but after all, it was hard to see what there was fishy about the baby who needed a bed.

We were questioned some more. We were taken upstairs and questioned some more. We sat in a room with a detective who was finger-printing some men, next to a room where some women were being held, and the questions went on. Perhaps we were not technically being held by the police, but in effect we were. We were questioned separately and together.

It was suggested that I had been wandering around the country with Mr. Joyce and the baby. This contribution to the case was made by the detective who alternately sneered at us and at the Catholic Charities, who had not taken care of the case though he donated his money to them. He remarked on this many times.

What had complicated the whole case was that Bernard had come to us in California, to our Los Angeles headquarters, when his wife had deserted him. There after much red tape, which took days, the baby was taken care of for a time and finally Bernard was sent back to West Virginia.

The fact that we had been concerned in his case before made the police confident that we were partners in his delinquency in running away from his ten dollar a month allowance in West Virginia. They distorted the story in their ugly imaginations and insinuations until it looked as though the charges were to be made against us of vagrancy, adultery, kidnapping and a few other sins and crimes. During the long hours we sat in the police station — and we were there until after midnight — the only response the Lieutenant made to the problem was sneers and suspicion. The detective upstairs was even worse.

Finally after hours of pondering on the part of the Lieutenant an ambulance doctor walked in, much to our surprise. He picked up the sleeping child, and, to our alarm and astonishment, examined the baby who refused to wake up and then handed him back to us.

"Nothing wrong with that baby," he said. We knew that before.

The interne was from the Flower Hospital, and being just a plain man he had a simple solution. "I'll say the baby is an undiagnosed case and bring him over to the hospital," he said. "He'll at least have a bed for the night."

"Then I'll have to arrest the father for vagrancy just to see that he doesn't desert him," the police decided. "And tomorrow the case will come up in the courts and they'll both be shipped back to West Virginia. We have enough problems of our own."

But this didn't seem any solution for us, so this idea was abandoned.

And then finally, after these hours of pondering, the great police department of the City of New York gave up. We had to take the baby back to Mott Street to find a bed for him there. The only contribution to our problem was that we were escorted back in the patrol wagon, and I am not yet decided whether we had this escort out of desire for our comfort or in order that the police might find out whether we really had a House of Hospitality.

In the wagon, our escort policeman was most sympathetic.

"It's a hard, cruel world," he said sadly.

We agreed.

"You've done wrong, young man, but still I can sympathize with your wanting to keep the child with you."

We were glad for his sympathy. He was a kindly man and he gave Bernard a dollar for the baby.

He helped us out carefully, escorted us to the rear tenement which we call home, and even insisted upon going upstairs. By this time I had decided on a solution. It would have saved us lots of time and worry if I had decided on it before.

We put the baby and the young father in my room where there are two single beds, and we woke up Teresa, aged twelve, and she and I went to a neighbor's apartment to sleep on the floor. (Our friend had one blanket on her bed that night and we had two, one under and one over us.) The next day we sent Bernard and Herbert, the baby, down to the farm at Easton to save them from being shipped back to West Virginia.

"I'm not a bum," Bernard had said sadly that evening. "I worked for three years in West Virginia until I got laid off and when I went to California, I went because I had a job there which lasted a year. This last summer I worked six months and I'm looking for work now, but I want to keep my baby."

2

"And they came to a farm called Gethsemane ... And Jesus said to them, 'My soul is sorrowful even unto death; stay you here and watch' [Matthew 26:36, 38].

"And when He had gone forward a little He fell flat on the ground. And He prayed that if it might be, the hour might pass from Him ... And being in agony, He prayed the longer. And His sweat became as drops of blood trickling down upon the ground" [Luke 22:41-42, 44].

Strangely enough there are objections and criticisms made by unbelievers in regard to the sufferings of Christ. There are some who believe that it is pathological and morbid to dwell on the agony of our Lord. There are others who say that there have been other martyrs who have suffered greater torments, and they cite cruel sufferings, sufferings that were prolonged for hours and even days, as in the case of the Jesuit martyrs here in New York state.

They cite the sufferings of little children, beaten, starved, crying in a premature and horrible despair, and they say with Ivan Karamazov that "the whole world of knowledge is not worth that child's prayer to 'dear kind God,' who does not seem to hear it."

They lose sight of the fact that in the Agony in the Garden, Christ took upon Himself the sins of the world and the sufferings due to those sins.

He withdrew from His friends and disciples. The three He had with Him slept (for their eyes were heavy). But even if they had been with Him, He would have suffered all the desolation and the loneliness and the utter desertion that anyone has ever suffered in all ages. He suffered not only the despair of one but of countless millions. The accumulated woe of all the world, through all the centuries, He took upon Himself. Every sin that was ever committed, that ever was to be committed, He endured the guilt of it. In His humanity, He was the I.W.W. who was tortured and lynched out in Centralia and Everett, and He likewise bore the guilt of the mob who perpetrated the horror on their victim. There was never a Negro fleeing from a maniacal mob whose fear and agony and suffering Christ did not feel. He Himself, in the person of the least of His children, has been hanged, tortured, afflicted to death itself, and He has at the same time been the one who has borne the guilt of the evil done. "Him, that knew no sin, for us He hath been made sin" [2 Corinthians 5:21]. He has suffered long years of imprisonment in jail, innocent and guilty; He has suffered the woe of a mother bereft of her child, and of a child bereft of all solace. "Who does not suffer and we do not suffer" [paraphrasing 1 Corinthians 12:26], St. Paul cried, voicing the dogma of the Mystical Body.

Who can measure the sufferings of Him Who died for our sins, in that hour He spent in Gethsemane, bent to the ground in His agony, His sweat becoming as drops of blood trickling down upon the ground, crying out "Father, if Thou wilt, let this cup pass from me!"

It is Christ in His humanity Who suffered, and since then suffering and death can no longer be victorious. "For we are saved by hope" [Romans 8:24], and even the natural man without faith can understand and realize hope.

Father McNabb[77] brought out in a recent book on our Lord that Christ's greatest temptation in the Garden of Olives was to hate his neighbor. Bernanos in his *Diary of a Country Priest* writes, "Hell is not to love any more."

I felt when I read this that the blackness of hell must indeed have descended on our Lord in His agony.

The one thing that makes our work easier most certainly is the love we bear for each other and for the people for whom we work. The work becomes difficult only when there is quarrelling and dissension and when one's own heart is filled with a spirit of criticism.

In the past, when I have spoken on the necessity of mutual charity, of self-criticism rather than criticism of others, the accusation has been made that I talk to the men as though they were angels, that I do not see their faults. Which is certainly not true.

The difficulty for me is not in *not* seeing the other person's faults, but in seeing and developing his virtues. A community of

---

77 Rev. Vincent McNabb, O.P. (1868-1943), Irish spiritual writer and supporter of Distributism, a movement encouraging small landholding and a return to agriculture as a "third way" between capitalism and communism. His writings were recommended to all Catholic Workers by Peter Maurin and deeply influenced Day's philosophy.

lay people is entirely different from a religious community like the Benedictines. We must imitate them by thinking in terms of work and prayer. But we must always remember that those who come to us are not there voluntarily, many of them, but because of economic circumstances. They have taken refuge with us. There is the choice of being on the streets, taking city care such as it is, or staying with us. Even many of the young "leaders" who give up home and position to come to help in the work are the rebel type and often undisciplined. Their great virtues often mean correspondingly great faults.

Yet those who are interested in the movement fail to see why it does not run as smoothly as a religious movement. They expect our houses and farms to be governed as a religious community is ruled, and in general they take the attitude that I am the one in authority who should rule with an iron hand, the others accepting this willingly. Truly the position of authority is the difficult one.

One of the difficulties of the work is to find those who are willing to assume authority. Leaders are hard to find. The very best in our groups who are members of unions for instance, are steadfast, humble, filled with the love of God and their fellows, and their very virtues make it hard for them to assume leadership. Often then, they leave it to the articulate ones who are often articulate about the wrong doings. They leave the foremost positions to those who like to talk rather than to do, to those who are aggressive and pugnacious and who do the movement harm rather than good. If they are not saying the wrong thing, enunciating the wrong ideas — being politicians in other words — then they are *saying* but not *doing*, and even doing contrary to what they are saying.

There are those leaders in the movement who think they believe in the idea of personalism, of everyone doing as he would have the other fellow do, being what he would have the other fellow be. They think they are doing right because they do not "give orders," or *dictate*. On the other hand, woe to anyone else who goes ahead and does something which he believes should be done. Such a show of initiative means that the offending one has not acknowledged their leadership by asking permission (and very often it would not be given, as not being the proper time for the activity in question). If the others meekly submit to this and stop doing, they are discontented and unhappy at not being able to work for the movement and feel that the idea of personal responsibility has been denied. If they argue the point there is dissension. And if I intervene, even unwittingly, not knowing that there has been a dispute, and say as I think about an activity, "Yes, go ahead, that is a splendid idea," then the immediate leaders claim that I am interfering with their authority and leading others to disregard it. My job is to smooth over differences and to get people to co-operate with each other, and not to be surprised that I am always putting my foot in it.

But the worst task of all is to try to correct people's wrongdoing in the way of direction and co-operation, by the positive method rather than the negative one of merely fault-finding; to uphold the ideal, to keep working toward that, rather than to discourage by pointing out all the things that are wrong.

It is human to dislike being found fault with. If you point out faults, rather than point out the better way of doing things, then the sting is there, and resentments and inactivity are the results. "What's the use of doing anything, it's all wrong!" Such childishness! But human beings are like that, and we must recognize their faults and try in every possible way to bring out their virtues.

On a visit to a group, there are always a half dozen who are filled with complaints (usually these are steady workers who have been with us for years and feel that they are a part of the whole movement). If you try to turn their criticisms so as to change their attitude of mind, you are refusing to listen to them. You don't give them a chance to show you how wrong everything is. You don't know what is going on. It is in vain that you assure them you do know what is going on, just how faulty different ones have been. No, that is not enough, if you treat all with equal patience, then you are not paying any attention to the complaints. Positive work to overcome obstacles such as people's temperaments is not enough for the fault-finders. They want recriminations and reprimands. "You are going to let him get away with that?" is the cry, when you try by courtesy and sympathy and respect to draw people together and induce co-operation.

It is very trying to receive so many complaints and not to be able to do anything about them. Those who do not complain and who try to work along the positive method are accused of being yes-men, and those who tell on each other and who always have some tale of woe, are informers. So in either case there is trouble.

If I were in a position of responsibility in charge of only one place, perhaps different methods could be used. I could be more definite, because I would be seeing all sides of the question and could speak from my own knowledge rather than from hearsay. There could be definite reproof and co-operation to bring about a change. But as I must visit so many headquarters and farms, I am never at the same House of Hospitality or farm long enough actually to take charge.

Oh yes, my dear comrades and fellow-workers, I see only too clearly how bad things are with us all, how bad you all are, and how bad a leader I am. I see it only too often and only too clearly. It is because I see it so clearly that I must lift up my head and keep in sight the aims we must always hold before us. I must see the large and generous picture of the new social order wherein justice dwelleth. I must hold always in mind the new earth where God's Will will be done as it is in Heaven. I must hold it in mind for my own courage and for yours.

The new social order as it could be and would be if all men loved God and loved their brothers because they are all sons of God! A land of peace and tranquility and joy in work and activity. It is Heaven indeed that we are contemplating. Do you expect that we are going to be able to accomplish it here? We can accomplish much, of that I am certain. We can do much to change the face of the earth, in that I have hope and faith. But these pains and sufferings are the price we have to pay. Can we change men in a night or a day? Can we give them as much as three months or even a year? A child is forming in the mother's womb for nine long months, and it seems so long. But to make a man in the time of our present disorder with all the world convulsed with hatred and strife and selfishness, that is a lifetime's work and then too often it is not accomplished.

Even the best of human love is filled with self seeking. To work to increase our love for God and our fellow man (and the two must go hand in hand), this is a life-time job. We are never going to be finished.

Love and ever more love is the only solution to every problem that comes up. If we love each other enough, we will bear with each other's faults and burdens. If we love enough, we are going to light that fire in the hearts of others. And it is love that will burn out the sins and hatreds that sadden us. It is love that will make us want to do great things for each other. No sacrifice and no suffering will then seem too much.

Yes, I see only too clearly how bad people are. I wish I did not see it so. It is my own sins that give me such clarity. If I did not bear the scars of so many sins to dim my sight and dull my capacity for love and joy, then I would see Christ more clearly in you all.

I cannot worry much about your sins and miseries, when I have so many of my own. I can only love you all, poor fellow travellers, fellow sufferers. I do not want to add one least straw to the burden you already carry. My prayer from day to day is that God will so enlarge my heart, that I will see you all, and live with you all, in His love.

CONCLUSION

1

AS I READ through the foregoing pages, I feel that I have given no adequate account of the work, that it is very much a day by day record of little events, of my own conflicts and meditations.

It is true that at times when much work was being done and progress was being made, little writing was done. There are large gaps in the account of our activities. In telling of the immediate works of mercy, I feel that I have neglected a great deal of our work in the labor field throughout the country from coast to coast. Naturally during those times when I was travelling and speaking before labor groups throughout the country, and when we were participating actively in strikes, there had to be gaps in the record.

Even in presenting a picture of life in a House of Hospitality, the story is not complete. I find the pages crowded with people, but in respecting their situation and their desire for privacy, I cannot go into details about them, what they look like, how they have come to be with us, their backgrounds and their tragedies. I must leave the book as it stands.

We have never faltered in our conviction during these six years of work that hospices such as our Houses of Hospitality are a vital necessity in times like these.

We do not deny that the State is bound for the sake of the common good, to take care of the unemployed and the unemployable by relief and lodging houses and work projects. Pope Pius XI pointed that out very clearly. He lamented that so much money was spent in increased armaments that should be spent on the poor. He urged the "press and the pulpit throughout the world" to fight the increase of armaments, and added sadly that "up to this time Our voice has not been heard."[78]

---

78   Pius XI, *Nova Impendent* (1931), para. 8.

No, we are not denying the obligations of the State. But we do claim that we must never cease to emphasize personal responsibility. When our brother asks us for bread, we cannot say, "Go be thou filled" [James 2:16]. We cannot send him from agency to agency. We must care for him ourselves as much as possible.

And we claim that as Catholics we have not sufficiently cared for our own. We have not used the material, let alone the spiritual resources at our disposal. We have not drawn upon our tremendous reserves of material and spiritual wealth. We have scarcely known or recognized that we possessed them.

Approximately twenty-five million Catholics in the United States! It would be interesting to know how many of them are on relief, trusting to State aid. If we took care of our own, and relieved the government of this immense responsibility, how conditions would be transformed! Then indeed people could say "See how they love one another!" [paraphrasing John 13:35]. Then indeed we would be "bearing one another's burdens" [Galatians 6:2]. But of course, we would not be limiting our care only to our own. We would inevitably be caring also for others outside the faith.

This would also point the way to a solution of the industrial problem. As Christian masters freed the slaves who had converted them, because they recognized their dignity as men made in the image and likeness of God, so the industrial slaves of today can find freedom through Christianity.

Certainly this is an upside-down way of looking at the problem from a worldly standpoint. But we are fools for Christ's sake. We are the little ones God has chosen to confound the wise. We are the least of His children, yet through us He has done great things. Surely the simple fact of feeding five thousand people a day, in all our houses month after month for a number of years, is a most astounding proof that God loves our work.

We are down in the slums, but we can never be as poor as Christ, or as those ragged and destitute ones who come to us in the mornings to be fed. We are constantly overcome with a sense of shame because we have so much more than these others.

Christ was a man so much like other men that it took the kiss of Judas to single Him out, as Mauriac says in his *Life of Jesus*. He was a man like those others on our bread line. We must see Christ in each of them.

Our work in the labor field takes place not only in the Houses of Hospitality. To reach the organized and the great masses of unorganized workers we have had to go out on the streets, to the public squares, to the factories, waterfronts and picket lines.

The hardships of the migratory worker and the sweatshop worker are even greater than those who are on the bread lines and in the lodging houses. They are the family men and women who are trying to care for others. They are those who are seeing their dear ones go without essentials in the way of medical care and food, who are seeing their children grow up to find unemployment awaiting them.

In the first chapter I gave a summary of the field covered by Houses of Hospitality. Here is a brief review of some of the labor issues we have dealt with during the past six years.

Again and again we have helped workers on strike regardless of all talk as to whether the strike was just or unjust. We have done this for two reasons: first, it is never wrong to perform the Works of Mercy; secondly, because in a time of industrial warfare it is easy to get in touch with the workers by meetings and by widespread distribution of literature. It is a time when the workers are thinking and struggling; they are enduring hardships and making sacrifices, they are in a receptive frame of mind.

The first number of the paper came out in May 1933. In that issue we featured a story of the Negro labor on the levees in the South which was being exploited by the War Department. We also wrote about women and children in industry and widespread layoffs of men.

In the second issue we took up the farmers' strike in the West and wages and hours of restaurant workers. In the third issue, child labor in the textile industry, as well as a two-page synopsis of labor struggles during the month. In the fourth issue we had front page stories on the coal strike and the milk strike. In these first issues of the paper there were also stories on the race issue and the condition of the Negro in industry and in professional work. In the sixth issue of the paper we were already combating anti-Semitism. In the same issue we showed up some profit-sharing plans of industrialists as a further move to exploit labor.

By the second year, our circulation had jumped from 2,500 to 35,000 copies, and our readers included workers and students throughout the country. In the second year, 1934, the seamen's strike on the West coast, the strike of the rural workers in the onion fields, a silk workers' strike in New Jersey, the textile strike, took up many columns in the paper. In New York City we helped Orbach's department store workers in their mass picketing, and called upon our readers not to patronize a store where such wages and long hours prevailed. We helped to defeat an injunction — one of the chief weapons of the employer to break strikes — which was handed down against the picketers. Our participation in this strike and in the National Biscuit Company strike cost us many readers. Our circulation was by now 65,000, but many church and school groups cancelled their orders because of the pressure of employers' groups. There were 3,000 on strike in the National Biscuit Company factory on 14th Street, and every day there were mass picket lines and scuffles with the police.

In the March 1935 issue there was printed a speech in regard to the Child Labor amendment which Dorothy Weston, Associate Editor, had made over the radio. Our endorsement of the Child Labor amendment also cost us many subscribers, as a majority of Catholics were opposed to it, for fear of government interference in the education of our youth. But in spite of the consistent opposition (which, as we have always pointed out, is very good for the clarification of thought), our circulation rose to 100,000 at the beginning of the third year.

When the Borden Milk Company the next year attempted to foist a company union on their workers, the editors took up their cause and called public attention to the unethical conduct of the employers. We called attention to the intimidation of Borden drivers by gangsters and thugs, and urged our readers not to use Borden's milk while unfair conditions prevailed. As a result of the story we ran, the employers attacked *The Catholic Worker* in paid advertisements in the *Brooklyn Tablet* and the *Catholic News*. This dispute also cost us some thousands of subscribers.

A few months later the spring strike of 1936 started among the seamen on the East coast. Because we had moved into our larger headquarters on Mott Street we were able to house about fifty of the seamen during the strike. In the fall strike, we not only housed some of them, but also fed thousands of them daily in the store we opened on Tenth Avenue, which we kept going for about four months. At that time we printed our "Stand on Strikes" which has been widely circulated in pamphlet form among labor unions throughout the country.

By publicity and moral support, we encouraged the organization of the steel industry when the C.I.O. began its activities. In the same year, our workers assisted the marble workers' strike in Vermont, the fishermen in Boston, the sharecroppers in Arkansas, the auto workers in Detroit. We covered the sit-down strike in Michigan, and the five and ten cent store strike in New York, the steel strike in Chicago. We also helped in the organization drive of the stockyards in Chicago.

That was the tragic year when ten workers were killed and scores more wounded in the Memorial Day massacre. One of our staff had a friend killed in that tragic episode. Our workers in Chicago had been helping in the soup kitchens and marching on the picket lines as well as distributing literature.

Many of these strikes I covered personally, in order to get a complete report to our readers, and also to speak to the workers at their meetings. I was one of the few newspaper reporters allowed into the Flint Fisher Body plant to visit the hundreds of sit-down strikers who had been in the plant for forty days. By this time we had groups of Catholic Workers in many big industrial centers throughout the country.

In the labor field the Pittsburgh group was most prominent, headed as it was by Fathers Rice and Hensler. They were the first priests to go out on the picket line and on sound trucks at street corners. Their example led many other priests to become active in the labor field.

The Lowell textile strike was interesting from several angles. When our workers began to distribute *The Catholic Worker* to the strikers and the public, and to start a food kitchen, the officials of the town telephoned the Chancery Office in Boston to find out if we were all right and were assured that we could go ahead. (On the other hand, we know of an occasion when a speaking engagement at a church in Jersey City was cancelled because of Mayor Hague's opposition to the paper.) The local paper proclaimed in their headlines that the entrance of *The Catholic Worker* into the Lowell strike marked the turning point in the conflict and led to prompt negotiations between the workers and the employers.

Often the immediate work in the House of Hospitality in caring for the unemployed kept us from work farther afield. It was of course impossible to answer all calls for help or to supply lay apostles wherever they were needed. We could only do the work which came to hand.

At the same time, we covered a pretty wide field. I notice in looking back over the old issues that Eddie Priest put in some months in a machine shop in Brooklyn, John Cort in a brass factory in New York, Julia in a five and ten cent store, where she did a good deal of indoctrinating and organizing by the distribution of literature and attendance at union meetings. Stanley Vishnewski covered many picket lines and Bill Callahan covered the Newspaper Guild strike in Brooklyn and the auto strike in Michigan.

We tried to cover not only city industrial plants, but also country plants. Certainly the Seabrook farm of four thousand acres in New Jersey with their own canning plant, is an industrial setup. The plant is so huge that two airplanes are used to fly over the fields to spray them against insects.

There is not much difference between this farm and the collective farms of Russia except that the latter are owned by the State. The Communists would make no changes in setup, admiring "bigness" as they do. They would merely take them over, they say, and run them for the benefit of the workers.

Some of the boys from *The Catholic Worker* farm in Easton went down to Seabrook and worked for a while, talking with union officials and workers and spreading literature. During the summer we plan to repeat this venture more intensively, giving almost a complete issue of the paper to discussing corporation farming as opposed to "farming as a way of life," and upholding the small landowner and co-operative owner against the State as well as against the industrialists. It is not only in California and in the South that horrible conditions exist for migratory workers and relief workers. We have them here in New Jersey, just outside the door.

An article on the natural and supernatural duty of the worker to join his union, appearing in the September 1937 issue found a widespread circulation. In New Orleans, where organization activities were bitterly fought at the time, it was circulated by the thousands, also in New England among the textile workers.

During this last year the truckdrivers' strike, the sharecroppers' strike, the Newspaper Guild strike in Chicago, the tanker strike and the miners' strike have been covered.

In the past six years we have had many interviews with Catholic industrialists and many of them were not too cheering. Not wishing to increase class war attitudes, we did not publish many of them.

During these past years, former Governor Murphy's stand in the auto strikes, and Sheriff Boyle's and Mayor Michael Sewak's stand in the steel strike in Johnstown were highlights. By moral force rather than by armed force, these men prevented violence and bloodshed and stood out not only against the industrialist but against a campaign of public vilification and condemnation. Because they resolutely refused to use armed guards against the workers, and insisted upon arbitration — because they upheld human rights above property rights — they were termed spineless and yellow-livered, not only by atheistic capitalists but by many of their fellow-Catholics. Their courage and leadership in public life have been an inspiration to others and a message of hope to the workers. May God raise up other men like them.

The great problems in the labor movement today are the conflict between the A. F. of L. and the C.I.O., and the unemployment situation. It is still a struggle to organize; in many industries only small beginnings have been made.

There is too much agitation about Communism in trade union ranks. This situation can be remedied only by education of the rank and file and by earnest and unambitious participation of Catholics in their trade unions. By "unambitious" we mean a participation which does not look towards personal advancement and official positions. There has been too much of that already on the part of Catholics in politics and trade unionism.

The day calls for a new technique. We must make use of the spiritual weapons at our disposal, and by hard work, sacrifice, self-discipline, patience and prayer (and we won't have any of the former without the latter), work from day to day in the tasks that present themselves. We have a program of action and a philosophy of life. The thing is to use them.

We have been criticized for holding up the counsels of perfection as norms of human conduct. It is sad that it is always the minimum that is expected of lay people. On the other hand, we get too much praise from some for performing work which is our plain duty. If we have a vocation for the work (and the joy we take in it is one of the proofs of our vocation), then we deserve no credit. Indeed we deserve censure for not having done more, and for doing what we have done so badly, given the opportunities we have had.

Through the help of His friends, God has given us the means and the opportunities to be closer to the poor and the outcast and the worker than any other group in the country today. That we have not effected more with those we have reached is our fault, which we must acknowledge and recognize without discouragement. We must make a greater use of prayer.

As Léon Bloy wrote: "There is only one unhappiness, and that is — *not to be one of the Saints.*"

And we could add: the greatest tragedy is that not enough of us desire to be saints.

2

It is a hot summer night, nearly ten o'clock. Here on Mott Street, the noise of children, of grown ups and of radios will continue until after midnight, so I might as well sit up and write. The telephone bell keeps ringing and visitors keep coming in, but Gerry Griffin and Joe Zarrella are downstairs to attend to both and I can sit upstairs here and finish this account. *Finish* is scarcely the word, however. An account of this kind is never finished. The work goes on, the little work of feeding people, and clothing them and housing them and talking to them. It continues here and in all the other houses throughout the country in one form or another. We may meet with failure on every side, but still the work goes on. And when I speak of failure, I am not cheerless about it. We have the failure of the Cross always before us. After all, we are sowing the seed and why should we be looking for any results. It may not be for us to reap a harvest. We are told to cast our bread upon the waters, which may seem a most profligate way of sowing, but we are assured that it will bear bread, so it is up to us to have confidence and to go ahead.

Gerry and Joe carry most of the burden of the New York house. Bill Callahan makes up the paper and does a lot of speaking; Eddie Priest has charge of the printing of pamphlets and leaflets and has gotten out 20,000 in the last year; Peter Carey and Victor Smith have charge of the Union of Unemployed which is made up of men from the bread line and has been going on for the past year. Through their Monday afternoon meetings they have kept a credit union going (a miracle when you consider it is made up of men who have come in from the bread line) and have started three cooperative hostels, one of which is named after St. Joseph and the other after St. Patrick. The men are off relief and support themselves by odd jobs, helping each other out in every way they can. Frank Datillo, Jim Smith and Kate Smith take care of the circulation department and right now Shorty, Kate Travis and John Pohl take turns in the kitchen. Peter Clark and a group of other men have charge of the bread line. But everybody helps everybody else and men come and go to take jobs and others take their places. Still, the ones I name have been with us for quite a time now.

The greatest inconvenience we suffer is lack of space. Out in the back yard these summer days we have set up a shoe repair shop and supply the leather and tools for each man to mend his shoes. We have a tailor who sets up his machine in any corner he can find and mends suits. The barber also operates in the back yard in the summer and in the store in winter. The card files, the letter files, the editorial office, the library, the reception room, are all one and the same apartment on the first floor and often it has to be a bedroom too when the house is crowded.

But somehow the work goes on. Here and everywhere is Peter Maurin, the guide, the teacher, the agitator. He has no office and shares his room with Joe and Gerry. He has a book case but no desk. He carries on his indoctrinating wherever he happens to be, in the office, on the street corner in the public square or on the lecture platform. These past eight months he has been travelling constantly throughout the far west and the south, and when the winter comes he will set out again, "stirring up the people". People are not the same, after meeting Peter. They read his book, *Easy Essays*, which is made up of many of his writings for *The Catholic Worker*, — or they hear him speak, and he stirs them to think, to read and to act. He never stirs them to unthinking action. The new social order with him is based on the knowledge and practice of the teachings of the Church and the study of the Gospels, history, and tradition.

One of these days we are going to write a book about Peter and call it "Conversations with Peter." All of us will write it and we will give the background of those conversations, the people with whom he is talking, the situations that have arisen to bring forth those conversations.

But right now as I contemplate the unanswered letters on the desk, the copy for the next issue which is coming out next week, the proofs for this book, a retreat on the farm in August for members of all the groups who can make it by the thumb route, a trip South in the fall and another to the far Northwest this winter, — it is hard to figure out when that piece of work will be done. I have scarcely written twenty-five pages in this note book the past year.

A few weeks ago I returned from a month's trip through the middle west where I visited fifteen of the houses. There has been news recently of two more houses opening in Baltimore and Buffalo and I shall have to visit them. Even now I have not visited the Troy and Burlington places.

I have found many things to cheer me on the way. For one thing, the utter poverty of the houses. They all depend on the voluntary and occasional contributions of the readers of the paper in those particular cities. In some cities there are only a few active workers who can contribute their time and some of the money they earn. For instance in Washington, the Blessed Martin House is run by a Negro, Llewellyn Scott, who works for the Government and earns about twenty dollars a week. Out of this he supports a mother and sister in a little apartment where they take in a roomer who helps bear the burden of the rent. He also supports the House of Hospitality there, putting up as many as twenty-five men and feeding about fifty every day. There are not only colored men but white men in the house. It is miserably poor and ramshackle and he somehow manages to find the twenty-five dollars a month rent. He wrote us the other day that just as all the food in the house gave out he went down to the alley where the entrance of the house is to tell the line of men that there was nothing else for them. And there just inside the door he found a big box of sandwiches that someone had left!

In Harrisburg the House of Hospitality has been used to shelter evicted families until they could be sheltered elsewhere. Mary Frecon who has charge of it is sheltering a mother and two children in her own home in addition to having the care of the House on her hands.

The House in Harrisburg sheltered Lucille, too. She was a colored girl, twenty-three years old. She was found dying in an empty house next door. She had grown up on the streets. She and her brothers and sisters had just prowled around, living as best they could. For the last few months, ravaged with syphilis and drink, Lucille had been cared for by an old colored man who lived in an abandoned shed down an alley. He gave her his cot — that and a chair were the only things he had — and he slept on the floor and waited on her as best he could. But the flies were eating her alive, huge horse-flies, and in her agony she crawled out and sought shade and relief in an abandoned house next to ours where another old colored man camping there had taken care of her. He too knew the uselessness of appealing to agencies. Then the neighbors told Mary Frecon about it and she found Lucille moaning and crying and trying to beat the flies away that fastened themselves upon her open sores.

She was brought to the clean bare rooms of the House of Hospitality and taken care of by the women of the Harrisburg group.

Not a hospital in Harrisburg would have her and it was only after five days that the doctor got an ambulance and sent her to the House of the Good Shepherd at Philadelphia where they deposited her without a word and with no papers about her case. The House of the Good Shepherd is not a hospital, but it is for such girls as Lucille had been. So they took her in, nursed her and there she died not many weeks later.

While she was lying in the Catholic Worker house she had been baptized and anointed by one of the priests at the Cathedral. Our slums are full of Lucilles.

In Cleveland there are two Houses and the one on the East Side in the Negro district was woefully poor. They had to pay twice as much rent as the House in the white neighborhood — this is always the case — and they didn't have one third of the room. The men there were sleeping in the cellar for lack of bed space upstairs and heavy rain had caused an open sewer pipe to overflow, filling the place with stench. As I went down the stairs to this desolate dormitory a rat brushed across my ankle. I was dizzied by the smell and by the contact with the rat and sat down on the edge of one of the neatly made-up beds. They had put linoleum down on the cement floor, and they had cleaned and whitewashed the place. They had put broken glass in the rat holes about the basement but even so as I sat there two more rats dashed across the room. It seemed unbelievable that these men, mostly colored, should welcome such a hole as a shelter. It indicated what they had been forced to accept before.

Poverty is one thing, and destitution still another. We have always made that distinction. Some of our houses have a decent poverty, which means that the men are reasonably fed and sheltered in a certain amount of poor comfort which they mainly make for themselves. The Houses in Toledo, Akron, Milwaukee, Chicago and St. Louis are a sample. There, through the work of the men themselves, who have come in to get help, the places have been improved. Plumbing has been repaired, heating has been provided through the mending of dilapidated furnaces, windows have been made fast, — and in some cases so much work has been done by the jobless that those who come to visit the houses think the men are living in too much comfort!

They do not see them as they come in, ragged, haggard and hopeless. They see only the comfortable House that they have made, they see now men who are halfway decently clothed and fed, men who bear some semblance to their own fathers and brothers and husbands, and they say,

"What are these men doing here, enjoying this comfort? Why don't they go away to make room for the destitute?" They do not realize that these same men were the destitute only a few weeks before.

It is true that these men have been removed from the class of the destitute. Now they are able by their initiative and their hard work, to feed and help others. They are the ones who keep the houses up, who do the cooking, the cleaning, the repairing.

In his book, *The Poor and Ourselves*, Daniel-Rops[79] points out clearly the distinction between the destitute and the poor. The destitute are so hopeless, so removed from ordinary life, that it is as though they had a wall around them. It is impossible to reach them, to do anything for them except relieve a few of their immediate needs. As soon as they have begun to work, to

---

79 Henri Daniel-Rops (1901-1965), French writer and historian. The work referenced is *The Poor and Ourselves* (trans. Barbara Wall; London: Burns, Oates and Washbourne, 1938).

think, to read, — no matter whether they are penniless or job-less, they are removed from the ranks of the destitute.

Yes, there are many things that cheer me, as I travel around the country. Down in Missouri, one of the CIO unions bought a piece of land for the evicted sharecroppers and has enabled them to make an experiment in cooperative farming. Here is an experiment in mutual aid, in personal responsibility, in education.

In Southern Illinois, a Chamber of Commerce in a little town has bought an abandoned mine, and removing some of the machinery which is expensive to operate, has put the miners back to work, giving them a chance to buy back the mine by deducting the price from their pay. Evidently this is being done with the cooperation of the miners' union, and is another example of mutual aid and personal responsibility.

Not everyone in the country is looking to the Federal government for help.

Certainly, leaving out of account Divine Providence, revolution is inevitable. But trusting to Divine Providence, may we not work with hope, that despite politics and the gigantic bureaucracy which is built up throughout the country, the people will themselves settle their problems?

Certainly without poverty, without an acceptance of poverty, and by that I mean decent poverty, with sufficient food, shelter and clothing, we cannot get out of the morass we are in. Certainly too, we can do nothing without the works of mercy, — an expression of our love for our neighbor to show our love for our God.

So we come back again to Peter Maurin's fundamental ideas. "Reach the people through voluntary poverty (going without the luxuries in order to have the essentials) and through the works of mercy (mutual aid and a philosophy of labor)."

It is hard for us ourselves to become simple enough to grasp and live with these ideas. It is hard for us, and hard for our readers and friends throughout the country. We still are not considered respectable, we still are combatted and condemned as "radicals".

"We are fools for Christ's sake ... we are weak ... we are without honor ... we are made as the refuse of this world, the offscouring of all, even until now" [1 Corinthians 4:10-13].

And following St. Paul, I am certainly praying that we continue so, because this is indeed "the downward path which leads to salvation."[80]

---

80   This quote, which also appears in Day's first attempt at autobiography, *From Union Square to Rome* (Maryknoll, NY: Orbis, 2006), p. 3, comes from F. P. Sturm's "Charles Baudelaire: A Study," in *The Poems of Charles Baudelaire* (London: Walter Scott, 1906).

For Further Reading

Throughout her life Dorothy Day was a prolific writer and has left a sizeable literary legacy for students of her life and thought.

Any study of her life must begin with her classic spiritual autobiography, *The Long Loneliness* (New York: Harper and Row, 1952). She continues the story of the Catholic Worker in *Loaves and Fishes* (New York: Harper and Row, 1963).

Robert Ellsberg has recently provided excellent editions of her diaries (*The Duty of Delight: The Diaries of Dorothy Day* [Milwaukee, WI: Marquette University Press, 2009]) and letters (*All the Way to Heaven: The Selected Letters of Dorothy Day* [Milwaukee, WI: Marquette University Press, 2010]).

The best biography, well-written and lavishly illustrated, is by Jim Forest, *All Is Grace: A Biography of Dorothy Day* (Maryknoll, NY: Orbis, 2011). It contains a full bibliography of Day's writings and the significant literature about her life and thought.

Dorothy Day died at St. Joseph Catholic Worker House on November 29, 1980. John Cardinal O'Connor, then-archbishop of New York, formally opened the investigation into Dorothy Day's sanctity in 2002. In November 2012, the United States Conference of Catholic Bishops, at the request of Timothy Cardinal Dolan, archbishop of New York, unanimously voted to forward Day's cause for canonization to the Congregation for the Causes of Saints in Rome. Those interested in supporting (through prayer or by financial contribution) the progress of her cause can visit The Dorothy Day Guild at dorothydayguild.org.

The Catholic Worker movement, which Day and Peter Maurin founded in 1933, continues her work in multiple houses on several continents. In keeping with her anarchist sympathies, if not with her theological convictions, each Catholic Worker community is autonomous, and some are considerably more independent of the Catholic theological tradition than others. The best source for learning more about the current Catholic Worker movement is http://www.catholicworker.org.

About the Editor

Lance Byron Richey is dean of the School of Liberal Arts and Sciences at the University of Saint Francis in Fort Wayne, Indiana. He holds doctorates in philosophy and theology from Marquette University.